First World War
and Army of Occupation
War Diary
France, Belgium and Germany

GUARDS DIVISION
4 Guards Brigade
Grenadier Guards
4th Battalion
2 February 1918 - 31 October 1918

WO95/1226/2

The Naval & Military Press Ltd
www.nmarchive.com
Published in association with The National Archives

Published by

The Naval & Military Press Ltd

Unit 10 Ridgewood Industrial Park,

Uckfield, East Sussex,

TN22 5QE England

Tel: +44 (0) 1825 749494

www.naval-military-press.com

www.nmarchive.com

This diary has been reprinted in facsimile from the original. Any imperfections are inevitably reproduced and the quality may fall short of modern type and cartographic standards.

© **Crown Copyright**
Images reproduced by permission of The National Archives, London, England, 2015.

Contents

Document type	Place/Title	Date From	Date To
Heading	WO95/1226/2 4 Bttn Grenadier Guards Feb-Oct 1918		
Heading	1226/2 4th Bttn Grenadier Guards W/Diary Feb 1918		
Heading	War Diary of 4th Battalion, Grenadier Guards. Vol. II, 1918. Period From Feb. 1st, 1918. To Feb. 28th, 1918.		
War Diary	H. 23. (Control).	02/02/1918	05/02/1918
War Diary	Arras	06/02/1918	11/02/1918
War Diary	Ecoivres	12/02/1918	16/02/1918
War Diary	Frleux B.II & 9.8	17/02/1918	17/02/1918
War Diary	B.11. d. 9.8	18/02/1918	21/02/1918
War Diary	Ecurie Camp	22/02/1918	24/02/1918
War Diary	B.10. d. 6.4 Villerval	25/02/1918	25/02/1918
War Diary	Baillevl Line.	25/02/1918	25/02/1918
War Diary	B.10. d. 6.4	26/02/1918	28/02/1918
Miscellaneous	G.D. No. 1208/6/A. App No. 3.	05/02/1918	05/02/1918
Operation(al) Order(s)	4th Battalion Grenadier Guards Order No. 157. App 164.	11/02/1918	11/02/1918
Miscellaneous	Account Of Raid On The Night Of The 19th. Feby, 1918 Made By Germans Against The 4th Battalion Grenadier Guards. Reference Map Maroeuil 1/20,000 and rough sketch attached. App 167.	23/02/1918	23/02/1918
Miscellaneous	A Form. Messages And Signals. App 169.		
Miscellaneous	A Form. Messages And Signals.		
Operation(al) Order(s)	4th Battalion Grenadier Guards Order No. 159. App 171.	24/02/1918	24/02/1918
Heading	31st Division. 4th Guards Brigade. 4th Battalion The Grenadier Guards. March 1918.		
Heading	4th Battalion The Grenadier Guards. Narrative of Events from March 21st to 31st 1918.		
Miscellaneous	4th Battalion Grenadier Guards Narrative of Events from March 21st to 31st 1918	21/03/1918	21/03/1918
Miscellaneous	4th. Battalion Grenadier Guards. List of Casualties 23/3/18 to 31/3/18	23/03/1918	23/03/1918
Miscellaneous	4th. Battalion Grenadier Guards. Roll of Officers who took part in the battle 21st./31st. Apl.1918	21/04/1918	21/04/1918
Heading	War Diary		
War Diary	Ecoivres	01/03/1918	01/03/1918
War Diary	Villers-Brulin	02/03/1918	09/03/1918
War Diary	Ecurie	10/03/1918	10/03/1918
Miscellaneous	Chelers	11/03/1918	11/03/1918
War Diary	Bethencourt	12/03/1918	21/03/1918
War Diary		21/03/1918	01/04/1918
Operation(al) Order(s)	4th Battalion Grenadier Guards Order No. 160	28/02/1918	28/02/1918
Operation(al) Order(s)	4th Battalion Grenadier Guards Order No. 161	01/03/1918	01/03/1918
Operation(al) Order(s)	4th Battalion Grenadier Guards Order No. 162	08/03/1918	08/03/1918
Map	Map E		
Miscellaneous	Record K.		
Heading	WO95/1226/2 4 Bttn Grenadier Guards War Diary April 1918		

Type	Description	Start	End
Heading	4th Guards Brigade 31st Division 4th Battalion Grenadier Guards April 1918 Appendices under separate Cover		
War Diary	Villers Brulin	02/04/1918	10/04/1918
War Diary	12 Midnight	11/04/1918	14/04/1918
War Diary	Borre	14/04/1918	16/04/1918
Miscellaneous	La Kreule	17/04/1918	18/04/1918
War Diary	De Tir Anglais	19/04/1918	21/04/1918
War Diary	Front Line	22/04/1918	22/04/1918
War Diary	Front Line As Per Map	23/04/1918	25/04/1918
War Diary	Farm Lcan Le Riest S Of H A 2 E8 Rouck	26/04/1918	26/04/1918
War Diary	Hondeghem	27/04/1918	30/04/1918
Miscellaneous	4th Battalion Grenadier Guards Particulars of Casualties period 17th to 25th April 1918.	17/04/1918	17/04/1918
Operation(al) Order(s)	4th Battalion Grenadier Guards Order No. S.G. 22	27/04/1918	27/04/1918
Miscellaneous	Some Lessons to be learnt Summarised.	16/04/1918	16/04/1918
Heading	4th Guards Brigade. 31st Division. 4th Battalion Grenadier Guards April 1918. Narrative Of Events. Casualties. Lists of Officers etc.		
Miscellaneous	4th. Battalion Grenadier Guards. List of Officers present with the Battalion on April. 2/1918. App 182.	02/04/1918	02/04/1918
Miscellaneous	4th Battalion Grenadier Guards. Casualty List For Period 12-13th April 1918.	12/04/1918	12/04/1918
Miscellaneous	4th Battalion Grenadier Guards List of Officers who Took Part in the Operations 11th to 13th April 1918	11/04/1918	11/04/1918
Miscellaneous	A Form. Messages And Signals.		
Miscellaneous	Clarence House, St James's. S.W. April 25th/18	25/04/1918	25/04/1918
Miscellaneous	Stand of 4th Guards Brigade near Vieux Berquin on 12th and 13th April 1918.	12/04/1918	12/04/1918
Miscellaneous	4th Battalion Grenadier Guards Narrative of Events from 10th. To 14th. April 1918.	10/04/1918	10/04/1918
Miscellaneous	XV Corps No. GOS /13/7 O Dated 23-4-1918 31D/211A.		
Miscellaneous	4th. Battalion Grenadier Guards. Distribution of Officers. 1/5/18. App 194.	01/05/1918	01/05/1918
Heading	4th Bttn Grenadier G April 1918 App 185 to War Diary 1226/2		
Heading	4th Guards Brigade. 31st Division. Action of 4th Battalion Grenadier Guards 12th to 14th April 1918. This Account Was Submitted By Lt.-Col W.S. Pilcher D.S.O. In Connection With Lys Operation.		
Diagram etc	4th Battalion at La Couronne Position on April 13, 1918		
Map	Sketch I		
Map	Croquis No. 3 Situation Ensemble Surle Pont Attaque De la IV Armee Allemande Le 10 April 1918 Au Matin. Legende.		
Miscellaneous	Staff Ride In France Action Of The 4th Battalion Grenadier Guards At The Battle Of Hazebrouck 12th To 14th April, 1918	12/04/1918	12/04/1918
Miscellaneous	List Of Officers Who Took Part In The Operations 12th and 14th April.	12/04/1918	12/04/1918
Miscellaneous	Stands For Description Of The Battle.		
Miscellaneous	Description Of The Battle-12th April.		
Miscellaneous	Message From General De Lisle (G.O.C. XV Corps.)		
Miscellaneous	Appendix II. Lessons To Be Learnt.		

Heading	WO95/1226/2 4th Battn Grenadier Guards War Diary May 1918		
War Diary	Hondeghem	01/05/1918	19/05/1918
War Diary	Hondeghem Saulty	20/05/1918	20/05/1918
War Diary	Saulty	21/05/1918	31/05/1918
Operation(al) Order(s)	4th Battalion Grenadier Guards Order No. 166	19/05/1918	19/05/1918
Miscellaneous	Extract of Divisional Routine Order 940/4063 D/may 24/1918. App 201.	24/05/1918	24/05/1918
Miscellaneous	4th Battn: Grenadier Guards. App. 202.	31/05/1918	31/05/1918
Heading	WO95/1226/2 4 Battn Grenadier Guards June 1918		
War Diary	Saulty	01/06/1918	10/06/1918
War Diary	La Cauchie	11/06/1918	17/06/1918
Operation(al) Order(s)	4th Battalion Grenadier Guards Operation Order No. 167	10/06/1918	10/06/1918
War Diary	La Cauchie	18/06/1918	30/06/1918
Miscellaneous	4th Battalion Grenadier Guards		
Miscellaneous	4th Battn Grenadier Guards Programme of Sports		
Miscellaneous	4th Battn Grenadier Guards Programme of Sports.		
Miscellaneous	4th Battalion Grenadier Guards List of Prizewinners in Sports Held At Saulty June 2nd 1918.	02/06/1918	02/06/1918
Miscellaneous	4th Battalion Grenadier Guards. Officers present with Battalion June 30/1918. App 208.	30/06/1918	30/06/1918
Miscellaneous	4th Battalion Grenadier Guards. Details of Variation in Strength for June. 1918. App 209.		
Miscellaneous	A Form. Messages And Signals. App 210.		
Miscellaneous	A Form. Messages And Signals.		
Heading	1226/2 War Diary 4 Bttn Grenadier Guards July 1918		
Heading	War Diary of 4th Bn. Grenadier Guards Vol. VII, 1918. From: 1st July, 1918 To:31st July, 1918.		
War Diary	La Cauchie	01/07/1918	08/07/1918
War Diary	Criel Plage	09/07/1918	31/07/1918
Operation(al) Order(s)	4th Battalion Grenadier Guards Order No. 168. App 211.	08/07/1918	08/07/1918
Miscellaneous	4th Battalion Grenadier Guards. Training Programme-14th July to 21st July, 1918	14/07/1918	14/07/1918
Miscellaneous	4th Battalion Grenadier Guards. App 213.		
Miscellaneous	4th Battalion Grenadier Guards List Of Officers By Seniority-1/8/18. App. 214.	01/08/1918	01/08/1918
Heading	WO95/1226/2 Aug 1918 4 Bttn Grenadier Guards		
Heading	War Diary 4th. Bn. Grenadier Guards. Volume. VIII (1918) Period August 1st To 31st 1918		
War Diary	Criel Plage	01/08/1918	31/08/1918
Miscellaneous	Brigade Championship. App. 216.		
Miscellaneous	Events & Times.		
Miscellaneous	4th Battalion Grenadier Guards. Training Programme- August 5th. to August 10th. 1918. App 217.	05/08/1918	05/08/1918
Miscellaneous	4th. Battalion Grenadier Guards. Training Programme August 12th. To August 17th. 1918. App 218.	12/08/1918	12/08/1918
Miscellaneous	4th Battalion Grenadier Guards Training Programme-19th August To 24th August 1918. App 219.	19/08/1918	19/08/1918
Miscellaneous	B.H.Q. Mess.		
Miscellaneous	4th Battalion Grenadier Guards. Novices Boxing Competition Held On 21st August, 1918 by kind permission of Lt-Colonel. W.S. Pilcher, D.S.O., Commanding 4th Bn. Grenadier Guards. App 220.		
Miscellaneous	Programme.		

Miscellaneous	4th Battalion Grenadier Guards. Prizewinners At Battalion Boxing Competition. App 220.	21/08/1918	21/08/1918
Miscellaneous	4th Battalion Grenadier Guards. Training Programme-26th August-31st August 1918.	26/08/1918	26/08/1918
Miscellaneous	4th Guards Brigade Novices Boxing Competition 2nd Day Light Weights. App 222.		
Miscellaneous	4th Guards Brigade. Novices Boxing Competition Held On Monday & Tuesday August 26th & 27th By Kind Permission Of Brigadier-General Hon. L.J.P. Butler, C.M.G., D.S.O., Commanding 4th Guards Brigade.		
Miscellaneous	Light-Weights. 1st Round.		
Miscellaneous	Welter Weights 2nd Round.		
Miscellaneous	Middle Weights. First Round.		
Miscellaneous	4th Battalion Grenadier Guards List Of Draft Proceeded 28/8/18 To Join 1st. Bn: Grenadier Guards. App 223.	28/08/1918	28/08/1918
Miscellaneous	4th Battalion Grenadier Guards Draft Proceeding To Guards Division-31/8/18.	31/08/1918	31/08/1918
Miscellaneous	4th Battalion Grenadier Guards.		
Miscellaneous	4th Battalion Grenadier Guards Distribution Officers. 1/9/18	01/09/1918	01/09/1918
Heading	1226/2 4 Bttn Grenadier Guard. War Diary Sep 1918		
Heading	War Diary of 4th Bn. Grenadier Guards. Vol. IX, 1918. Period: From: 1st September, 1918 To: 30th September, 1918.		
War Diary	Criel Plage	01/09/1918	24/09/1918
War Diary	Hiermont	24/09/1918	28/09/1918
War Diary	Bray-Sur-Somme	29/09/1918	30/09/1918
Miscellaneous	4th Guards Brigade Training Programme For Company Of Young Officers Attached To 4th Bn. Grenadier Guards. App 26.	07/09/1918	07/09/1918
Miscellaneous	4th Guards Brigade Training Programme For Company Of Young Officers Attached To 3rd Bn. Coldstream Guards.	07/09/1918	07/09/1918
Miscellaneous	4th Guards Brigade Training Programme For Company Of Young Officers Attached To 2nd Bn. Irish Guards.	07/09/1918	07/09/1918
Miscellaneous	4th Guards Brigade Training Programme For Company Of Young Officers Attached To 4th Bn. Grenadier Guards.	16/09/1918	16/09/1918
Miscellaneous	4th Guards Brigade Training Programme For Company Of Young Officers Attached To 3rd Bn. Coldstream Guards.	16/09/1918	16/09/1918
Miscellaneous	4th Guards Brigade Training Programme For Company Of Young Officers Attached To 2nd Bn. Irish Guards From 16th Sept. To 21st Sept.	16/09/1918	16/09/1918
Miscellaneous	4th Battalion Grenadier Guards. Scheme For Training Week Ending 14th Septr. 1916. App. 227.	14/09/1918	14/09/1918
Operation(al) Order(s)	4th Battalion Grenadier Guards Order No. 169. App 228.	23/09/1918	23/09/1918
Miscellaneous	4th Battalion Grenadier Guards Order No. 170. App 231.	27/09/1918	27/09/1918
Operation(al) Order(s)	4th Battalion Grenadier Guards Order No. 171. App 233.	28/09/1918	28/09/1918
Miscellaneous	4th Battalion Grenadier Guards. Variations Of Strength September 1918.		
Miscellaneous	4th Bn Grenadier Guards List Of Officers By Seniority Sept. 30th 1918.	30/09/1918	30/09/1918

Heading	WO95/1226/2 War Diary Oct 1918 4 Bttn Grenadier Guard.		
Heading	War Diary of 4th Battalion, Grenadier Guards Vol. X, 1918 Period From 1st October To 31st October, 1918.		
War Diary	Bray Sur Somme	01/10/1918	02/10/1918
War Diary	7Rise	03/10/1918	07/10/1918
War Diary	Frise Poueilly BellenGlise	08/10/1918	08/10/1918
War Diary	Brancourt	09/10/1918	09/10/1918
War Diary	Montigny	10/10/1918	10/10/1918
War Diary	Gouy	11/10/1918	15/10/1918
Miscellaneous	Combles	16/10/1918	25/10/1918
War Diary	Criel	26/10/1918	31/10/1918
Operation(al) Order(s)	4th Battalion Grenadier Guards Order No. ?2. App 238.	02/10/1918	02/10/1918
Miscellaneous	No 1 Coy. App 243.	15/10/1918	15/10/1918
Miscellaneous	A Form. Messages And Signals.		
Operation(al) Order(s)	4th Battalion Grenadier Guards Order No. 175	24/10/1918	24/10/1918
Miscellaneous	4th Battalion Grenadier Guards List Of Draft Proceeding To Join 2nd Bn. Grenadier Guards.		
Miscellaneous	4th Battalion Grenadier Guards. List Of Draft Proceeding To Join 1st Bn. Grenadier Guards.		
Miscellaneous	4th Battalion Grenadier Guards. Training Scheme.		
Miscellaneous	4th Battalion Grenadier Guards. N.C. Os" Course Of Instruction.		
Miscellaneous	4th Battalion Grenadier Guards Officers Present With Battalion 31/10/18.	31/10/1918	31/10/1918
Miscellaneous	4th Battalion Grenadier Guards Strength Of Battalion October 1918. App. 249.		
Heading	Guards Division 4th Gds Bde 4th Bn Gren Bde June-Oct. 1918		

WO 95
1226/2
4 Bttn Grenadier Guards
Feb - Oct 1918

1226/2

4th Bttn Grenadier Guard

W/Diary Feb 1918

CONFIDENTIAL.

WAR DIARY.

OF

4th Battalion,   Grenadier Guards.

Vol. II, 1918.

Period:
From Feb. 1st, 1918.
To   Feb. 28th, 1918.

Army Form C. 2118.

WAR DIARY
or
INTELLIGENCE SUMMARY.
(Erase heading not required.)

Instructions regarding War Diaries and Intelligence Summaries are contained in F.S. Regs., Part II. and the Staff Manual respectively. Title pages will be prepared in manuscript.

Place	Date	Hour	Summary of Events and Information	Remarks and references to Appendices
J.23.Cahal	Saturday 2/2/18	9.30 a.m	Brigade on right carried out raid from bombers capture. One enemy killed on front line & two fine guns & visibility. Battalion looked as serving a mist gave progress in improving the trenches. Captain A.H. Steepe & 110 joined the Battalion and is posted to No 3 Company.	
H.23.Cahal	Sunday 3.2.18		Little activity on front. Our Artillery carried out a shoot on the enemy's emplacement. Enemy L.G. also bomber shown a light with yr own field battles fire. Battalion continued to L.N on trenches.	
H.23.Cahal	Monday 4.2.18		All quiet on Battalion front. On R. continued on trenches heather fine.	
H.23.Cahal	Tuesday 5.2.18		Enemy shelled Battalion Headquarters in the morning. One man wounded. Pte Yardley. Battalion ordered to be laid on to H.R.H.S. Battalion Operation Orders getting out as H.H. Brigade Administration for the Line.	A.Pb.16a & Feb.18
		8 P.M	Battalion reached billets	

Army Form C. 2118.

WAR DIARY
or
INTELLIGENCE SUMMARY.
(Erase heading not required.)

Instructions regarding War Diaries and Intelligence Summaries are contained in F.S. Regs., Part II. and the Staff Manual respectively. Title pages will be prepared in manuscript.

Place	Date	Hour	Summary of Events and Information	Remarks and references to Appendices
ARRAS	Wednesday 6.2.18		Battalion Moved Clean Billets weather fine. C.O. went round billets. Lt. Greenwood and 2/Lt Burt joined the Battalion from the Employment Battalion. Both have been employed outside the Battalion at Divisional HQs & other Employment. Order from Division Headquarters attached.	APP/62
ARRAS	Thursday 7.2.18 9 A.M - P.M		Companies at disposal of Company Commanders for training. The following policy of officers took place. Weather fine. Visit G.C. Bent to No 1 Co. Visit J.S. Greenwood to No 4 Co. 2/Lieut R.H.S. Stevenson-Gore to No 3 Co. Lieut J.C. Rolfe to No 2 Co. Lieut J.C. Glyn for No 4 Co No 3 Co	
ARRAS	Friday 8.2.18		Companies trained under Company Commanders. The Battalion left the 3rd Guards Brigade and joined the 4th Guards Brigade under the Command of Brigadier General Lord Ardee C.B. Some rain during the day	

Army Form C. 2118.

WAR DIARY
or
INTELLIGENCE SUMMARY.
(Erase heading not required.)

Instructions regarding War Diaries and Intelligence Summaries are contained in F. S. Regs., Part II. and the Staff Manual respectively. Title pages will be prepared in manuscript.

Place	Date	Hour	Summary of Events and Information	Remarks and references to Appendices
ARRAS	Saturday 9.2.18		Company Training under Company Commanders. Weather fine. Men from Divisional - Brigade Bug log returned to their Battalion	
ARRAS	Sunday 10.2.18		Battalion had Baths in ARRAS. Weather fine. Voluntary Service at 5 P.M.	
ARRAS	Monday 11.2.18		C.O. inspected Battalion. Battalion very clean. Company training. Draft of 1 N.C.O. & 14 men arrived. Company farewell dinner. All N.C.O's & Men of B Coy from Grenadier Batt. Battalion farewell dinner. Referred Lord Henry Seymour present and B-General Brooke and B-General	
ECOIVRES	Tuesday 12.2.18		Battalion marched over to 31st Division into Divisional Reserve. Brigade Order attached as A ------ Battalion was taken by Brigadier 3rd Grenade Brigade at the Saluting Point. the Drums of 1st and 2nd Batt Grenadier Guard and the Pipers started playing the 2nd Batt. Scots Guards and the Irish Guards B and	App. 163. App. 164

Army Form C. 2118.

WAR DIARY
or
INTELLIGENCE SUMMARY.
(Erase heading not required.)

Place	Date	Hour	Summary of Events and Information	Remarks and references to Appendices
ECOIVRES	Wednesday 13.2.18		Played the Battalion out. The G.O.C. 3rd Guards Brigade Congratulated the Battalion on their splendid appearance on Parade and on their marching past. The Transport was also praised for their magnificent appearance again. Company Training carried out. The weather being very much against many not more relating to routine etc resumed. Numerous fatigue parties formed.	
ECOIVRES	Thursday 14.2.18 11 A.M.		Corps Commander (XIII) inspected the Battalion and expressed himself very pleased with the appearance of the Battalion on parade and marching past. No 2 Company fired on Mont St Eloi Range, lecture for Instruction on Parade. H.M. The King awarded the late Lieut (A Captain) P.H.T. PATON the VICTORIA CROSS	
ECOIVRES	Friday 15.2.18		Company Training to-day. Company Commanders No 3 - 4 Coys Carried out Firing Practice on range. Weather still very cold. Early C.O and Company Commanders visited line at AR LEUX RD General Platoon arrange Relief with 18th &c. D.L.I.	

Army Form C. 2118.

WAR DIARY
or
INTELLIGENCE SUMMARY.
(Erase heading not required.)

Instructions regarding War Diaries and Intelligence Summaries are contained in F.S. Regs., Part II. and the Staff Manual respectively. Title pages will be prepared in manuscript.

Place	Date	Hour	Summary of Events and Information	Remarks and references to Appendices
ECOIVRES	Saturday 16.2.18		Company Commanders to view of their Companies ta views of their Companies No 1 & 2 Coys shot on range. Brusts class on Lewis.	
ARLEUX B11a.98	Sunday 17.2.16	18 to 05	Battalion relieved Durham Light Infantry in the line. Relief Completed without incident except shelling on ARLEUX LOOP. Brigade orders attached as Appendix. Battalion and letter from Major-General Lewis Division attached. Kim. Kim. Kim. Battalion leaving the Sunken Trenches relieved. Coy in advanced support-sunken line.	App 165 App 166
	30.07 F.O.R.M		Quiet night on Battalion front. Some slight shelling. and Continues settled d no ration parties taking on line. Much shelling during night. No casualties	
R.11.A.98	Monday 18.2.18		A quiet day on Battalion sector. Battalion carried on with trenches and wiring line to his Battalion. both flanks to 2,300 yards. Much work required Hard frost.	

A 5834   Wt. W4973/M687   750,000   8/16   D. D. & L. Ltd.   Forms/C.2118/13

WAR DIARY
or
INTELLIGENCE SUMMARY.
(Erase heading not required.)

Army Form C. 2118.

Place	Date	Hour	Summary of Events and Information	Remarks and references to Appendices
B.11.a.5.8	Tuesday 19.2.18		Quiet day on Front. Weather Cold.	
		5.0 P.M	O.C. 2nd Bt. Irish Guards went round line with C.O.	
		9.0 P.M	Just as C.O. arrived back at B⁺ HQrs the Enemy put down a very heavy barrage all along Battalion front and attacked ARLEUX Post in two waves the objective being Company Headquarters in BRITANNIA TRENCH. Lewis Company sent to Battalion Headqrs. Casualty report. Message of Congratulation sent to B Battalion attacked as :-	App 167.
B.11.a.5.8	Wednesday 20.2.18		G.O.C 31st Div best round of trenches with C.O. Plenty Artillery activity. Quiet day.	
B.11.a.5.8	Thursday 21.2.18		Battalion relieved by 2nd Bt. Irish Guards Brigade orders for Relief attached. Wounded No 29395 Pte J. White steel	App 168. App 169.

A 5634 Wt W4973/M687 750,000 8/16 D.D. & L. Ltd. Forms/C.2118/23

Army Form C. 2118.

WAR DIARY
or
INTELLIGENCE SUMMARY.
(Erase heading not required.)

Place	Date	Hour	Summary of Events and Information	Remarks and references to Appendices
ECURIE CAMP	Friday 22.2.18		Battalion "turned clean". A good Camp with plenty of accommodation. Weather fine. Battalion at 2 hours notice. C.O. inspected Transport.	
ECURIE CAMP	Saturday 23.2.18	3.30 p.m - 4.30 p.m	C.O. addressed Battalion with reference to German raid on night 19th & 20th. He conveyed to the troops by the Army Commander and congratulated them on their fine performance and fighting qualities shown. Some Coy Commanders and Coys marched under Coy Commanders. Three hundred men on Fatigue Belloy Belleua — — —	App 170
ECURIE CAMP	Sunday 24.2.18	3.0 p.m	C.O. and Company Commanders visited sites to arrange attack for taking over from 2nd Bn Coldstream Guards. Football Match v 3rd Divnl Train Battalion won 2 — 1. Weather a little rain and cloudy.	

Army Form C. 2118.

WAR DIARY
or
INTELLIGENCE SUMMARY.
(Erase heading not required.)

Place	Date	Hour	Summary of Events and Information	Remarks and references to Appendices
B.10.a.6.4 MINERVA TRENCH LINE	Monday 25.2.18		Battalion relieved 3rd Bn Coldstream Guards in the line. Relief complete 12 Midday. Quiet day. Fatigue party 100 men attached Battn. No Casualties but Carried on improving trenches during little rain in morning. See rest of day attached Battalion order for Relief attached Brigade	App 171 App 172
B.10.a.6.4	Tuesday 26.2.18		Quiet day on Battalion front. Working Carried on improving trenches. Fatigue party of 175 men found at night for R.E. and working in front line, under 3rd Bn Coldstream Guards. A lot of wiring done on Battalion front.	
B.10.a.6.4	Wednesday 27.2.18		Quiet day. Some shelling of our Batteries. One Bosche Aeroplane brought down behind No 1 Company or the line. Work Carried on as before and the usual Fat. The Parties found.	

Army Form C. 2118.

WAR DIARY
or
INTELLIGENCE SUMMARY.
(Erase heading not required.)

Place	Date	Hour	Summary of Events and Information	Remarks and references to Appendices
B.10.a.6.4	Thursday 28.2.18		Some shelling of our Batteries. Our aerial activity very marked. Much work done round Harry Wood. Zep gas parties. Officers of 2nd Bn K.O.Y.L.I. arrived + were attached to Coys. armies preparatory to taking over. No Conf. as officers are present with the Battalion. The following Officers left for Palestine with the Battalion. B.2nd — Lt.-Colonel Fas. Pilcher D.S.O. Commanding. " Major C.J.A. Walker M.C. 2-i-c " Captain R. Gerard D.S.O. Adjutant " " H. Chapman M.C. Intelligence " " J.H. Inglefield-Anneslees A/Q.M.R. R.O. 2/Lt. J.R. Pelly Harrods T.O.	
			No.1 Co Captain H.H. Sloan Stanley M.C. No.2 Co Captain C.E. Benson D.S.O.	
			Lieut C.E. Isby M.C. Lieut Hon C.L.S. Codrigne M.C.	
			" E.H. Tuckwell M.C. " J.J. Pryce	
			" R.B. Osborne " H.P.B. Knox	
			" H.G. Pilkey " H.P. Rodger	
			2/Lt F.C. Bart 2/Lt R.L. Munay-Lines	

WAR DIARY
or
INTELLIGENCE SUMMARY.
(Erase heading not required.)

Army Form C. 2118.

Place	Date	Hour	Summary of Events and Information	Remarks and references to Appendices
			No 3 Co Captain C.H. Greville D.S.O. " P.L. Gunn Munro Lieut F. Lyon " Hn. H.F.L. Hardinge M.C. " M.J. Thomas " C.J. Towson-Green 2/Lieut Lieut E.R.V. Stowe T/c R at Stoke. "/Lieut R.M. Heikel "has rest to Aylwood" under orders of Ba Office. Strength attached on Apl —	No 4 Co Mickle H.B Lieut J.K. " N.R. Halsey " J.S. Greenwood " R.D. Richardson 2/- Apl 1/3

[signature]
LIEUT.-COL.
COMMANDING 4th BATTN. GRENADIER GUARDS.

App 163

SECRET.　　　　　　　　　　　　　　　G.D. No. 1208/6/A.

1st Guards Brigade.　　　　"G".　　　　　　4th Gds Brigade
2nd Guards Brigade.　　　　D.A.D.O.S.
3rd Guards Brigade.　　　　A.D.M.S.
4th Guards M.G. Coy.　　　Divisional Train.

1. The following Battalions will move on February 8th 1918 to the 31st Division to form the 4th Guards Brigade, under Brigadier-General R. le N. Lord ARDEE, C.B. :-

　　　　4th Bn. Grenadier Guards.
　　　　3rd Bn. Coldstream Guards.
　　　　2nd Bn. Irish Guards.

2. The above Battalions will move complete with 1st Line and Train Transport and all authorized stores, including accoutrements, steel helmets, Box Respirators, full scale of clothing and necessaries, and two blankets per man.

3. Officers and Other Ranks attending Courses of Instruction will not accompany these Units but will rejoin them later on completion of the Course.

4. All men of the above Battalions, who are detached or employed in the Corps Area will be recalled and rejoin their Units.

Nominal Rolls as pro-forma will be rendered to reach this office by 6 p.m. on 6/2/18 :-

Regtl. No.	Name.	Unit.	Nature of Employment.

5. All men attached to Machine Gun Companies and Trench Mortar Batteries will return to their Units under arrangements to be made by O.C. Units concerned.

A limited number of specially selected men, attached to Machine Gun Companies who are fully qualified Machine Gunners, will be transferred to the Machine Gun Guards.

6. The above named Units will forward to D.H.Q. Nominal Rolls of all Officers, Warrant Officers, N.C.O's and men returning from leave, or Courses in the United Kingdom, who will return to this Country on or after the 7th February 1918, to reach this Office not later than 6 p.m. on 6th instant.

7. All Officers, W.O's, N.C.O's and men proceeding on leave now onwards, will be warned that their destination on return will be 31st Division Railhead and NOT Guards Division Railhead.

H.Q. Guards Division.　　　　　　　　　Lieutenant-Colonel,
5th February, 1918.　　　　　　　　　　A.A. & Q.M.G., GUARDS DIVISION.

SECRET. Copy No. XI

4th. Battalion GRENADIER GUARDS' Order No. 157.

Ref. Maps (sheet 51.b.N.W.
         (sheet 51.c.
                                                        February 11/1918.

---

1. 4th. Guards Brigade (less 3rd. Battn. Coldstream Guards) will move into the 31st. Divisional Area on the 11th. and 12th. insts., and from 12 noon, 12th. inst. will be in Divisional Reserve.

2. (a). The Battalion will march on 12th. inst. to VILLAGE CAMP, ECOIVRES, (F.15.b.2.4) by road ANZIN St. AUBIN – CHAUSSEE BRUNEHAUT – road junction F.9.c.3.1 – road junction F.14.a.8.8 – road junction F.13.b.5.6.
   (b). The Head of the Battalion will pass the Starting Point – ROND POINT, ARRAS – at 9/40.a.m.
        Order of March:-
             B.H.Q.,
             Drums,
             No. 1 Coy,
             " 2 "
             " 3 "
             " 4 "
             Transport.
   (c). Dress – Service Dress Marching Order.....Steel helmets and Jerkins will not be carried.
   (d). After the first halt an interval of 100 yards will be maintained between Companies, and between the Battalion and the Transport.
   (e). Supply & baggage wagons of Guards Divl. train will march with Transport

3. (a). All blankets (rolled in bundles of ten), steel helmets and jerkins will be collected at Company Headquarters, and a guard of 1 man left in charge, with rations for the following day.
   (b). Officers' kits and surplus stores will be collected under arrangements to be made by the Quartermaster, who will communicate same direct to all concerned.

4. A billeting party under Captain V. CHAPMAN, M.C., will meet the Staff Captain at the Road Junction F.21.b.60.95. at 9/0.a.m.

5. Battalion Headquarters will close at ARRAS at 9/0.a.m and re-open at the new billets on completion of the move.

                                            A. Hardinge
                                                           Lieut.,
Issued at 2/30 pm   Asst. Adjt. 4th. Battalion Grenadier Guards.

Copies Issued to:-

        1. No. 1 Company.   2. No. 2 Company.
        3. No. 3 Company.   4. No. 4 Company.
        5. 2nd-in Command.   6. Quartermaster.
        7. 4th. Gds. Bde.   8. Captain V. Chapman, MC.
        9. Medical Officer.   10. Sergeant Major.
       /11. War Diary.   /12. War Diary.

Account of raid on the night of the 19th. Feby,1918,
made by Germans against the 4th. Battalion
GRENADIER GUARDS. Reference Map MAROEUIL 1/20,000
and rough sketch attached.

The 4th. Guards Brigade, which had been formed on the 11th. Feb,1918, came under orders of the 31st. Division on the same date, and moved into the new Divisional area. The 4th. Battalion was billetted in VILLAGE CAMP, ECOIVRES.

On the 17th. February, the 4th. Battalion Grenadier Guards moved into the front line at ARLEUX en GOHELLE, relieving the 18th. Battalion Durham Light Infantry.

The 2nd. Battalion Irish Guards moved into the RED Line, and were in support.

This was the first tour in the trenches of the newly formed Brigade, and the 4th. Battalion Grenadier Guards were the first battalion of the new Brigade to go into the front line.

The event is of historical interest to the Regiment, but has importance in other respects.

The new line that was taken over from the D.L.I. was an example of the new system of holding in depth.

The Brigade frontage was 2000 yards in length and held by one battalion, which constituted an outpost line.

The original continuous front line of trenches was held very lightly by posts at long intervals supported some thousand yards in rear by a trench known as the ARLEUX LOOP SOUTH & NORTH, where Battalion Headqrs. was situated, with No. 3 Company less one platoon, and a platoon of No. 4 Company.

The portion of the line selected by the enemy for his attack was in the area held by No. 2 Company. The purpose of his attack was to secure identification, and, if possible, capture company headquarters at the junction of BENEDICTINE & BRITANNIA trenches.

The Commanding Officer was aware that the arrival of a fresh battalion in the line would be likely to be observed by the enemy, and that therefore a raid was highly probable - further, a prisoner who came into the lines of the D.L.I. before relief took place stated that the enemy suspected the presence of the Guards, and intended to shortly make a raid to confirm the fact. Nothing however was definitely observed to indicate the exact time or locality.

The Commanding Officer of the 2nd. Battalion Irish Guards went the round of the trenches with the Commanding Officer, they being shortly due to relieve, at about 7.p.m on the 19th.

The night was fine with a slight mist. The moon had already risen.

The two Commanding Officers were actually at posts 13 & 14 at 8.p.m, and from there returned to their respective Battalion Headquarters.

At 8.p.m a concentrated bombardment was put down on the front line from OAK POST on the left to the junction of ALBERT & TOMMY on the right.

The shells used were 5.9, 4.2, 77.mm and light and heavy trench mortars. Numbers 7,8,13 & 14 posts were subjected to shrapnel, but not trench mortar or H.E.

The bombardment was of such an intense character on BRITANNIA & BENEDICTINE and SEVERN, that great portions of the trenches were obliterated.

Standing at Battalion Headquarters in ARLEUX LOOP South, a clear view of the front line was obtained. The first S.O.S rocket went up on the left of OAK POST, and brought down our barrage with very little delay opposite the S.O.S. - the conclusion drawn was that the battalion on our left was attacked - later, an S.O.S. went up from No. 2 Company's Headquarters, and was repeated by Battalion Headquarters. The Liaison artillery officer suspected that the first S.O.S. was a false alarm, and confirmation was obtained by telephoning to No. 4 Company on the left.

This enabled the endangered area to be protected by an adequate concentration of artillery, but valuable time had been lost, and the raiders reached our line, having passed through an unnecessarily thin barrage.

The artillery fire of both sides continued till 9/45.p.m, when it died away, and was succeeded by complete quiet.

The Intelligence Officer was sent up at 9/30.p.m to report on the situation, and obtain identification if any, and was followed shortly afterwards by the Commanding Officer.

Evidence of the single surviving prisoner, and the statements of our own men enables the whole episode to be reconstructed accurately.

-2-

The raid, which was planned by the Regimental Staff of the 469th. I.R., was carried out in two sections, each of one offizier stellvertrepen and about 28 O.R. - in all the raiders numbered sixty.

Practice trenches made from aeroplane photographs had been dug in BEAUMONT, and the party were repeatedly trained in the attack. All the men who took part had been withdrawn from the line three weeks before the event, and well fed and looked after. Every man was specially selected for the enterprise, and the raiders were the pick of the 469th I.R. in physique and other qualities making them suitable for the work in hand. Their equipment was of high quality, and carefully thought out, consisting of short light rifle, 1917 pattern with leather sling, trench dagger, automatic pistol, wire cutters, watches and canvas bag for carrying stick bombs.

The instructions issued, and confirmed on a captured map, were to raid the junction of TEE & BRANDY, Nos. 13 & 14 Posts, Company Headquarters and Nos 7 & 8 Posts.

Shortly after the enemy barrage came down, the men in No. 8 post saw a strong party advancing down BRANDY from TEE, and a fierce fight commenced. Seeing the they were outnumbered, the garrison of No. 8 fell slowly back on No. 7 post.

Captain BENSON, at Company Headquarters, shortly after the bombardment commenced, sent Lieut. WRIXON to find out the exact position: this officer arrived, having passed through the heavy barrage, just as No. 8 was falling back on No. 7, and took charge.

He concentrated the men of Nos. 7 & 8 in No. 7 Post, and a short length of BEER, and prepared to defend the post to the last. He now had a combined bombing and Lewis gun post at his disposal, 2 NCOs and twelve men in all.

The enemy advanced along BRANDY, split into two parties and some continued to bomb up the trench; but the major portion got out of the trench and made across the open towards BEER, roughly moving parallel to BRANDY.

Private FLETCHER, No. 1 of the Lewis gun team in No. 7 post, saw the party, and fired at them. Several dropped, and the remainder disappeared carrying some of their wounded with them. At the same time, the enemy bombing party in BRANDY ceased bombing, and it is presumed joined their comrades in flight.

Hardly was the party disposed of than Lieut. WRIXON saw another party advancing up BEER: the danger appearing from this unexpected quarter decided Lieut WRIXON to meet it half-way - he advanced down BEER to attack the enemy and shot the first man dead with his revolver. His next opponent threw a bomb at him, which burst within a few feet without wounding him.

Pte. COLES, who was behind Lieut. WRIXON, killed the second man with his rifle at point blank range, after which a note was sounded on a bugle, and the enemy made off. The bugle was captured.

During the fight, the Germans attempted a ruse by calling out in English, "Take off your gas respirators and return to your support line"

Lieut. WRIXON heard some of our men repeat these instructions, which they thought came from an officer, and quickly countermanded the supposed order.

A totally distinct fight had taken place at Nos. 13 & 14 posts, generally known as ALTON POST.

This position was generally held by a machine gun protected by a bombing post. On the night of the 19th., a R.E. officer was working with a party of his men at the M.G. dug-out. The machine gun was knocked out by the first few shells of the barrage, and a small party of Germans rushed at the post out of the dark immediately afterwards.

Corporal HORAN, who was in charge of the bombing post, disabled three of their number with well-directed bombs, but one very tall German, and possibly some more, broke through and proceeded to throw bombs down the entrance of the dug-out, nearly killing the R.E. officer.

This officer ran round to another exit, and again narrowly escaped a second bomb before he got out into the open. In the meantime, a Grenadier named Pte. MOORE, attached to the R.E., closed with the German and was stabbed to death.

Corporal HORAN arrived on the scene with his rifle, and shot the German, after which no more was seen of the enemy.

This wounded German, refusing to surrender, was killed.

The casualties suffered were - one man of the battalion attached to the R.E. killed in ALTON Post by trench dagger - one man wounded by bomb, and five by shell fire, one of whom subsequently died.

The enemy left two dead and five wounded in our line; of the latter, four died of their wounds, and the sole survivor was a Sergeant Major (Acting Officer), and he was also very dangerously wounded, and who afterwards gave valuable information. He has survived his wounds.

A German deserter who came over to the IRISH Guards after the Battalion had been relieved reported that the enemy losses were 5 killed, 10 missing, 18 severely wounded.

It is clear that the enemy incurred heavy additional losses by our Lewis machine gun fire and bombing as he retired to his own line.

Apart from the bravery of Lieut. WRIXON and Corporal HORAN and Pte. COLES, several men distinguished themselves in various ways.

Pte. TAYLOR, who had been sent back from No. 8 post to fetch bombs from No. 7 post ran into a party of Germans round a traverse, and was taken prisoner. He was told on pain of death to lead the Germans to No. 14 post, and feigned to be willing to do so. Suddenly, the Germans changed their minds, and told him to lead them to their own lines.

Instead of doing so, he led them to No. 8 post, and when a few yards off, shouted a warning to the garrison and threw himself on the ground.

The men of the garrison threw bombs and advanced; the Germans abandoned their prisoner and fled.

Pte. CUNLIFFE, a stretcher-bearer, behaved with great gallantry, helping to rescue Pte. TAYLOR, and repeatedly passed through heavy shell fire to bring in wounded, and dress their wounds.

The Germans failed to obtain an identification of any kind, either in the form of a prisoner or any equipment which would tell them anything of value.

They lost probably half their number in casualties, and generally received a very severe blow to their moral.

The Officer, 2 NCOs and 12 men had defeated an attack by four officers and 60 specially trained and selected Germans after a preliminary bombardment of exceptional severity.

The reasons for the failure of the Germans cannot be attributed to their lack of courage or foresight; the enemy were extremely brave and determined, and the operation was carried out with vigour and astuteness.

Among the causes that led to their defeat were the presence of bombs in every post, whether a bombing post or Lewis gun post, and the ability of all ranks in their use. The keenness of our men to come to close quarters instead of acting purely on the defensive, and the able manner in which Lieut. WRIXON handled his men, and the splendid example of personal bravery he set to all ranks, and to the good Trench Discipline which prevailed in No. 2 Company.

G Pilcher.
Lt.Colonel.

Febry.23/1918.   Commanding 4th. Battalion Grenadier Guards.

"A" Form
MESSAGES AND SIGNALS.
Army Form C. 2121

SECRET

App 16.9

TO:
No 1 — Q — 1.0
2 —
3 — 45th Bde — War Diary
4 — 2. J. Gds

Sender's Number: S.D.15
Day of Month: 20
AAA

1. (a) The 2 S.G will relieve the Batt. on 21st in the FRONT LINE.

(b) No 3 Cy (2 S.G) will relieve No 3 Cy (4 G.G) Support
    2 — 4 — OAK
    4 — 2 — ARLEUX
    1 — 1 — TOMMY

(c) C.H.Q and 1 guide per platoon (4 plat guides for No 1 Cy 2 Cy, 4 unarmed) will report to CAPT. CHAPMAN at Batt. H.Q at 10.30am. He will conduct them to the junction of THIRD & ARLEUX LOOP SOUTH where they will meet 2 S.G.

(d) The relief will be carried out by day except for ARLEUX & OAK POSTS.

	"A" Form		Army Form C. 2121
	MESSAGES AND SIGNALS.		(in pads of 100). No. of Message.........

Prefix......Code.........m. Office of Origin and Service Instructions.	Words	Charge.	This message is on a/c of	Recd. at.........m.
	Sent At.........m.		.................Service.	Date.........
	To......... By.........		(Signature of "Franking Officer.")	From .... By.........

TO { (2)

Sender's Number.	Day of Month.	In reply to Number.	AAA
*SD 15	20		

Troops for the posts will remain in ARLEUX LOOP until dusk.

(c) Dinners will be at 11.30 am.

3 (a) B HQ, No 1 Co and No 4 Coy (less OAK POST platoon) will move off to DAINVILLE RAILHEAD via TIBET when ready.
Train leaves 4.30 pm.
Take over ECURIE Hutted CAMP at A.27.c.07.

(b) No 3 Coy will take over line at BRIERLEY HILL B.14.a.5.5. when relieved (see TIBET rules).

From
Place
Time

The above may be forwarded as now corrected. (Z)

.... Censor. Signature of Addressor or person authorised to telegraph in his name
* This line should be erased if not required.

"A" Form
MESSAGES AND SIGNALS.

Army Form C. 2121 (in pads of 100).

Sender's Number.	Day of Month.	In reply to Number.	AAA
*S.D. 15	20		

(c) No 2 Coy & OAK POST PLAT. will move off to LONGWOOD B.15.a.3.4 when they will entrain at 9 p.m.

(d) Interals of 100' between platoons.

3. Maps, stores and 12 L.G. drums taken over in FOREST POST will be handed over and receipts sent to B. H. Q. by 12 noon 22nd.

4. Kits, stores for all coys (less No 3) will be sent down by ration train to-night with 15 petrol tins per coy.

5. Relief complete will be sent to B.H.Q by BAB and runner.

Ref. Map MAROEUIL 1/20,000

From N.A.C.
Place
Time 4 p.m.

S.E.C.R.E.T. WD Appx 171   Copy No 11

4th Battalion Grenadier Guards Order No 152.

Reference Map Sheet:- MARQUILL. 1/20,000.   24th February, 1918.

1. The Battalion will relieve the 3rd Battalion COLDSTREAM GUARDS in the
   BAILLEUL - WILLERVAL line tomorrow, 25th instant.

2. (a) The head of the Battalion,(less No 3 Company),will pass DAYLIGHT
       RAILHEAD at 9-0.a.m.
   (b) Order of march :-

                No 1 Company.
                Battalion Headquarters.
                No 4 Company.
                No 2 Company.

   (c) Dress:- Service Dress Marching Order with Gas Helmets at the "ALERT".
   (d) Intervals :- 200 yards between Companies West of DAYLIGHT RAILHEAD.
                     50 yards between Platoons East of DAYLIGHT RAILHEAD.
   (e) One days rations will be carried.

3. (a) No 1 Company (4th Bn Gren Gds) will relieve No 1 Company (3rd Bn C.Gds)
    " 4   "   "   "   "   "   "   "   " 4   "   "   "   "
    " 2   "   "   "   "   "   "   "   " 2   "   "   "   "
    " 3   "   "   "   "   "   "   "   " 3   "   "   "   "

   (b) No 3 Company will follow in rear of No 2 Company after No 2 Company
       has passed PRIESTLY HILL.

4. 3 Lewis Guns of No 3 Company will go on in advance under arrangements
   to be made by O.C.No 3 Company to take over the anti-aircraft position
   in ARLEUX LOOP SOUTH.

5. (a) 2 Guides for B.H.Qrs, 1 guide per Company H.Q.,and 1 guide per
       platoon for Nos 2, 3 and 4 Companies will be at B.C.B.C.O. at the
       Water Point in TIRED ALLEY.   Guides for No 1 Company at the
       junction of TOMMY ALLEY and SUGAR POST, B.16.b.8.4.
   (b) B.H.Qrs, Nos 2, 3 and 4 Companies via TIRED ALLEY.
       No 1 Company via TOMMY ALLEY.

6. Lewis Guns, fuel and dixies will be at DAYLIGHT RAILHEAD at 8-45.a.m.
   under arrangements to be made by the Transport Officer.   Guns, etc,
   will be laid out to ensure of no checking in picking up.

7. Kits, Mess stores, etc, will be collected under arrangements to be
   made by the Quartermaster, who will issue orders for their collection.

8. (a) Maps,stores,etc,will be taken over and receipts sent to B.H.Qrs
       by 2-0.p.m.25th.
   (b) The usual daily reports will be sent in by Companies.

9. Relief complete will be sent by B.A.B.Code and runner.

10. Battalion Headquarters will close at BOURIN WOOD CAMP at 9-0.a.m.
    and re-open in BAILLEUL - WILLERVAL line on completion of the relief.

Issued at ..Q... p.m.
                                                            Captain,
                                     Adjutant 4th Battalion Grenadier Guards.

Copies to :-
   1 - 4. Companies.   5. 4th Guards Brigade.
       6. Quartermaster.   7. Transport Officer.
       8. Intelligence Officer.   9. Drill Sergeant.
      10. War Diary.   11. War Diary.
  12 - 14. Retained.   15. Details.
      15. 3rd Bn Coldstream Guards.

31st Division.
4th Guards Brigade.

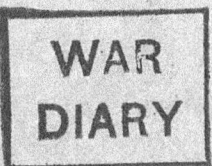

4th BATTALION

THE GRENADIER GUARDS.

MARCH 1 9 1 8

Appendices attached :-

    Report on Operations 21st to 31st
    Operation Orders.
    Map showing Corps Defence Line.

4th Battalion The Grenadier Guards.

Narrative of Events from March 21st to 31st 1918.

4th. Battalion Grenadier Guards.

Narrative of Events from March 21st. to 31st.1918.

On March 21st. the 4th. Battalion GRENADIER Guards was in billets in the CAUCOUS - SAINTREVILLE - BUNEAUCOURT Area.
During the day a heavy bombardment was heard in the distance.
The 4th. Guards Brigade, as part of the 31st. Division, was in General Headquarters reserve.
About midnight, an order was received from Brigade warning the battalion to be ready to embus on the 22nd. at 8.a.m: this warning was later confirmed, but the time of embussing was changed to 10.a.m.
The Battalion completed e-bussing by 10/30.a.m, and the complete 4th. Guards Brigade was moved to BLAIRVILLE via St.POL and DOULLENS.
During the early morning, shells were heard passing over at a great height: when passing through St.POL, it was discovered that the enemy had commenced a systematic bombardment of the back areas with his high velocity guns, paying special attention to St.POL.
The busses arrived at BEAUMETZIRI about 6/30.p.m, and remained there for an hour and a half whilst the Commanding Officer and Brigadier went forward in a motor to reconnoitre.
On receipt of a message from the Commanding Officer, the busses moved forward through BLAIRVILLE, and the troops debussed at the cross-roads west of BOISLEUX au MONT.
The Transport, which had left IDICOURT at 8.a.m in the morning, proceeded by a cross-country route to BLAIRVILLE, and the cookers arrived at the cross-roads and distributed hot food to the troops about 10.p.m.
The Commanding Officer called in company commanders, a conference was held and the situation explained.
The weather was fine and cold, with a bright moon.
Standing at the cross-roads, a large fire could be seen burning on the sky-line: this proved to be the canteen at BOISLEUX au MONT which was destroyed together with many thousands of pounds worth of food to prevent provisions falling into the hands of the enemy. - looking at the event afterwards, it seemed an improvident step to have taken, as many of the British troops in the neighbourhood had had no rations, and the enemy never reached this point until four days later.
The Battalion was guided to its new position by the Commanding Officer through HAMELINCOURT, and Battalion Headquarters were established in a ravine east of the ERVILLERS-BOYELLES Road on the morning of the 23rd. of March at 3/30.a.m.
The line occupied by the Brigade ran through JUDAS FARM, and to the east of ERVILLERS: St.LEGER was in the German hands.
The IRISH Guards and the 4th. GRENADIER Guards held the front line, and the 3rd. COLDSTREAM Guards were in support.
The dispositions were as per map attached.
During the morning, messages arrived from the Brigade that the enemy had broken through at MORY, and that our right flank was in danger: this was contradicted in the afternoon, and our troops were in touch with troops on their right in the Army line throughout this period.
An order issued to the Battalion to feel their right and take over from the 40th. Division was never carried out because the troops on our right refused to move, stating they had no orders.
On the morning of the 23rd., there commenced a most harassing shelling of our trenches by our own guns, causing the IRISH Guards and the 4th. GRENADIER Guards casualties: every effort was made to stop the shelling, but without avail:(2nd.Lt.A.J.NIBBY was wounded during this shelling).
About 10.p.m on 23rd. Brigade issued orders for a side step to the right of a thousand yards, the object being to close any gaps which might be forming at the threatened area near MORY: the 3rd. COLDSTREAM Guards dug a new line in support of the new position: this side-step to the right was eventually carried out by the 2nd. IRISH Guards, who were in position on the morning of the 24th, but found no troops on their right, and were then in a very precarious condition.
Short-shooting by our guns continued all day intermittently.

-2-

An inter-company relief was ordered, and took place on the night of the 24th., Nos. 1 & 4 Coys. occupying the switch line, and 2 & 3 the Army line. Nos. 2 & 3 Coys. had undergone a very severe test during their occupation of the switch line: they had been heavily shelled by the Germans and our own artillery - they had fired 20,000 rounds of S.A.A. and inflicted heavy losses on the enemy, who were moving about their front.

During the whole day, rumours of trouble on the right succeeded each other, and, finally, the news arrived that the 40th. Division would retire during the night to a new line, and be relieved by the 42nd. Division, which latter would still remain in touch with the 51st. Divn. All troops were warned against spies dressed as British Officers spreading false reports.

The weather was still fine.

About 10.p.m. Battalion Headquarters moved to a quarry in the SENSEE valley about 1000 yards to the right of the original position: the dug-out occupied was a deep one, and shell-proof.

The original headquarters was taken over by a battalion of the Durham Light Infantry under Colonel CARTER.

The weather was still fine with a bright moon.

On arrival at the new Headquarters the quarry was put into a state of defence, and Battalion Headquarters dug themselves fire protections facing towards MORY.

The Headquarters of the 3rd. COLDSTREAM Guards was situated 200 yards further to the right, and communication was established between the two headquarters, and a line run back from the COLDSTREAM to Brigade.

During the morning of the 25th., the companies were warned of a possible retirement under cover of darkness, and, as the day proceeded, this step seemed to become more certain.

About noon, men from line battalions began coming back from the direction of MORY towards ERVILLERS, followed by platoons led by officers, and it became certain that the line on our right had given way.

At 1.p.m the IRISH Guards Intelligence Officer, who went with the Commanding Officers IRISH & COLDSTREAM Guards to reconnoitre, reported Germans coming over the ridge on the right in large numbers: this information was passed on to the Brigade, and eventually orders were received to evacuate the line at 2.p.m. and fall back to a line N.W. of COURCELLES.

The situation when the order came for retirement was extremely difficult. It was clear that the right had given way completely.

The enemy were advancing directly against the Headquarters of the GRENADIERS & COLDSTREAMS, and there seemed little to prevent them getting behind the IRISH Guards and GRENADIER Companies in the line. The Commanding Officer withdrew Nos. 2 & 3 Companies from the army line, and placed them on the high ground behind Battalion Headquarters, where they were available under his hand to use for counter-attack in case of need.

When carrying out this order, Captain REASON, (commanding No. 2 Coy.) was wounded, but successfully evacuated owing to the gallantry of one of his sergeants - Sergeant MARSH.

The evacuation of the wounded of all ranks of the 4th. Guards Brigade was a noticeably fine piece of work - no one was allowed to fall into the enemy's hands, although the battalion Sick Sergeant of the Grenadiers and the Medical Officers of the COLDSTREAMS & IRISH Guards remained after their battalions had marched off, and with the enemy within a few hundred yards of their aid-post.

A company of the COLDSTREAM Guards was ordered to counter-attack and were being formed up, when, without any warning, our own heavy artillery poured shells onto their Battalion Headquarters and the spot where they were assembling.

This successfully defeated a counter-stroke which might have inflicted a severe blow on the enemy, and, in addition, caused many casualties to our men.

The enemy seemed unwilling to press forward against our line and defensive flank, and when it became dark on the night of the 25th., the 4th. Guards Brigade was still in its same position, with a strong defensive flank drawn back on the right.

The companies were warned to assemble at Battalion Headquarters at 9.p.m: at 9/30.p.m our own heavies commenced bombarding Battalion Headquarters, and severely wounded Captain O'BRIEN of the 2nd. Bttn: IRISH Guards.
Runners were sent slightly changing the assembly point for companies, so saving many casualties.
2/Lieut. DAWSON-GREENE, No. 2 Coy, was wounded at the assembly point.
The Battalion formed up in a sunken road to the rear of Headquarters, and moved off in perfect order at 10/30.p.m.
The march was continued to the Crucifix at MOYENVILLE, which was reached about 1.a.m on the morning of the 26th.
The battalion immediately dug a new line of trenches east of the village, and the men were supplied with hot food from the cookers, which had been sent up.
During this period the enemy shelled MOYENVILLE with his heavies, but inflicted no casualties.
At 4/30.a.m on the 26th. an order was received to fall back to AYETTE, and hand over trenches to troops in front of us.
At 6 o'clock, the battalion moved back through AYETTE to DOUCHY les AYETTE, where Battalion Headquarters was established.
At noon on the 26th., an order arrived from Brigade assigning a special role to the 4th. Battalion, namely, to occupy and fortify GURNOY Farm, and the battalion moved to the new position about 2.p.m. Nos. 3,4 & 1 Coys, in order from left to right, dug in east of the farm in a line commanding a fine field of fire, and disposed in depth. No. 2 Company was in support behind the farm, in a disused trench, near Battalion Headquarters.
An alarming message of undoubted German origin was received advising that the enemy had broken through at MOYENVILLE with armoured cars: this was later refuted.
The night of the 26th. and the morning of the 27th. passed quietly. About 2a.m, the battalion I.O. reported that troops were retiring on our left, and enquiries showed these troops to be the 93rd. Brigade. Steps were taken to warn the Brigade Headquarters.
At 4/30.p.m orders were received to reinforce the 93rd. Brigade - these were cancelled, and orders substituted to place one company each at the disposal of the 2nd. IRISH Guards and 3rd. COLDSTREAM Guards: these companies, namely nos. 1 & 2, marched off about 5.p.m, and did not come under the orders of the 4th. Battalion again until the night of relief.
The enemy had every intention, after the retirement of the 93rd. Brigade, of following up their advantage, and commenced to mass near the aerodrome outside AYETTE to the number of about 2 battalions. Our artillery, who had perfect observation, allowed the movement to be completed, and then concentrated all their fire on the spot - this force was practically annihilated, and the remainder fled in disorder.
Nos. 1 & 2 Coys., who had been placed under the IRISH Guards, now had their period of hardships. The weather became cold and wet, but despite all difficulties, they dug and improved their line, and wired in their position, and, when relieved, handed over a system of trenches which were a formidable obstacle to any further advance. Since the relief the enemy has made no further attempts on this part of the front.
On the 28th., Battalion Headquarters and the remaining two companies moved to the left, and occupied trenches dug and vacated by the 3rd. COLDSTREAM Guards.
The fine spell of weather had commenced to break, and there was a fine drizzling rain.
About midnight, Battalion Headquarters moved back into some gun pits 200 yards further back, where they stayed for the remainder of the period under review.
The 29th., 30th. & 31st. passed quietly: the artillery shelled AYETTE, otherwise there was nothing of importance to report.
The weather continued uncertain with a good deal of mist and rain.
On the night of the 31st. March/April 1st. the battalion was relieved by the 16th. Battalion Lancashire Fusiliers, and marched back to ADINFER.

—4—

The Battalion, when relieved, had completed ten days of strenuous fighting, digging and marching. The comforts of an established trench line had been unavailable, the whole period being spent in open warfare of the kind associated with the autumn of 1914.
A rearguard action had been fought amidst disconcerting rumour of disaster, and with constant threats to the flanks.
The Brigade, at times, was holding practically the entire 31st. Division's front, yet there was no sign of depression amongst the men on their arrival at BIENVILLERS - they were tired, but confident and cheerful.
It is of great regimental interest to note that in the last phase, the 4th. Guards Brigade found themselves in touch with the GUARDS DIVISION on their left, and a feeling of relief passed through all ranks when they realized that their left flank was secure, and heard how the German attacks on the Guards Division had been shattered.
The casualties incurred in view of the length of period under fire, and the close fighting, were light: namely... 4 officers and 75 other ranks.... see attached casualty list and rôll of officers engaged in the action;

Apl. 2/1918.

L. Rowe
Lt. Colonel.

Commanding 4th. Battn: Grenadier Guards.

4th. Battalion GRENADIER Guards.

List of Casualties 23/3/18 to 31/3/18.

KILLED.	26403	L/C.	Mills	L. Killed in action	23/3/18.
	24902	Pte.	Clarke	A.	"
	26154	:	Rowley	J.	"
	23239	L/C.	Brailsford	W.	24/3/18
	20679	Pte.	Cornwell	T.	"
	24957	:	Bland	H.	"
	29788	:	Woodall	H.	"
	14723	:	Ward	A.	29/3/18.
	20346	Cpl.	Keep	P.	"
DIED OF WDS.	27349	Pte.	Ayres	G. Died of Wounds	23/3/18.
WOUNDED.	23974	Pte.	Bevan	J. Wounded.	23/3/18.
	28151	:	Logie	H. "	23/3/18.
	28837	:	Wilson	J. "	23/3/18.
	30616	:	Speight	E. "	24/3/18.
	28763	:	Atkinson	H. "	"
	25650	:	Jagger	F. "	"
	28005	:	Mellor	S. "	"
	25046	L/C.	Bass	S. "	"
	26522	Pte.	Broughton	W. "	"
	29061	:	Clarke	W. "	"
	28614	:	Rees	C. "	"
	22079	:	Brown	J. "	"
	29973	:	Newman	A. "	25/3/18.
	20247	L/C.	Bullock	S. "	"
	28800	Pte.	Croker	D. "	"
	29725	:	Black	E. "	"
	10859	:	Drabble	T. "	"
	14113	:	Billings	J. "	"
	17032	Sgt.	Carpenter	L. "	"
	28098	Pte.	Goodall	A. "	"
	25935	L/C.	Moore	A. "	"
	16135	Pte.	Pellett	C. "	"
	26959	:	Jones	J. "	"
	30057	:	Ask	A. "	"
	27298	L/C.	Peters	E. "	"
	25593	Pte.	Drew	G. "	"
	28935	L/C.	Bradley	W. "	"
	23998	L/S.	Dolphin	A. "	"
	21285	L/C.	Slade	H. "	"
	26402	:	Williams	A. "	"
	23479	Pte.	Dendridge	E. "	"
	27365	:	Craig	B. "	"
	30039	:	Bonham	G. "	"
	29758	:	Hollands	G. "	"
	24246	:	Savage	A. "	"
	12945	:	Kingston	A. "	"
	28776	:	Harrison	A. "	"
	20496	L/C.	Sawyer	W. "	"
	28336	Pte.	Watts	E. "	"
	28324	:	Mawdsley	C. "	"
	26917	:	Williams	J. "	"

16939	L/C.	Smith	W.	29/3/18.	24800	Pte.	Humphries	W.	29/3/18.
28137	Pte.	Naylor	E.	29/3/18.	16498	L/C.	Buchanan	C.	29/3/18.
22351	L/C.	Nippers	W.	29/3/18.	24315	Pte.	Duffield	R.	29/3/18.
27514	Pte.	Nuttall	F.	29/3/18.	24653	:	Campkin	W.	29/3/18.
27502	:	Crewdson	F.	29/3/18.	15187	Spl.	Ellis	W.	29/3/18.
21230	Cpl.	Heyes	R.	29/3/18.	28856	Pte.	Waring	A.	29/3/18.
30594	Pte.	Fell	L.	29/3/18.	28685	:	Rose	E.	29/3/18.
26470	:	Pepall	G.	29/3/18.	24907	:	Rolph	L.	31/3/18.
25445	:	Norris	C.	31/3/18.					

Captain C.E.Benson,DSO. wounded 25/3/18.
2/Lieut A.J.Gilbey..... wounded 25/3/18.
2/Lieut C.J.Dawson-Greene..wdd. 25/3/18.
WOUNDED) Lieut. R.H.Rolfe.... wdd. at duty. 25/3/18.
AT DUTY.) 23402 Pte. Dawson G............. 25/3/18.

4th. Battalion Grenadier Guards.

Roll of officers who took part
in the battle 21st./31st.Apl.1918.

Headquarters: Lt.Colonel W.S.PILCHER, DSO. Commanding.
Captain C.R.GERARD, DSO. Adjutant.
Captain M.CHAPMAN, MC. Intelligence offr.
Captain I.H.INGLEBY. Quartermaster.
Lieut.G.W.SELBY LOWNDES. Transport officer.
Lieut.G.R.GREEN. attached for duty.

No.1 Company.

Captain H.H.Sloane Stanley, MC.
Lieut C.E.Irby, MC.
Lieut E.H.Tuckwell, MC.
2Lieut A.J.Gilbey.(Wounded).

Lt.Tuckwell came out to rear B.H.Q.,
and was replaced by 2/Lt.R.B.Osborne
26/3/18.
Lt.G.C.Burt replaced 2/Lt.Gilbey.

No.3 Company.

Lieut. F.C.Lyon.
Lieut. N.D.Thomas.
2Lieut.C.J.Dawson-Greene.(Wdd 25th).
2Lieut.I.Macdonald.(To Hospital Sick,25th).

Captain.G.C.Sloane Stanley replaced
Lt.Lyon 26/3/18, latter officer returning
to rear B.H.Q.

No.2 Company.

Captain C.E.Benson, DSO.
Lieut R.H.Rolfe.
Lieut R.L.Murray Lawes.

Lieut.Murray Lawes came out to
rear B.H.Q. and was replaced
by Lt.Hon.C.S.Rodney.
Lt.T.T.Pryce, MC went up & took
over command of Coy. 26/3/18.

No.4 Company.

Lieut.T.W.Minchin,DSO.
Lieut.N.R.Abbey.
Lieut.J.E.Greenwood.
2/Lt.R.D.Richardson.

Lt.Colonel,
Commanding 4th. Battalion Grenadier Guards.

Apl. 2/1918.

WAR DIARY

Army Form C. 2118.

WAR DIARY
or
INTELLIGENCE SUMMARY.

(Erase heading not required.)

4 Gren. Gds
Nov. 1918

Place	Date	Hour	Summary of Events and Information	Remarks and references to Appendices
ECOIVRES	Friday 1st March	12:30 AM	Battalion relieved in the line and proceeded to ECOIVRES by train. A good relief and quiet. Weather very cold. Casualties during the tour in the trenches. The details under Major Barker joined the Battalion — also the Transport. Relief orders attached as —	App 174
VILLERS-BRULIN	Saturday 2nd March	3.0 PM	Battalion moved by train to VILLERS-BRULIN area — the Division became G.H.Q. Reserve. Billets fair but scattered. Poor Training Grounds. Weather overcast — cold, misty. Scheme for training attached — Order (Battalion) for journey attached —	App 175
VILLERS-BRULIN	Sunday 3rd March		C.O. rode around Billets and made improvements. Weather showed a "clean" Rain most of the day. Battalion cleaning issued and attached on Much Rain	App 176
VILLERS-BRULIN	Monday 4th March		Adjutant's parade. Training as per Programme. Weather Col d & misty	
VILLERS-BRULIN	Tuesday 5th March		Adjutant's parade. Training as per Programme. Weather — some rain & misty. Lt. Horne returned for the Base Hospital. A draft of 48 O.R. found from the Household Battalion which had been this bombed	

Army Form C. 2118.

WAR DIARY
or
INTELLIGENCE SUMMARY.
(Erase heading not required.)

Instructions regarding War Diaries and Intelligence Summaries are contained in F.S. Regs., Part II. and the Staff Manual respectively. Title pages will be prepared in manuscript.

Place	Date	Hour	Summary of Events and Information	Remarks and references to Appendices
VILLERS – BRULIN	Wednesday 6th March	10 AM	The Major-General Commanding 31st Div. inspected the Battalion on Company Parade grounds & expressed himself very pleased with the appearance of the Battalion and Transport.	
		11 AM	Battalion received Lewis Gun Company Commanding	
		2 P.M.	No 1 & 3 Coys Musket'y Bathts at TINCQUES.	
"	Thursday 7th March		Battalion trained as per programme. Nos. 2 & 4 Coys and Transport went to TINCQUES for Baths. Battalion found a working party of 500. O.R. to relieve Irish Guards.	
"	Friday 8th March		Battalion trained as per programme. 2 i/c Command went to H. Hqs. of 2nd Bn Irish Guards at ECOIRIE to arrange details for taking over trenches on the "Brown Line" – FARBUS – BAILLEUL. Very fine weather.	

Army Form C. 2118.

WAR DIARY
or
INTELLIGENCE SUMMARY.
(Erase heading not required.)

Instructions regarding War Diaries and Intelligence Summaries are contained in F.S. Regs., Part II. and the Staff Manual respectively. Title pages will be prepared in manuscript.

Place	Date	Hour	Summary of Events and Information	Remarks and references to Appendices
VILLERS BRULIN.	Saturday March 9th	1.25 P.M.	Battalion under Lt in Command marched off from VILLERS BRULIN to entrain at TINCQUES at 3.0 P.M. for ECURIE Rl. Ht.	
		4.30 P.M.	Arrived at RLwer Stn & guides of 9th Infantry Brigade were met and Staff Guides conducted companies to their billets in dug-outs near "Brown Line" from Battalion Hq: at ECURIE just North of FARBUS to South of BAILLEUL. Lewis Guns arriving with Transport shortly afterwards were kept after leaving Transport just left VILLERS BRULIN for BR4Y and ECURIE at 12.0 midnight. Details under Capt with part of Transport under Captain G.C. Sherwin Shanley encamped at QUESTREVILLE for training. Brigade and Battalion orders	A+F. 176
ECURIE.	Sunday March 10th	9.0 A.M.	Very fine hazy morning. 2 Lt in Command with 6rd kits.	
		6.P.M.	Wire received from XIII Corps to embus at MADAGASCAR CORNER. Buses	

WAR DIARY
or
INTELLIGENCE SUMMARY.
(Erase heading not required.)

Army Form C. 2118.

Place	Date	Hour	Summary of Events and Information	Remarks and references to Appendices
			to be at MADAGASCAR CORNER at 9.0 P.M. Battalion bus immediately ordered to rendez-vous at MADAGASCAR CORNER.	
		10.45 P.M.	All embussed. Neuville 2nd in Command went to H.q. 63rd Div: to ascertain destination of Battalion. Destination proved to be CHELERS.	
		10.30 P.M.	Transport started to reach CHELERS at 5.30 A.M. having dropped No.1 Coy. at BETHENCOURT and No.2 Coy. at TINQUETTE. Battalion reached CHELERS about 3.0 A.M. Batt: Hq: established with Brigade in Chateau, CHELERS. Batt: got settled in Billets by 4.0 A.M.	
CHELERS.	Monday 11th March 1918		Very fine day. Battalion rested. 2nd in Command had round Billets & decided to collect them next day.	
		4.0 P.M.	Battalion H.q. moved to BETHENCOURT	

Army Form C. 2118.

WAR DIARY
or
INTELLIGENCE SUMMARY.

(Erase heading not required.)

Instructions regarding War Diaries and Intelligence Summaries are contained in F. S. Regs., Part II. and the Staff Manual respectively. Title pages will be prepared in manuscript.

Place	Date	Hour	Summary of Events and Information	Remarks and references to Appendices
BETHENCOURT	Tuesday March 12th		Details rejoined companies and Battalion took over billets as detailed in Batt: Orders attached.	APP. 177.
			No: 2 & 3 Coy & 100 men of No 1 had billets at TINCQUES. Billets fairly good but very scattered.	
"	Wednesday March 13th		Training to her programme in orders attached. Remainder of Battalion billeted at TINCQUES.	APP. 178.
		3:0 pm	Bct: beat Brigade Hq: at Football in Div: Competition.	
"	Thursday March 14th		Training as per programme in orders attached.	APP. 179
BETHENCOURT	Friday March 15th		Coys trained as per Training Scheme heads Time. Battalion played 3rd Batt: Coldstream Guards in Final Football Competition. Batt: drew 2 all. The Field Marshal C-in-C awarded for gallantry in the field the Military Cross. the Distinguished Conduct Medal to Lieutenant M P.S. NIVEN. No 20177 Sergeant M. HORAN. No 28835 Pte. L. TAYLOR. No 21495 " J. CUNLIFFE. No 14228 " T. FLETCHER.	

Army Form C. 2118.

WAR DIARY
or
INTELLIGENCE SUMMARY.
(Erase heading not required.)

Instructions regarding War Diaries and Intelligence Summaries are contained in F. S. Regs., Part II. and the Staff Manual respectively. Title pages will be prepared in manuscript.

Place	Date	Hour	Summary of Events and Information	Remarks and references to Appendices
	March		The Corps Commander awarded the Military Medal to 8663 Pte Cole, 29983 Pte Temple for gallantry in the field. All the above awards were for the Raid on the Battalion on night 15th Feb - 20th Feb.	
BETHENCOURT	March 16th Saturday		Companies trained under Training Scheme. Football match v 1st Batt? Coldstream Guards. Draw 2 - all. 2/Lieut J. Macdonald joined the Battalion. Weather fine.	
BETHENCOURT	March 17th Sunday		Voluntary Services. Divisional Running Competition. Battalion was 4th. Rugby match v Divisional Artillery. Result 2A-14 pnts: Batt? 12 points. Weather fine.	App 18o
BETHENCOURT	March 18th Monday		Training as per scheme attached as App. Football match v 3rd Batt? Coldstream Guards. Battalion beaten by 1 - 0. Weather fine and warm.	
BETHENCOURT	March 19th Tuesday		Training as per Scheme. Weather fine. Much rain.	

Army Form C. 2118.

WAR DIARY
or
INTELLIGENCE SUMMARY.
(Erase heading not required.)

Instructions regarding War Diaries and Intelligence Summaries are contained in F. S. Regs., Part II. and the Staff Manual respectively. Title pages will be prepared in manuscript.

Place	Date	Hour	Summary of Events and Information	Remarks and references to Appendices
BETHENCOURT	March 31st		Training as per programme. Some rain. at C.R.D. Stand took over command of 4th G.B. T.M.B.	
BETHENCOURT	March 31st		Brigade Field Day. Orders attached as App. German Bombardment of our lines served to the same Brigade order to move at once received.	App 18.
	11.30 P.M.			
	21st March to 1st April		Operations from March 22nd to April 1st will be attached as Narrative with Casualty reports when etc.	

b. S. Fletcher
Major 4th Battalion
Grenadier Guards

War Diary

SECRET.   Copy No. 15

4th. Battalion GRENADIER GUARDS' Order No. 160.

Reference Map sheet:- MARŒUIL 1/20,000.   28th. Feb, 1918.

---

1. (a). The Battalion will be relieved by the 8th. Bttn: King's Own Yorks.
   Light Infantry on March 1st. in the Support Line.
   (b). Companies will be relieved in the following order:-
       'A' Company, K.O.Y.L.I. will relieve No. 1 Coy.(4/G.G.) via TOMMY.
       'D'   .... 4 .... via TIRED.
       'B'   .... 2 ....
       'C'   .... 3 ....
   (c). 1 guide for Battalion Headquarters, 1 for Company Headquarters and 1
       per platoon (except for No 1 Coy, who will send 5 guides under an
       officer to be at DAYLIGHT RAILHEAD at 9/30.a.m via TOMMY) will report
       at Battalion Headquarters at 8.a.m; Lieut. M.D.THOMAS will conduct
       the guides to DAYLIGHT RAILHEAD.

2. Maps, Stores, Schemes etc will be handed over, and receipts obtained,
   which will be sent to Battalion Headquarters by 12 noon, March 2nd.

3. Relief complete will be reported to Battalion Headquarters by S.A.B. and
   runner.

4. (a). After relief, companies will proceed to DAYLIGHT RAILHEAD (No. 1 Coy.
       via TOMMY, remainder via TIRED) where they will entrain at 1/30.p.m.
   (b). Companies that arrive before the entraining time will form up as
       follows:-
              No. 1 Company along No. 1 Post,
               " 2   "   " 2 "
               " 3   "   " 3 "
               " 4   "   " 4 "
       Care will be taken to remain concealed as much as possible.
   (c). Detrain at ECOIVRES (F.14.c.80.55) at 3.p.m, and march to VILLAGE
       CAMP, F.13.b.2.4.
              Order of March:-
              Bn. H.Qrs,
              No. 1,
              No. 2,
              No. 3,
              No. 4.

5. Lewis guns and dixies will be carried out to DAYLIGHT RAILHEAD; separate
   orders for kits, etc have been issued.

6. O.C., Details will send a party of 1 Officer, 1 NCO. for Battalion Hqrs.,
   and 1 per Company to report to Staff Captain at VILLAGE CAMP, F.13.b.2.4
   at 11.a.m on 1st. March.
   Guides will meet the battalion at the place of detrainment.

7. (a). Transport will be relieved by 187th. Infantry Brigade.
   (b). Lines will be notified in the ECOIVRES Area.
   (c). They will be clear of present lines by 10/30.a.m.

8. Details at the Transport will march to ECOIVRES under orders to be issued
   by O.C. Details.

9. Orders for the 22 other ranks from each company to be attached to 2nd.
   Battalion IRISH Guards will be issued separately.
   Lieut. T.T.PRYCE, M.C, will command the party.

10. Battalion Headquarters will close in the BAILLEUL - WILLERVAL Line on
    completion of relief, and re-open at VILLAGE Camp, ECOIVRES after the move

                                                                    Captain,
Issued at 2/10.p.m.   Adjutant 4th. Battalion Grenadier Guards.

Copies issued to all concerned.

SECRET.   Copy No. 12.

4th. Battalion GRENADIER GUARDS' Order No. 161.

Reference Map: LENS 11.1/100,000.   March 1/1918

1. The Battalion will proceed to the VILLERS BRULIN area tomorrow, 2nd. March, and will come into G.H.Q. reserve.

2(a). The Battalion will march to ECOIVRES Station, where it will entrain. The head of the Battalion will leave the camp at 2/15.p.m.
 (b). Order of March:-
                Bttn:Hqrs.
                    1,
                    2,
                    3,
                    4.
 (c). Interval of 100 yards between companies.
 (d). Dress:- Service Dress Marching Order.

3. Officers' kits, Stores etc, and Lewis guns will be at the Transport lines by 11/15.a.m.

4. Dinners will be at 11/30.a.m.

5. On arrival at TINQUES, the Battalion will detrain, and march off in the following order to places as stated:-
        Battalion Headquarters)
        No. 2 Company.   )   VILLERS BRULIN.
        No. 4 Company.   )
        No. 3 Company.   BETHONSART.
        No. 1 Company.   OUESTREVILLE.
    Intervals.......... 100 yards between companies.

6. Transport will move to OUESTREVILLE under orders to be issued by O.C. Transport.

7. A billeting party, under Captain M.CHAPMAN,MC, will parade at Battalion Headquarters at 11/25.a.m. 1 NCO. from Battalion Headquarters, and 1 NCO. per company. Company strengths will be brought.

8. Lieut. T.T.PRYCE, MC, will report to Captain FURZE, 4th. Guards Brigade at 2.p.m at ECOIVRES Station. He will take 1 NCO. from his company with him.
   Entraining stat will be sent to Battalion Headquarters by companies by 11.a.m.

9. Battalion Headquarters will close at VILLAGE Camp, ECOIVRES at 2.p.m, and re-open at VILLERS BRULIN on completion of the move.

                                            C. Stead
                                                        Captain,
Issued at 11.p.m.   Adjutant 4th. Battalion Grenadier Guards.

Copies issued to:-
    1. No. 1 Company.   2. No. 2 Company.
    3. No. 3 Company.   4. No. 4 Company.
    5. Captain M.Chapman, MC.   6. Lieut.T.T.Pryce, MC.
    7. Transport Officer.   8. Quartermaster.
    9. 4th. Guards Brigade.   10. Sergeant Major.
    11. War Diary.   12. War Diary.

SECRET.

Copy No. 12.

4th. Battalion GRENADIER Guards' Order No. 162.

Ref. LENS Map 1/100,000. March 8/1918

1. (a). The Battalion (less Details) will replace the 2nd. Bn. IRISH Guards in the forward area for work under XIII Corps tomorrow, 9th. inst.
   (b). Each company will find 125 other ranks.

2. (a). The Battalion (less Details) will march to TINCQUES Station, where it will entrain for ECURIE.
   (b). The head of the Battalion will pass the starting point (junction of VILLERS BRULIN - GUESTREVILLE and VILLERS BRULIN - BETHONCOURT roads) at 1/25.p.m.
   (c). Order of March:-
   > Battalion Hqrs.
   > No. 2 Coy,
   > No. 4 Coy,
   > No. 3 Coy,
   > No. 1 Coy.

   Intervals. 100 yards between companies.
   Dress. Service Dress Marching Order with Steel helmets, and Gas respirators at the ALERT.
   Each man will carry one blanket rolled in the waterproof cape, and 150x rounds.

3. On arriving at the detraining point, companies will march direct to their respective positions, with 100 yards between platoons.

4. (a). Officers' kits, stores, dixies, Lewis Guns and 20 magazines per company will be collected at Company Headquarters at about 8.a.m. tomorrow under arrangements to be made by the Quartermaster, and taken to ECURIE Station, where they will be picked up by companies)
   (b). All surplus kits, blankets, etc. will be collected under arrangements to be made by the Quartermaster, and stored at GUESTREVILLE.

5. All ranks left behind will be billeted in GUESTREVILLE: companies will arrange that their parties are marched there under an officer after the remainder of the company has gone; if no officer is available, under the senior N.C.O.
   Captain G.C.Sloane Stanley will allot billets to companies.

6. The Transport will move to BRAY under orders of the Transport Officer.

7. Dinners tomorrow will be at 12 noon.

8. Battalion Headquarters will close at VILLERS BRULIN at 2/30.p.m, and re-open at ECURIE on completion of the move.
   All correspondence (except URGENT, which will be sent by cycle orderly) will be marked D.R.L.S., and be sent via usual channels.

(signed) Captain.

Issued at 10/30.p.m. Adjutant 4th. Battalion GRENADIER Guards.

Copies to....
1 No. 1 Company.   2. No. 2 Company.
3 No. 3 Company.   4. No. 4 Company.
5 2nd in Command.   6. Quartermaster.
7 Transport Officer.   8. Captain G.C.Sloane Stanley.
9 4th. Gds Bde.   X. Sgt. Major.
11 War Diary.   12. War Diary.

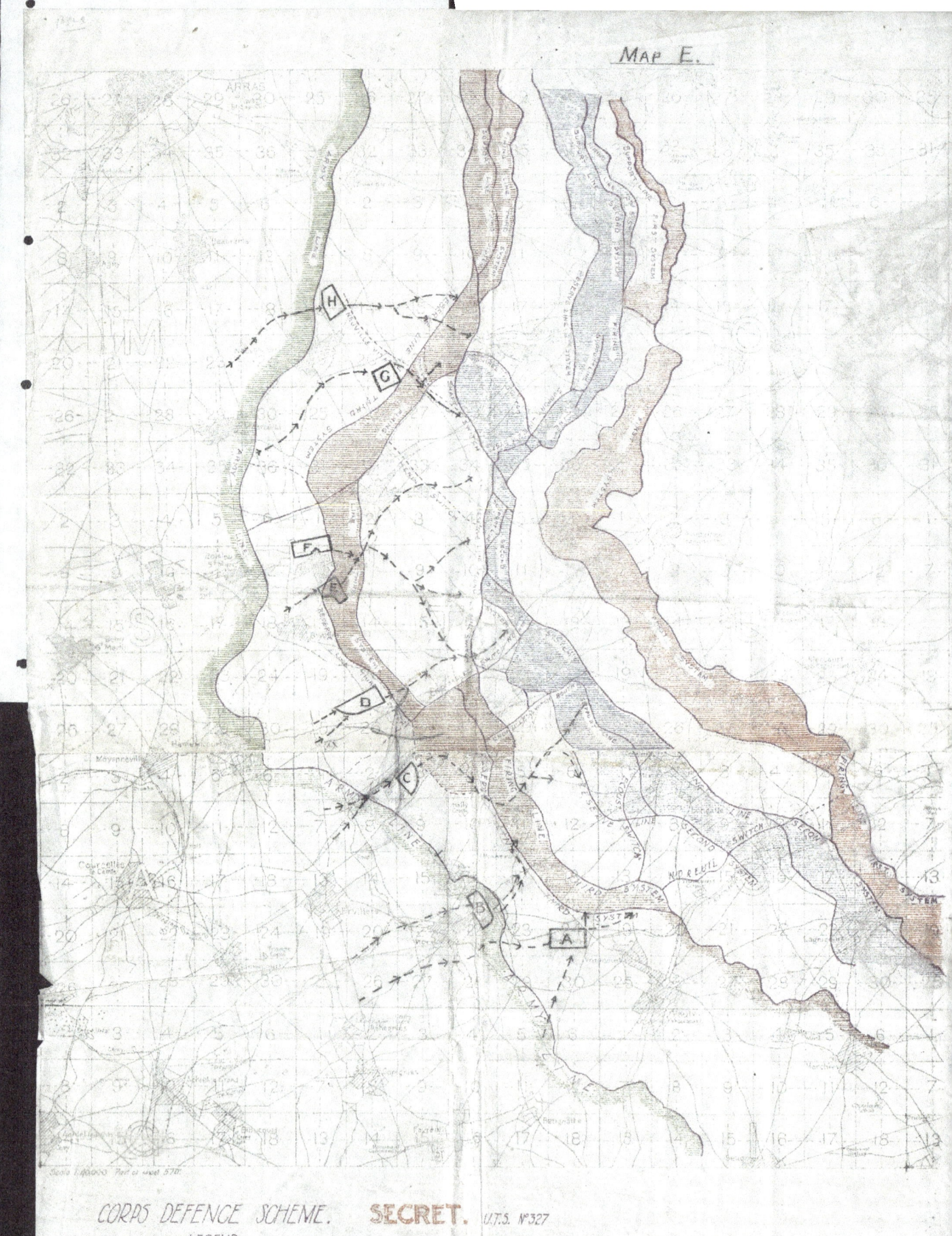

WO 95
1226/2

4 Btth Grenadier Guards
War Diary
April 1918

4th Guards Brigade.

31st Division.

WAR DIARY

4th BATTALION

GRENEADIER GUARDS

APRIL 1918.

Appendices under separate cover

4 Gds / 31

Army Form C. 2118.

4 Grenadier Gds

S.1 4 0

WAR DIARY
or
INTELLIGENCE SUMMARY.
(Erase heading not required.)

20.

Places	Date	Hour	Summary of Events and Information	Remarks and references to Appendices
VILLERS BRULIN	2nd April		Battalion moved by Bus from SOHERN. Weather fine. Visit T.T. Pryce M.C. took over command of No 2 Company from 2nd Lieut [?] was the first time with the Battalion and strength of Battalion attached. Heavy officers & recruits attached to Battn. details attached.	App 882 App 15?
VILLERS BRULIN	3rd April		Battalion general clean. Kit inspection. Officers [?] inspected by Two Coys (No 2 – No 4) to VILLERS BRULIN. Two Coys (No 1 – 3) JETHOUSART. Captain G.H. Knowles D.S.O. was transferred as 2nd in command to 1st Battn.	
VILLERS BRULIN	4th April		Companies trained under Coy Commanders. Adjutants Parade of No 2 – 4 Coys. Weather fine dull.	
VILLERS BRULIN	5th April		Adjutants Parade. Conference. General weather fine. Battalion platoon football match.	

Army Form C. 2118.

WAR DIARY
or
INTELLIGENCE SUMMARY.
(Erase heading not required.)

Place	Date	Hour	Summary of Events and Information	Remarks and references to Appendices
VILLERS BRULIN	6th April		Adjutants Parade – Company Training – Men rank & shaft of 930. O's arrived, all men who had previous service with the Battalion gas helmet inspection by Div Gas Officer. Battalion went to Baths at TINCQUES	
VILLERS BRULIN	7th April Sunday		Voluntary Church Service. C.O's Conference at Brigade H.Q. Some rain. Battalion went to Baths at TINCQUES. Lieut C.S. Nash M.C. Lieut R.H. Est 2/Lieut R.P. Philipps } Joined the Battalion 2/Lieut H.V. Stratford Army Commanders message attached as	App 183
VILLERS BRULIN	8th April Monday	Roth offences	C.O's parade. 2 Trained with Company Commanders	
VILLERS BRULIN	9th April Tuesday		Battalion paraded for a Practice Ceremonial under the Brigadier at TINCQUES. Advance Party of 10 men under Major Walker M.C. proceeded. Afterwards Missing Rifles	

Army Form C. 2118.

WAR DIARY
or
INTELLIGENCE SUMMARY.
(Erase heading not required.)

Place	Date	Hour	Summary of Events and Information	Remarks and references to Appendices
VILLERS BRULIN	10 April Wednesday		Review by G.O.C. 31st Div at TINCOURT of 4th Guards Brigade. The G.O.C. complimented the Brigade on its appearance. Sound of very heavy firing from the BETHUNE - ESTAIRES district. Captain G.C. Sloane Stanley allowed to proceed to April Captain XIII Corps Agricultural officer for duty. Orders for Brigade Reviews attached Batts received orders to entrain that evening to proceed northwards to take part in the battle around MERVILLE and ARMENTIERES.	App 184
12 Midnight April 10th - 11th April			Account of entrain of Battalions with Casualties Reports, Maps, Messages etc attached as	App 185

WAR DIARY
or
INTELLIGENCE SUMMARY.

(Erase heading not required.)

Army Form C. 2118.

Place	Date	Hour	Summary of Events and Information	Remarks and references to Appendices
BORRE	14th April Sunday		Left Brigade HQ at 2.30 AM with Batt. HQ arrived 1500 hrs. Battalion stopped at GRAND-LE-SEC-BOIS till 7.15 AM. Arrived BORRE 8.15 AM. not at TURKELING. On conducted MTBetts to billets between BORRE and HAZEBROUCK. Battalion has organised into 3 Companies of 3 Platoons each and has been asked to consider No 1 Coy Captains No 10 2 E NEEDHAM and be known as No 1 Coy P.P. Signor Ellen	
BORRE	15th April Monday		Battalion Cleaned up and reorganised dur[ing] day. Made up. C.O.'s Conference at Brigade H.Q. where the to be held is case of attack were pointed out. Battalion Church service when ser[mon] practice under Lt. Tuckwell.	
BORRE	16th April Tuesday		Lewis gun team practice under Lt. Tuckwell Physical Exercise for rest of Battalion	

WAR DIARY or INTELLIGENCE SUMMARY

Army Form C. 2118.

Place	Date	Hour	Summary of Events and Information	Remarks and references to Appendices
			Battalion Shelled in Billets. Third hit with no shell which killed 3 men & wounded 5 men including C.S.M. PETTITT. Batt moved in afternoon about 2 miles away to LA KREULE. Weather fine. Casualties attached as App.	App 82
LA KREULE	17th April Wednesday		Left LA KREULE and marched to Billets near LA HALTE just South of HAZEBROUCK. C.O. in conference with Brigadier. When orders were given. Brigade and Batt Orders Fr 16 to Fr 17 th attached. A Composite Battn formed of 8 Batts with 2 R.B. Constituting the 2nd line to the history of the Brigade - as under 4th & Suffolk formed Regiments - to be Commanded by O-448 Suffolks. Coy booked in supporting 2nd line around HAZEBROUCK	App 87
LA HALTE	18 April Thursday		Coys booked in supporting 2nd line around HAZEBROUCK. Quiet day. Some rain.	

Army Form C. 2118.

Army Form C. 2118.

WAR DIARY
or
INTELLIGENCE SUMMARY.
(Erase heading not required.)

Instructions regarding War Diaries and Intelligence Summaries are contained in F. S. Regs., Part II. and the Staff Manual respectively. Title pages will be prepared in manuscript.

Place	Date	Hour	Summary of Events and Information	Remarks and references to Appendices
LE TIR ANGLAIS	19th April Friday		Battalion took over from 2nd Australian & 9th Battns. Coys moved off a.m. Billets LE TIR ANGLAIS. Batt. HQrs. Reg. Shelter also 3 Coys being found. Cover with Cos as 2nd in Command. Batt. as Support to the Brigade. Batts. order and Brigade order attached as Map	App 88
LE TIR ANGLAIS	20th April Saturday		Battalion found working parties. Commander kept round front line. 2/Lt. Richardson severely wounded, the other offrs. also reported to died of wounds on 23.4.April	
LE TIR ANGLAIS	21st April Sunday		Coys a Fat. Sue keen front line. Enemy shelled by day shell by night	Funk holes

WAR DIARY
or
INTELLIGENCE SUMMARY.
(Erase heading not required.)

Army Form C. 2118.

Place	Date	Hour	Summary of Events and Information	Remarks and references to Appendices
			The Corps Commander awarded Military Medals to the following N.C.O's and Men for gallantry in the field during recent operations above of ST LEGER and South of ARRAS and of ERVILLERS	
			No 20356 L-Sgt A Marsh No 24343 Pte J Smith No 21884 Pte J Long	
			No 28442 L/Cpl A Perrin No 27952 Pte H Read No 28383 Pte J.R. Gee	
			No 12911 Pte J Varlington No 20123 Pte G Bone	
			No 23665 Pte R.L. Saunders 26620 Pte D. McCoog 22014 Pte E. Parry	
Fontaine	21st Apr Monday		Lt ROLFE was killed by an Enemy shell during the night. Heavy Enemy bombardment with gas = H.E. Battn relieved 12 RoyIr in front line. References as per map to App 188. Battn a d Brigade orders attacked as t The Composite Battn ceased to Exist ? at 12 p.m and 4 Shropshire, Fusiliers and 3 Bn Essex made separate Battns	App/169

Army Form C. 2118.

WAR DIARY
or
INTELLIGENCE SUMMARY.
(Erase heading not required.)

Instructions regarding War Diaries and Intelligence Summaries are contained in F. S. Regs., Part II. and the Staff Manual respectively. Title pages will be prepared in manuscript.

Place	Date	Hour	Summary of Events and Information	Remarks and references to Appendices
Montluc as before	2.3rd April		Quiet. Relief but one Battn obliging a Coy Rds No Casualties. Relief complete 11.30 p.m though impeded by fire shells. searchlights	
			Quiet day. Rival guards had a successful raid. Capturing prisoners. Battn co-operated by sending forward a Lewis gun in the right flank. There lay Russian On Range. was excellent. Some shelling retaliation	
	24th April		Quiet day on our front 3rd CLG relieved 2nd on 18. Our left Our Artillery put down normal counterpreparation Hostile Artillery light.	
	25th April		Quiet day. On Artillery active. Heavy gun fire in distance. Batts relieved by 12th R.Oxford LI in evening. Relief complete by 12 midnight.	

WAR DIARY or INTELLIGENCE SUMMARY

Army Form C. 2118.

Place	Date	Hour	Summary of Events and Information	Remarks and references to Appendices
			Batt^n r Brigade orders attacked as —	App 19c
			list of Casualties during the 5 days in the line	App 19
			The Battn has formed into 2 Coys of 3 Platoons ea.	
			The following officers went up with the Battery:	
			Battn H^Qs Lieut Colonel H.S. Pilcher Adjutant Captain C.R. Gerard	
			Lieut Henry Lowe	
			No 1 Coy No 2 Co	
			Captain Hinde P.E. Needham Lieut C.E. Irby	
			Lieut E. Thelwell Mr Gregor-Ellis	
Farm nr 26th Apr 16			Battalion viewed Gas & Foot Inspection and has	
PRIEST s of HAZEBROUCK			to End few shell been Batt Hqs 2 men	
			wounded.	

A.5834 Wt. W4973/M687 750,000 8/16 D.D. & L. Ltd. Forms/C.2118/13.

Army Form C. 2118.

WAR DIARY
or
INTELLIGENCE SUMMARY.
(Erase heading not required.)

Place	Date	Hour	Summary of Events and Information	Remarks and references to Appendices
HONDEGHEM	27 April		Battalion moved off to HONDEGHEM as a relief by 1st Battn. Dublin Fusiliers. Battn. and Brigade Relief orders Billets fair. Weather fine	App 192
HONDEGHEM	28 April Sunday		C.O's inspection of Billets. Divine Service by Coy. Routine attached Battn. Orders showing	App 193
HONDEGHEM	29 April Monday		Battn. found working party of 200 o.R. and 3 officers. Rest of Battalion trained in the instruction of Lieut Trethewell to learn from training. The following Officers joined the Battalion — are posted as follow:- 2/Lieut Ho. S.E. Markam No 1 Co. Officer A.H. Morris No 2 Co.	

A.5834 Wt. W4973/M687 750,000 8/16 D. D. & L. Ltd. Forms/C.2118/13.

WAR DIARY
or
INTELLIGENCE SUMMARY.
(Erase heading not required.)

Army Form C. 2118.

Place	Date	Hour	Summary of Events and Information	Remarks and references to Appendices
			The Corps Commander under authority granted by His Majesty the King awarded the MILITARY MEDAL to the following NCOs and men for gallantry in the field - operations on 11th, 12th, 13th April	
			No 15985 Sgt. H. Hodkinson No 21811 Pte. T. Jennison No 26304 Pte R.	
			No 13279 L/Sgt T. Tapp 21744 " T. Katzenett Newport	
			No 20907 Cpl. B. Newell 21851 " I. Askey 26394 Pte J.	
			No 17358 L/Cpl A. Louth 23402 " J. Dawson Pbern	
			No 21465 Pte H. Round 26281 " St. Smith 26887 Pte T. Robinson	
30 Alfred Houdain Tuesday			Coy Training under Company Commanders. Inspired exercise. Full Scheme for Platoon Lewis Gun Training. Weather fine. The following awarded by Granted for gallantry Italian Bronze Medal for Military Valour No 11511 C.Q.M.S. Price late No 1 Co	

Army Form C. 2118.

WAR DIARY
or
INTELLIGENCE SUMMARY.
(Erase heading not required.)

Place	Date	Hour	Summary of Events and Information	Remarks and references to Appendices
			List of Officers serving with the Battalion Strength of Battn. 2/Lieut A.F. Huington joined the Battn. and is posted to No. 2 Co.	App 194 App 195

B Pilcher
LIEUT.-COL.
COMMANDING 4TH BATTN. GRENADIER GUARDS.

4th Battalion Grenadier Guards.

Particulars of casualties period 17th to 25th April 1918.

Killed:

	Lieut. R.M.Rolfe.	Killed in Action.	22-4-18.
17127	L/C F.Dean.	do	do
23892	Pte J.Dyer.	do	do

Died of Wounds.

	2/Lieut.R.D.Richardson.	Died of Wds.	26-4-18.	Wounded.	21-4-18.
15531	Sergt.H.Hackett.	do	22-4-18.	Wounded.	22-4-18.

Wounded.

8748	Sgt.F.Darton.	Wounded.	22-4-18.	25254	Pte Stenner C.	Wd.	22-4-18
26500	Pte J.Wilson.	do	do	24957	Pte J.Thurston.	do	
27611	Pte R.Dickinson.	do	do	25649	Pte W.Flayle.	do	
25641	Pte J.Knight.	do	do	27427	Pte B.Kersey.	do	
25975	Pte C.Crayford.	do	do				

Gassed.

12954	Sgt Foxon H.	Wd.Gas 23/4/18.	11846	Sgt W.Waters.	Wd.Gas 24th.
21882	L/C F.Clapton.	do	27362	Pte G.Hodgson.	do
29621	Pte A.Barnes.	do	21547	Pte J.Mayo.	do
26517	Pte H.Smart.	do	25074	Pte T.Dore.	do
29673	Pte C.Thorpe.	do	20630	Pte F.Phillips.	do
21465	Pte H.Round.	do	22184	Pte E.Haynes.	do
29724	Pte W.Rawson.	do	23641	Pte G.Humphries.	do
21511	Pte J.Wilkinson.	do	28357	L/C F.Petford.	do
25528	L/C H.Haynes.	do			

26th April,1918.

Lieut-Colonel,
Commanding 4th Battalion Grenadier Guards.

Copy No .....8....

4th Battalion Grenadier Guards Order No S.O.22.

Reference Map Sheets:- 36.c.N.E. 1/20,000.
27.S.E.1/20,000.   27th April, 1918.

1. The Battalion will be relieved today, 27th inst by 2 Companies 1st Battn Royal Dublin Fusiliers.

2. (a) After relief the Battalion (less details and transport) will march to HONDEGHEM.(V.2.d.5.9.).
   (b) Order of March :-

      Drums.
      B.H.Q.
      No 1 Company.
      No 2 Company.

   (c) Starting point:- On road 100 yards West of Battalion Headquarters.
   (d) Time :- As soon as relieving unit arrive - probably about 5 p.m.
   (e) Guides meet the Battalion cross roads V.7.b.4.5.
       Distances 100 yards between companies.
   2 cookers Dress :- Service Dress Marching Order, steel helmets to be worn.
   (f) Lewis Gun limbers, Bomb and S.A.A. limbers will accompany the Battalion.

3. (a) Details, transport, etc, (less Lewis Gun limbers, bomb and S.A.A. limbers, will leave their billets at 3.p.m. and be conducted to the new area by their billetting N.C.O's.
       100 yards interval between every six vehicles will be maintained.
   (b) O.C. Details will leave one N.C.O. to hand over to incoming unit.

4. A billetting party under Lieut R.L. Murray Lawes will report to B.H.Q. at 9-30.a.m.

5. Kits, stores, blankets, etc, will be collected at 1-p.m.
   Lewis Gun limbers will report loaded to B.H.Q. at 2-p.m.

6. On arrival in the new area the Battalion will come into Corps Reserve and will be under 1 hour's notice to move.

7. Battalion Headquarters will close at E.6.d.8.8. after relief and re-open at HONDEGHEM (V.2.d.1.9.) on completion of the move.

Issued at ...8.45 a.m........   _____ Captain,
                                              Adjutant 4th Battalion Grenadier Guards..

Copies issued to :-

   1. O.C. No 1 Coy.   2. O.C. No 2 Coy.
   3. Quartermaster.   4. Transport Officer.
   5. O.C. Details.   6. 4th Guards Brigade.
   7-8. War Diary.   9-12. Retained.

Some lessons to be learnt...... Summarised.

(i). Ammunition to be pushed up at all costs; the battalion fired over 110,000 rounds.

(ii). The use of rifle grenades in this enclosed country.

(iii). Stokes Mortar would have been useful.

(iv). The necessity of bold action with Lewis guns.

(v). Snipers in considerable numbers to be pushed forward in front of our lines.

(vi). The necessity of concealing trenches. This is due to the fact that the Germans bring up their field guns, and fire over open sights.

(vii). The urgent necessity of training of officers and men in open warfare.

(viii). That 70% of the men should carry shovels as part of their equipment.

(ix). The holding of roads over the streams at all costs as a form of strong points.

(x). The pushing forward of our field guns to deal with advanced German field guns.

(xi). F.O.O. with a line and telephone; this proved invaluable to the battalion.

16th. April, 1918.

Lt. Colonel,
Commanding 4th. Battalion Grenadier Guards.

4th Guards Brigade.
31st Division.

4th BATTALION

GRENADIER GUARDS

APRIL 1918.

NARRATIVE OF EVENTS.
CASUALTIES.
Lists of Officers etc.

App. 182

4th. Battalion Grenadier Guards.

List of Officers present with the Battalion on April. 2/1918.

```
Lt.Colonel W.S.Pilcher, DSO.      Commanding.
    Major C.F.A.Walker, MC.       2nd.in Cmmd.
    Captain C.R.Gerard, DSO.      Adjutant.
    Captain M.Chapman, MC.        Intllgce. Officer.
    Captain I.H.Ingleby.          a/Quartermaster.
    Lieut. G.W.Selby Lowndes.     Transport Officer.
    Lieut. E.H.Tuckwell, MC.      I/c. Lewis Guns.

Captain H.H.Sloane Stanley,MC.    Commdg. Company.
Captain G.C.Sloane Stanley.       Commdg. Company.
    Lieut. T.W.Minchin, DSO.      Commdg. Company.
    Lieut. T.T.Pryce, MC.         Commdg. Company.
    Lieut. F.C.Lyon.
    Lieut. Hon A.H.L.Hardinge,MC. Assistant Adjt.
    Lieut. C.E.Irby, MC.
    Lieut. Hon.C.C.S.Rodney.
    Lieut. N.R.Abbey.
    Lieut. M.D.Thomas.
    Lieut. G.R.Green.
    Lieut. G.C.Burt.
    Lieut. J.E.Greenwood.
    Lieut. R.H.Rolfe.
    Lieut. R.L.Murray Lawes.
    2/Lieut R.D.Richardson.
    2/Lieut R.B.Osborne.
```

<u>Detached</u>. Lt.(a/Capt).C.G.Keith,MC.....attd. 3rd.Gds.Bde.HQ.
    2/Lieut. D.J.Knight........attd. 4th.Gds.Bde.HQ.
    Lieut. M.P.B.Wrixon,MC....Hospital (Gas poisoning).
    2/Lieut.I.Macdonald........Hospital (Sick).

4th Battalion Grenadier Guards.

Casualty List for period 12 - 13th April 1918.

Officer Casualties.

Captain J. Chapman, M.C.	Killed in Action.	12-4-18.
Captain H.H. Sloane Stanley, M.C.	do.	12-4-18.
Lieut. V.R. Abbey.	do.	12-4-18.
Captain J.T. Minchin, D.S.O.	Wounded.	12-4-18.
Lieut. C.E. Nash, M.C.	do.	12-4-18.
Lieut. R. Treen.	do.	12-4-18.
Lieut. J.L. Greenwood.	do.	12-4-18.
Lieut. D.C. Burt.	do. & Missing	12-4-18.
2/Lieut. M.D. Osborne.	Wounded	12-4-18.
Captain T.T. Pryce, M.C.	Missing.	13-4-18.
Lieut. Hon. C.C.S. Rodney.	do.	13-4-18.
Lieut. P.J. Cox.	Wounded & Missing.	13-4-18.
Lieut. J.D. Thomas.	do.	do	13-4-18.
Lieut. P.O. Lyon.	do	do	13-4-18.
2/Lieut. T.T. Millions.	do	do	13-4-18.
2/Lieut. E.D. Stratford.	do	do	13-4-18.
2/Lieut. T.W. Sich.	do	do	13-4-18.

Other Ranks.

Killed.

28847	L/C	Allen	P.	K/A. 12-4-18.	20723	Pte	Beesley	C. " 12-4-18.
10404	Sgt	Buckle	E.	" 12-4-18.	25401	Pte	Broughton	G. " 12-4-18.
20348	Pte	Brown	G.	" 13-4-18.	25037	Pte	Bridges	F. " 13-4-18.
28063	Pte	Collings	A.	" 13-4-18.	24203	L/C	Cadman	J. " 13-4-18.
28078	Pte	Attridge	G.	" 13-4-18.	28775	Pte	Davies	D. " 13-4-18.
21835	L/C	Deade	G.	" 13-4-18.	10901	Pte	Darlington	" 13-4-18.
20718	Pte	Frence	W.	" 12-4-18.	28804	Pte	Harris	G. " 13-4-18.
18308	L/S	Hinks	P.	" 13-4-18.	20505	Pte	Gittus	" 13-4-18.
20379	Pte	Jarvis	J.	" 12-4-18.	21860	Pte	Gallagher	J. " 13-4-18.
20170	Pte	Griffiths	M.	" 13-4-18.	24740	Pte	Pitcher	J. " 13-4-18.
	Pte	Judy	G.	" 13-4-18.	26507	L/C	Swallow	H. " 13-4-18.
20086	Pte	Smith	T.	" 13-4-18.	20138	Pte	Thayre	R. " 13-4-18.
27082	Pte	Willis	L.	" 12-4-18.	25110	L/C	Wilton	A. " 14-4-18.
14049	Sgt	Brewster	A.	" 13-4-18.				

Wounded.

11511	C.Q.M.S.	Price	W.	Wdd. 12-4-18.	13312	2nd	Greenhar	A. W/dd 13-4-18.
22430	L/C	Lang	B.	" 13-4-18.	20197	L/C	Houston	R. " 13-4-18.
37247	L/C	Price	R.	" 12-4-18.	25847	L/C	Taylor	R. " 13-4-18.
27582	L/C	Marshall	A.	" 13-4-18.	25705	Pte	Burns	R. " 13-4-18.
28854	Pte	Haverstock	J.	" 12-4-18.	27757	Pte	Cowley	G. " 13-4-18.
13825	Pte	Clayton	W.	" 13-4-18.	21411	Pte	Dicker	R. " 13-4-18.
19122	Pte	Dixon	J.	" 12-4-18.	24970	Pte	Cunliffe	T. " 13-4-18.
12502	Pte	New	R.	" 12-4-18.	20691	Pte	Hall	J. " 13-4-18.
25820	Pte	Harris	C.	" 12-4-18.	21000	Pte	Hilton	J. " 13-4-18.
20061	Pte	King	W.	" 12-4-18.	18355	Pte	Medhurst	" 13-4-18.
23502	Pte	Longridge	A.	" 13-4-18.	10002	Pte	Newton	J. " 13-4-18.
25030	Pte	O'Neill	J.	" 13-4-18.	17346	Pte	Peaty	A. " 13-4-18.
20580	Pte	Pepper	W.	" 13-4-18.	27130	Pte	Reeves	E. " 13-4-18.
26506	Pte	Smallwood	J.	" 13-4-18.	25644	Pte	Slogrett	R. " 13-4-18.
29703	Pte	Terry	H.	" 13-4-18.	10535	Pte	Burns	M. " 13-4-18.
13834	Pte	Barfitt	T.	" 13-4-18.				
13317	Cpl	Swambrill	H.	" 13-4-18.	17297	L/C	Scott	C. " 13-4-18.
30292	Sgt	Wood	S.	" 13-4-18.	15703	Sgt	Drake	F. " 13-4-18.
11041	Cpl	Moore	J.	" 13-4-18.	22177	L/C	Moran	H. " 13-4-18.
26606	Cpl	Watts	H.	" 13-4-18.	28154	L/C	Chappell	F. " 13-4-18.
6730	L/C	Wilkins	C.	" 13-4-18.	18704	L/C	Odle	C. " 13-4-18.
20198	L/C	Wilkins	H.	" 13-4-18.	27814	Pte	Butterworth	" 13-4-18.
20055	Pte	Britton	A. Susp.	12-4-18.	9776	Pte	Chilten	W. " 13-4-18.
10949	Pte	Ireland	J. Wdd.	14-4-18.	25161	Pte	Elsworth	W. " 13-4-18.
7010	Pte	Krager	B. "	13-4-18.	24697	Pte	Fisher	L. " 13-4-18.

Sheet 2.

Wounded.(contd).

25400	Pte	Halliday	A.	Wdd.	12-4-18.	28519	Pte Huggins	J. Wdd.	12-4-18.
27690	Pte	Halstead	J.	"	12-4-18.	29864	Pte Hutchins	J. "	12-4-18.
26040	Pte	Hawse	A.	"	12-4-18.	27547	Pte Johnson	D. "	12-4-18.
27532	Pte	Hoad	J.	"	12-4-18.	29550	Pte Jellock	R. "	12-4-18.
12410	Pte	Moore	H.	"	12-4-18.	29199	Pte Lee	S. "	12-4-18.
29711	Pte	Preston	W.	"	12-4-18.	29677	Pte Poynter	H. "	12-4-18.
11173	Pte	Richardson	A.	"	12-4-18.	29526	Pte Reay	J. "	12-4-18.
15818	Pte	Smith	J.	"	12-4-18.	28034	Pte Standish	L. "	12-4-18.
27403	Pte	Todd	W.	NYD(N)	12-4-18.	29991	Pte Thomas	D. "	12-4-18.
28292	Pte	Tatlock	J.	Wdd.	12-4-18.	27720	Pte Trethowan	R. "	12-4-18.
9805	Pte	Whitney	W.	"	12-4-18.	28529	Pte Watson	J. "	12-4-18.
18175	C.S.M	Eastorman	G.	"	12-4-18.	9192	L/C Smith	M. "	12-4-18.
21173	Pte	Asbury	P.	"	12-4-18.	26872	Pte Bancroft	J. "	"
24817	Pte	Bizzell	N.	"	"	29133	Pte Chambers	A. "	"
25570	Pte	Clayton	J.	"	"	29107	Pte Dale	D. "	"
29249	Pte	Glover	A.	"	"	21272	Pte Gill	J. "	"
28511	Pte	Jones	R.	"	"	29747	Pte Saviére	J. "	"
25541	Pte	Searle	R.	"	"	28401	Pte Silvester	W. "	"
29825	Pte	Nutter	L.	"	"	29405	Pte Turner	O. "	"
29751	Pte	Vince	B.	"	"	30899	Pte Willcocks	A. "	"
28729	Cpl	Henton	T.	"	"	17223	L/C Hatley	S. "	"
17200	Pte	Bagshaw	J.	"	"	27622	Pte Bracknool	J. "	"
21041	Pte	Bishop	A.	"	"	28049	Pte Craft	J. "	"
24942	Pte	Corlett	R.	"	"	29078	Pte Cumming	R. "	"
29249	Pte	Clutterbuck	F.	"	"	29890	Pte Cooper	H. "	"
12776	Pte	Hodgson	A.	"	"	29214	Pte Holmes	R. "	"
27488	Pte	Knight	G.	"	"	28464	Pte Mason	A. "	"
26704	Pte	Lunford	R.	"	"	27761	Pte Patrickson	W. "	"
29027	Pte	Richardson	J.	"	"	26900	Pte Simpson	A. "	"
27357	Pte	Shuttleworth	B.	"	"	25722	L/C Sleeman	A. "	"
✱ 11550	L/Cpl	Barrett	G.	"	12-4-18.	15850	L/C. Oddy	C. "	"
10599	L/Cpl	Pettitt	T.	"	16-4-18.	30252	Pte Peers	G. "	16-4-18.
26228	Pte	Warburton	N.	"	"	29722	Pte Robinson	W. "	16-4-18.
23235	"	Harris	W.	"	"	29169	- Bolton	E. "	"

Wounded (at duty)

30240	Pte	Brooks	G.	at D.	12-4-18.	12608	Pte Scott	W. at D.	"
27326	Pte	Wheeler	A.	"	"	26721	Pte Starling	J. "	"

Killed.

31177	Pte	Johnson	B.	K/A.	15-4-18.	26550	Pte Tideswell	J. K/A. 15-4-18.
			10680	Pte Tweddle	R.	K/A. 16-4-18.		

✱ Died of Wds 13/4/18.

Sheet 4.

Missing.

No 1 Company.

20019	Sgt	Trotter	J.	13th.	15580	L/S	Mulvey	J.	13th.
30327	Cpl	Whitehurst	T.	"	20224	L/C	Lee	A.	"
28845	L/C	Partington	W.	"	25631	L/C	Parker	J.	"
12404	L/C	Atkins	A.	"	16732	L/C	Shipman	W.	"
30024	L/C	White	F.	"	23015	L/C	Hidden	G.	"
30307	L/C	Ling	A.	"	21573	L/C	Rastall	C.	"
37853	L/C	Buxton	S.	"	29378	Sgt	Taylor	G.	"
34002	L/S	Fesey	J.	"	27440	Pte	Astleford	C.	"
20794	Pte	Atkins	T.	"	27449	Pte	Barker	J.	"
16804	Pte	Branchflower	W.	"	27813	Pte	Bancroft	R.	"
24654	Pte	Boswell	R.	"	28480	Pte	Burton	R.	"
31770	Pte	Barber	G.	"	26316	Pte	Carter	L.	"
27470	Pte	Cox	H.	"	27687	Pte	Courtenay	W.	"
80005	Pte	Christiansen	S.	"	29783	Pte	Crook	F.	"
18009	Pte	Clarke	J.	"	30093	Pte	Clarke	J.	"
24071	Pte	Davey	H.	"	29842	Pte	Denny	F.	
27494	Pte	Evans	E.	"	28859	Pte	English	W.	(now Wdd)
30035	Pte	Erdeser	L.	"	18925	Pte	Cook	J.	"
28825	L/C	Prince	J.	"	25926	L/C	Edwards	C.	"
30117	L/C	Broadfoot	J.	"	25833	L/C	Saunders	W.	"
25752	Pte	Fancourt	F.	"	26474	Pte	Gibson	G.	"
27510	Pte	Gardiner	F.	"	20029	Pte	Goodsell	D.	"
30596	Pte	Gower	E.	"	30021	Pte	Glaister	H.	"
20400	Pte	Herrington	C.	"	20154	Pte	Hobson	C.	"
20574	Pte	Heath	C.	"	29002	Pte	Handover	R.	"
18581	Pte	Hindman	R.	"	16600	Pte	Hogg	S.	"
29051	Pte	Harrison	W.	"	20101	Pte	Ingram	W.	"
23448	Pte	Jay	H.	"	27409	Pte	Jackson	J.	"
37831	Pte	Jarvis	W.	"	29080	Pte	Lawey	J.	"
29791	Pte	Lindop	J.	"	30601	Pte	Langley	G.	"
22303	Pte	Munn	J.	" (now wdd)	25220	Pte	Moseley	B.	"
26691	Pte	Milburn	J.	"	30609	Pte	Montague	G.	"
18946	Pte	Moody	H.	"	28035	Pte	Patch	H.	"
85551	Pte	Packer	R.	"	27434	Pte	Parker	P.	"
26808	Pte	Sewkill	S.	"	21590	Pte	Small	L.	"
17909	Pte	Sanderson	C.	"	28770	Pte	Stafford	C.	"
20414	Pte	Sporton	E.	"	33665	Pte	Saunders	R.	"
30712	Pte	Taylor	W.	"	27076	Pte	Thew	C.	"
29954	Pte	Towill	A.	"	26075	Pte	Taberner	C.	"
26894	Pte	Walker	C.	"	27457	Pte	Wooldridge	S.	"
29957	Pte	West	G.	"	30621	Pte	Wilkins	A.	"
30624	Pte	Walkley	S.	"	25702	Pte	Street	C.	"
24343	Pte	Smith	T.	" (now Wdd)	30817	Pte	Stephenson	H.	"

No 2 Company.

17116	Sgt	Ferris	W.	13th.	20556	L/S	Marsh	H.	13th.
21778	L/S	Ainscow	H.	"	19274	L/C	Ratcliffe	A.	"
30245	L/C	Newbury	H.	"	21361	Pte	Askey	L.	"
28705	Pte	Atkins	F.	"	28255	Pte	Barton	R.	"
28925	Pte	Barrett	W.	"	30125	Pte	Bent	J.	"
0563	Pte	Coles	W.	"	~~29713~~	~~Pte~~	~~Cumbria~~	~~G.~~	~~"~~
28176	Pte	Chadwick	F.	"	27253	Pte	Clarke	J.	"
29390	Pte	Lunny	E.	"	31650	Pte	Dale	A.	"
8184	Pte	Evans	J.	"	31739	Pte	Fullard	J.	"
26122	Pte	Fuller	C.	"	28432	Pte	Gill	R.	"
27823	Pte	Harvey	A.	"	29389	Pte	Harrison	E.	"
30041	Pte	Harper	W.	"	18925	Pte	Joyce	A.	"
17720	Pte	Jones	D.	"	25654	Pte	Kitchingham	H.	"
29062	Pte	Lilham	F.	"	20172	Pte	Lees	F.	"
28992	Pte	Lockley	A.	"	24448	Pte	Lane	A.	"
20516	Pte	Marsh	D.	"	28195	Pte	Moore	J.H.S.	"
30362	Pte	Newstead	J.	"	15937	Pte	Price	A.	"
24463	Pte	Prior	A.	"	26982	Pte	Park	T.	" (now Wdd)
14932	Pte	Powell	A.	"	27482	Pte	Rowbotham	S.	"
30795	Pte	Ray	T.	"	28029	Pte	Richardson	S.	"
25631	Pte	Roden	H.	"	26261	Pte	Smith	E.V.	"
29709	Pte	Shanks	C.	"	29925	Pte	Sumner	C.	"
30044	Pte	Skidmore	J.	"	24393	Pte	Thorpe	L.	"
28251	Pte	Taylor		"	24294	Pte	Thornton	A.	"

Sheet 4.

Missing.No 2 Company.(cont).

21309	Pte	Threlfall	T. 13th.	27755	Pte	Whitelock	J. 13th.
26090	Pte	Wills	W. "	26006	Pte	Warburton	W. "
~~21151~~	~~Pte~~	~~Wood~~	~~A. "~~	29856	Pte	Wilks	J.W. "
30620	Pte	Westall	J.O. "	21095	Pte	Waller	R. " (now Wdd)
29600	Pte	Whitbread	W. "	27309	Pte	White	T. "

No 3 Company.

10918	Sgt	Bull	H. 13th.	11121	Sgt	Blackmore	H. 13th.
7395	Sgt	Palethorpe	T. "	21175	Cpl	Kemp	C. "
21868	Cpl	Pearson	A. "	18706	Cpl	Orpwood	W. "
25692	L/C	England	V. "	19514	L/C	Boulton	F. "
26651	L/C	Jones	C.T.R. "	28126	L/C	Taylor	H. "
25626	L/C	Backhouse	A. "	16339	L/C	Norris	C. "
17304	L/C	Oakden	F. "	19978	L/C	Wathern	R. "
25152	L/C	McCormack	M. "	13764	L/C	Birch	W. "
19566	L/C	Hennessey	L. "	21754	L/C	Harkin	A. "
25133	L/C	Janes	W. " (now wdd)	26559	L/C	Donegani	K. "
26504	Pte	Alderson	J. "	21751	Pte	Arrowsmith	R. "
25157	Pte	Brignall	J. "	16625	Pte	Bond	J. "
29019	Pte	Berry	W. "	26905	Pte	Beetle	M. "
21565	Pte	Barrow	A. "	19703	Pte	Barrell	T. " (now Wdd)
29806	Pte	Bussey	G. "	20194	Pte	Brown	W. "
26393	Pte	Bennett	H. "	27312	Pte	Cooper	A. "
29486	Pte	Coyne	T. "	25575	Pte	Chambers	A. "
29967	Pte	Dimmick	H. "	15296	Pte	Evans	J. "
30693	Pte	Earnshaw	A. "	29021	Pte	Finch	C. "
28081	Pte	Griffen	E. "	27508	Pte	Gilham	R. "
29320	Pte	Gover	A. "	30016	Pte	Griffiths	J. "
30014	Pte	Grief	R. "	26816	Pte	Gould	H. "
18721	Pte	Maycock	S. "	25820	Pte	Hollobone	F. "
29995	Pte	Hawkridge	L. "	9580	Pte	Harris	H. "
29064	Pte	Haines	A. "	25231	Pte	Huntley	R. "
26582	Pte	Heyne	E. "	29687	Pte	Jones	H.W. "
29972	Pte	Jackson	I. "	26766	Pte	Jones	L. "
25059	Pte	Kean	R. "	30702	Pte	Kitchen	J. "
26964	Pte	Lawrenson	J. "	21768	Pte	Langford	A. "
20522	Pte	Millward	J. "	26193	Pte	Miller	G. "
29409	Pte	Mortimer	W. "	26874	Pte	Middleditch	J. "
29449	Pte	Mottram	T. "	27117	Pte	Meaker	A. "
28999	Pte	Nunn	W. " (now Wdd)	27053	Pte	Nuttall	G. "
29760	Pte	Prebble	J. "	27320	Pte	Parsons	L. "
27346	Pte	Perkins	F.J. "	27302	Pte	Potts	A. "
26290	Pte	Partt	S. "	1129	Pte	Roberts	J. "
29785	Pte	Russell	A. "	26444	Pte	Roberts	H. "
25377	Pte	Rouse	L. "	21646	Pte	Shopstone	P. "
27550	Pte	Scott	H. "	25241	Pte	Smallwood	G. "
29297	Pte	Sutterby	A. "	30025	Pte	Sketcher	F. "
26102	Pte	Stott	J. "	21522	Pte	Shotbolt	W. "
21739	Pte	Shaw	W. " & Hosp. 11/4/18.	15493	Pte	Toon	E. "
24593	Pte	Tranter	W. "	26557	Pte	Tomlinson	H. "
24079	Pte	Tracey	L. "	30022	Pte	Thomas	K. "
17233	Pte	Treherne	W. "	29727	Pte	Vickers	J. "
26883	Pte	Wilson	F. "	27512	Pte	Wooliscroft	W. "
30783	Pte	Warrell	G. "	26470	Pte	Webber	E. "

Sheet 5.

Missing (continued).

No 4 Company.

19475	L/S	Barton	R.	15th.	27464	L/S	Ayres	A.	17th.
20002	Sgt	Stafford	R.	"	15067	Sgt	Streeter	E.	"
24776	L/S	Swift	N.	"	22148	L/C	Curtis	C.J.	"
24263	L/C	Clements	T.	"	24920	L/C	Chalmers	J.	"
23841	L/C	Cattanach	A.	"	10550	L/C	Charnley	L.	"
27030	L/C	Jibson	J.	"	25508	L/C	Honewood	A.	"
15443	Cpl	Hammond	H.	"	17401	L/C	Lane	F.	"
20049	L/C	Ludlow	J.	"	21705	L/C	Lomas	C.	"
24198	L/C	Milton	W.	"	16617	L/C	Raynor		"
24866	L/C	Rowbotham	S.	"	23604	L/C	Theile	E.	(now wounded)
30017	Pte	Abery	S.	"	30522	Pte	Archer	H.C.	"
23023	Pte	Bradley	S.	"	25076	Pte	Bloor	E.	"
25132	Pte	Baker	A.	"	20945	Pte	Butcher	E.	" (now Wdd)
30279	Pte	Ayers	C.R.	"					
10711	Pte	Bloor	E.	" (now Wdd)	20215	Pte	Bailey	W.	"
25522	Pte	Baldwin	S.	"	25677	Pte	Berrington	L.	"
23905	Pte	Bateman	W.	"	22713	Pte	Baxter	L.	"
29701	Pte	Barnes	J.	"	20425	Pte	Baker	E.	" (now Wdd)
29979	Pte	Brooks	G.	"	29415	Pte	Billinghurst H.		"
19718	Pte	Brown	H.	"	26548	Pte	Burnham	F.	"
26403	Pte	Brown	A.	"	26149	Pte	Brain	H.	"
26105	Pte	Crozier	C.	" (now Wdd)	28674	Pte	Cook	F.	"
24791	Pte	Capper	A.	"	24847	Pte	Crowhurst	A.	"
24475	Pte	Clarke	C.J.	"	24625	Pte	Carter	C.	" (now Wdd)
30891	Pte	Christopher F.		"	50082	Pte	Clarke	W.	" (now Wdd)
17876	Pte	Dale	C.	"	26299	Pte	Dalby	A.	"
29989	Pte	Douglas	R.	"	24659	Pte	Mimrose	A.	"
17273	Pte	Edwards	S.	"	21246	Pte	Elloway	C.	"
11277	Pte	French	W.	"	26881	Pte	Fletcher	S.	"
29937	Pte	Fox	J.	"	22091	Pte	Gooch	E.	"
29999	Pte	Gaston	L.H.	"	20507	Pte	Griffiths	W.H.	"
23997	Pte	Green	A.	"	26171	Pte	Gee	H.	"
25125	Pte	Gutter	A.J.	"	15122	Pte	Hampton	J.	"
30187	Pte	Holbrook	J.	"	20045	Pte	Howarth	C.	"
10822	Pte	Hall	J.	"	15085	Pte	Harrison	W.H.	"
26080	Pte	Howarth	C.	"	20928	Pte	Hesketh	J.	"
29411	Pte	Hilliard	L.	" (now Wdd)	22912	Pte	Hollis	A.	"
19008	Pte	Hill	C.D.	"	26498	Pte	Jones	W.	"
30105	Pte	Jones	R.A.	" (now Wdd)	29920	Pte	Jackson	G.	"
25891	Pte	Kellett	G.	"	25596	Pte	Kavanagh	A.	"
30000	Pte	Kitt	A.	"	21854	Pte	Lomas	J.	"
23296	Pte	Laking	S.	"	23962	Pte	Long	S.V.	"
29141	Pte	Lindley	H.	"	29705	Pte	Lakin	E.	"
19324	Pte	Longhurst	J.	" (now Wdd)	28891	Pte	Mello	A.	" (now Wdd)
29881	Pte	McIvoy	D.	" (now Wdd)	23616	Pte	Mitchell	J.L.	"
21805	Pte	Neal	H.	"	11260	Pte	Palin	A.	"
18511	Pte	Perkins	J.	"	29696	Pte	Phillips	C.	"
9083	Pte	Roberts	R.	"	29063	Pte	Richardson	J.	"
30014	Pte	Robinson	J.	"	28830	Pte	Sands	A.	"
26486	Pte	Spackman	J.	"	27891	Pte	Sturdy	C.	"
23652	Pte	Seabrook	A.	"	25022	Pte	Snickett	A.	"
29102	Pte	Saunders	W.	"	29416	Pte	Shayer	C.	"
24215	Pte	Spiby	T.	"	27573	Pte	Smith	M.	"
27560	Pte	Stimpson	A.	"	14004	Pte	Seagraves	C.	"
30912	Pte	Smith	S.R.	"	30090	Pte	Smith	W.	"
26464	Pte	Taylor	E.A.	"	24901	Pte	Tudor	C.	"
25515	Pte	Thomas	J.	"	25786	Pte	Taylor	C.	"
27860	Pte	Tuck	A.	"	22964	Pte	Thurlby	W.	"
17382	Pte	Woosey	S.	"	27240	Pte	Wells	R.	"
29617	Pte	Walker	A.	"	26025	Pte	Whitehead	C.	"
10023	Pte	Wood	H.	"	11205	Pte	Wood	H.	" (now Wdd)
20719	Pte	Yates	J.	"					

4th Battalion Grenadier Guards.

List of Officers who took part in the operations 11th to 13th April. 1918.

Lieut-Colonel	W.S.Pilcher, D.S.O.	Commanding.
Captain	C.R.Gerard, D.S.O.	Adjutant.
Captain	M.Chapman, M.C.	Intelligence Officer
Lieut.	N.R.Abbey	Attached B.H.Q.
Lieut.	R.L.Murray Lawes	From 12th to take place of Capt M. Chapman, M.C. Killed

No 1 Company.

Capt. H.H.Sloane Stanley, M.C.

2/Lieut R.B.Osborne.

2/Lieut H.D.Stratford.

Lieut G.C.Burt.(from 12th inst.)

No 2 Company.

Captain T.T.Pryce, M.C.

Lieut Hon.C.C.S.Rodney.

Lieut R.H.Rolfe. (attached 4th Guard Bde)

2/Lieut G.P.Phillipps.

No 3 Company.

Lieut. C.S.Nash, M.C.

Lieut. M.D.Thomas.

Lieut. P.H.Cox.

Lieut. F.O.Lyon.(from 12th inst)

No 4 Company.

Lieut. G.R.Green.

Lieut. J.E.Greenwood.

2/Lieut.G.W.Sich.

Captain.T.W.Minchin, D.S.O.(from
~~2/Lieut. R.D.Richardson.~~ (12th
(inst.

Lieut-Colonel,

Commanding 4th Battn Grenadier Guards.

"A" Form
MESSAGES AND SIGNALS.

(In pads of 100.)

No. of Message................

Prefix......Code......m.	Words.	Charge.	This message is on a/c of:		Recd. at......m.
Office of Origin and Service Instructions		Sent			Date..............
....	At.............m.		...............Service.		From..............
....	To..............				
....	By..............	(Signature of "Franking Officer.")		By..............

TO { No 1 Cy

Sender's Number.	Day of Month.	In reply to Number.	AAA
S.D.6	12		

No 1 will push two platoons into shell VIEW HOUSE as soon as that is occupied push forward patrols to K.18.c.6.6. AAA 3 C.G. are advancing on your right endeavouring to advance to College K.23.d. If ~~~~~~ VIEW HOUSE - MERVILLE road is inclusive for 3 C.G. AAA No 1 must establish touch & keep free to flank on MERVILLE - NEUF BERQUIN road by advancing a platoon behind the scouts AAA. Advance will commence at 11 a.m. AAA Artillery barrage will be put down on NEUF BERQUIN - MERVILLE road

From ....A...O.C....
Place
Time 7.45 A M.

The above may be forwarded as now corrected.   (Z). Sender
                                                      Censor.   Signature of Addressor or person authorised to telegraph in his name.

* This line should be erased if not required.

Copy.

Clarence House,
St James's, S.W.
April 25th /18.

My dear Pilcher,

I have heard from the Lt-Col: of Regt: of the magnificent fight set up by our 4th Battalion on April 11th, 12th and 13th and I feel that I must write to you, as its Commanding Officer, to express my admiration of the conduct of all ranks in a time of supreme peril not only for the Battn:, but also for the 4th Guards Brigade and possibly the whole of the British Troops on that front.

I have read with pride of the gallantry and endurance shown by all companies of your Battn: but especially of No 2 Company so ably led and commanded by Capt: Pryce — most deeply do I mourn the loss of so many fine Grenadiers who have so nobly maintained the traditions of the 1st Regt: of Guards — I wish you would let the men know from me how highly I admire their splendid bravery and devotion to duty in one of the hardest fought battles the Grenadier Guards have ever been engaged in.

The 4th Battn: seems to have vied with the Coldstream and Irish Guards in their splendid defence against the terrible onslaughts of the masses of the enemy, who in many cases seem to have been quite round them.

I congratulate you on commanding such a Battn:.

I have seen and spoken to Capt: Minchin in hospital, he was going well when I saw him.

Hoping you and all ranks of the Battn: are having a rest after your 3 days frightful exertions.

Believe me

Yours very sincerely

ARTHUR.
F.M.
Col. Grenadier Guards.

Stand of 4th Guards Brigade near Vieux Berquin
on 12th and 13th April 1918.

On 10th April 1918 the Germans attacked the British and Portugese line from Armentieres southwards in overwhelming force. Troops were hurried up from all directions to stem the German on-rush, but in spite of this by nightfall on 11th April the Germans had advanced about 10 miles forcing back our troops before them, and there appeared to be nothing to prevent the enemy reaching the important town of Hazebrouck next day. Such was the situation at the moment when the 4th Guard Brigade, consisting of 4th Battalion Grenadier Guards, 3rd Battalion Coldstream Guards, and 2nd Battalion Irish Guards, arrived in Motor Busses at Strazeele at 9 p.m. on 11th April 1918. The Brigade had spent the previous night lying along the roadside in column awaiting the Busses. It had spent some 10 hours of the 11th packed in the Motor Busses. All the men and Officers were therefore tired and stiff.

The orders given to the Brigade were to stop the German advance towards Hazbrouck at all costs. After a short rest and a meal the battalion moved forward towards the enemy through the dark night, lighted only by the flashes of the German shells as they burst. Each man carried a shovel in addition to his arms, for experience had taught these veterans to value their shovels immediately after their rifles bayonets and ammunition.

By dawn the brigade was in position in touch with the enemy and holding an extended front of about $2\frac{1}{2}$ miles with the 3rd Battalion Coldstream Guards on the right, the 4th Battalion Grenadier Guards on the left, and the 2nd Battalion Irish Guards in reserve.

As soon as it was light the Germans opened a heavy fire with Field Guns rifles and Machine Guns, and under cover

of/

of this fire they recommenced their advance. About 1800 yards
in front of them they could see the trees of the forest of
Nieppe. Once they could gain a footing in this forest, they
knew they would have a covered approach which would lead
them to within striking distance of Hazebrouck, and so they
pressed forward eagerly intent on sweeping aside all opposition.
But as they advanced the thin and scattered line of Guardsmen
opened an accurate fire and drove them back. Again they
pressed forward, supported this time by their light field guns
firing at point blank range, for these had been worked up behind
hedges to within 300 yards of the British trenches. But again
they were driven back although the guardsmen suffered heavily
from their fire. At this moment it was decided to deliver
a counter attack along the brigade front. For this purpose
two companies of the Irish Guards were brought up on the right
flank of the brigade front, and at 11 a.m. the line composed
of two companies 2nd Battalion Irish Guards on the right, 3rd
Battalion Coldstream guards in the centre, and 4th Battalion
Grenadier Guards on the left, advanced and attacked. Although
this attack met with heavy opposition and was unable to progress
very far, yet it fulfilled its chief object of delaying the
enemys further advance for several hours. It was on the left
of the brigade line that the best progress was made. This
flank was attacking down a broad main road leading from Vieux
Berquin to Neuf Berquin. No 2 Company, 4th Battalion
Grenadier Guards, under the command of Capt. T.F. Pryce, M.C.
formed this flank. This company attack with marked skill
and determined gallantry, covering its own advance with the
fire of its own rifles and rifle grenades. They captured the
small hamlet of Pont Rondin through which the main road ran,
killing 30 Germans, and capturing 2 Machine Guns and 2 prisoners.
Capt. Pryce, the gallant command of this company himself
killed 7 of the 30 Germans.

At/

At about 3 p.m. the enemy renewed his attacks all along the line and the situation again became very critical, for the enemy succeeded in driving in a portion of the brigade front.   But an immediate counter-attack, carried out without superior orders, but No.2 Company of the 3rd Battalion Coldstream Guards, and a company of 2nd Battalion Irish Guards, drove back the enemy and re-established the situation.

About an hour before dusk the Germans made one more determined effort to gain their goal.   But the spirit of discipline of the Brigade of Guards stood firm, and in spite of heavy losses from the fierce artillery, trench mortar, and Machine Gun Fire, the Guardsmen drove back the Germans.

Darkness brought a welcome respite from the intense firing, but it brought no further relief or rest to the 4th Guards Brigade.   Orders were sent to them to continue their resistance at all costs.   The fate of the British Army seemed to hang on their being able to carry out these orders for the last available reinforcements, the 1st Australian Division were being hurried up into the battle to form a solid defensive line which would stop the German onrush effectually.   The plan was for the Germans to be held back at all costs while this fresh division formed a well organised and strong line of resistance about 1,000 yards behind the fighting line.   It was reckoned that the Australians would require until the following evening to complete this task and it was therefore the duty of the 4th Guards Brigade to hang on until that time.

The night was therefore spent by the Guardsmen in readjusting their line and replenishing their ammunition and preparing themselves in every way for the grim conflict which they knew would recommence at dawn.   Although the 4th Battalion Grenadier Guards had lost 8 Officers and 250 other ranks, and the Battalions had lost proportionately heavily yet it was found necessary to increase the frontage occupied by the brigade in

order/

order to cover the required ground.

With the first streak of dawn the German attacks were renewed. A thick fog during the early hours of daylight enabled the Germans to work forward their light Machine Guns into the intervals between the scattered British posts. They also brought up an armoured Motor Car against a portion of the Coldstreams line. Throughout the morning the enemy made repeated attacks. These were met and driven back by the gallant determination of the small and scattered bands of heroic Guardsmen. The story of Guardsman Jacotin of 3rd Battalion Coldstream Guards is typical of the spirit shown by all these gallant men. He was one of the Garrison of the left post of No.3 Company 3rd Battalion Coldstream Guards. All the men in the post except himself were killed or wounded, but yet he fought on by himself, and stopped the German advance until he was killed by a hand grenade thrown by a German who had crept up behind the trench while Guardsman Jacotin was shooting at the Germans in front of him and holding the trench single handed.

And so the fight went on until shortly after noon, when the troops on the left of the 4th Guards Brigade, who had been holding the village of La Couronne immediately on the left of the Grenadiers, were driven back by a heavy concentrated German attack. The Germans at once occupied La Couronne and under cover of the houses they were quickly able to attack the left of the Grenadiers, both from the flank, and from the rear. The left Company of 4th Battalion Grenadier Guards was No.2 Company, commanded by Capt. Pryce, the Company which had counter attacked so successfully on the previous day. The Company was thus surrounded. They continued fighting on, and by so doing they succeeded in delaying the Germans, although they sacrificed themselves. What subsequently happened to this Company was told by its one survivor, a Corporal who worked his way back to the Australian Lines on the following night.

He/

He related how at 6.15 p.m. Capt. Pryce realised that the situation was hopeless as his ammunition was all expended and the Germans were all round him and were being reinforced. At this time a party of the enemy approached to within 80 yards of his trenches.

Captain Pryce ordered his Company, which was then 18 strong, to charge with the Bayonet. The enemy were luckily unable to fire from the front, as their own troops were behind our men, and the charge was completely successful in driving back the Germans. Again the enemy worked forward to close quarters, and again Capt. Pryce and his gallant band drove them back. But meanwhile the enemy were receiving reinforcements, and these eventually turned the scale against this indomitable defence. Captain Pryce was one of the last of this band of heroes to die. He was last seen fighting in a hand-to-hand struggle against overwhelming odds. By their noble self-sacrifice in their country's cause they kept the Germans at bay long enough to allow the Australians to form a strong line of defence, which the Germans never succeeded in penetrating. By their gallant deaths they all earned for themselves undying fame. His Majesty King George V granted a posthumous award of the Victoria Cross to their gallant leader, Capt. Pryce.

The remainder of the thin scattered line of the 4th Guards Brigade was almost as this left flank, and thus it came about that by nightfall the Germans were able to call themselves masters of the field where these bloody encounters had taken place, but only to find that in front of them the 1st Australian Division had securely established themselves as an impenetrable barrier, a result which had only been made possible by the spirit of determination and of devotion to duty of the Brigade of Guards.

4th. Battalion Grenadier Guards.

Narrative of Events from 10th. to 14th. April, 1918.

The Battalion, billetted at VILLERS BRULIN, received orders to embuss on April 10th., the time fixed for embussing at TINCQUES being 11/45 p.m. The busses did not arrive until 11/30.a.m the 11th., when the battalion proceeded to STRAZEELE via St.POL.

The Battalion debussed at about 9/30.p.m and marched down to a field by STRAZEELE Station, near Le PARADIS.

The Brigadier there had a conference of Commanding Officers, and the Battalion had orders to take up a position with the 3rd. Battalion COLDSTREAM Guards on the right from K.6.b.5.8 to L'EPINETTE, K.11.a.3.4, a frontage of 2000 yards. There were supposed to be elements of another division on the Battalion's left, and in front.

Companies got to their positions just about dawn, marching off from Le PARADIS about 2/30.a.m.

There was a considerable shortage of tools, and, when daylight came, the companies were very insufficiently dug in.

No. 1 Company was on the right, No. 4 in the centre, No. 2 on the left and No. 3 in support. Battalion Headquarters at GARS BRUGGHE, K.5.b.5.8.

Immediately it was light, the Germans fired very heavily at any movement with machine guns and light field guns, both of which they had a very considerable number.

At about 9/30.a.m the Brigadier came up to Battalion Headquarters and ordered that the battalion with the 3rd. Battalion COLDSTREAM Guards should advance and push forward with two companies as far as possible. Nos. 1 & 2 Companies were detailed to send forward two platoons each. No. 1 to seize VEIRHOUCK, No. 2 to seize PONT RONDIN. The attack started about 11.p.m: No. 1 Coy. was unable to progress at VEIRHOUCK owing to very heavy intense machine gun and artillery fire, which swept the only road over the stream down which they had to advance: they suffered severe casualties. No. 2 Coy. made a most skilful advance to PONT RONDIN, the two platoons personally led by Captain T.T.PRYCE,MC worked down the road from house to house, all of which were occupied by small parties of Germans with light machine guns. Many Germans were killed, Captain PRYCE killing seven himself, giving out fire orders and directing his rifle grenade and rifle fire in a most skilful manner. In the houses captured by this company some 30 dead Germans were found: two machine guns and two prisoners were captured, one of which was a NCO. decorated with the Iron Cross.

The bravery shown by the Company Commander and these platoons was beyond all praise, as they were heavily shot at, and there was a battery of enemy field guns some 300 yards down the road south of PONT RONDIN, firing over open sights, also several trench mortars. This company had some 20 casualties.

At about 2/30.p.m the line remained the same: at 3.p.m. Captain PRYCE reported that his left flank was in the air and Germans could be seen in F.25.d which was some 1000 yards to the rear of his left flank, and were shooting at him with Trench mortars and field guns over open sights and also the machine gun fire was intense.

The whole of his advance could be seen quite plainly from Battalion Headquarters.

He decided to re-adjust his line with his left at K.6.b.5.8: even then the Germans were well behind his left flank. This he did, and held on till dusk, when the line was re-adjusted from Brigade, though suffering the severest casualties. His company lost 80 NCOs & men and 1 officer during this fighting out of 120 who went into action.

During the day, from 9.a.m till dusk, Battalion Headquarters was fired on by 2 field guns in the open about L.7.a.3.3 and by a Trench mortar, and very heavily by machine guns. The farm was set on fire, and Captain M.CHAPMAN,MC and Lieut. N.R.ABBEY, of Battalion Headquarters, were killed.

To some extent, this fire was kept down by the skilful and gallant work of Lieut. LEWIS, of 152nd. Brigade,RFA, who exposed himself continuously to get direct observation, and mended his line in the open under heavy fire and no doubt inflicted heavy casualties on the Germans of whom many were seen to fall.

The rest of the battalion front remained intact all day although attacked several times, and badly enfiladed in places, No. 4 Company having some 70% casualties, including all its officers.

The Battalion casualties for the day were about 250, including 9 officers: about 50% of its effectives.

Owing to the left flank being in the air, the Brigadier gave orders for the battalion to re-adjust its line. The right was to be about K.5.b.6.2 where it would be next to 3rd. Battalion COLDSTREAM Guards' left.....the battalion left to rest 300 yards south of La COURONNE, where it was to be in touch with 12th.Bn.K.O.Y.L.I.

The battalion, during the day, fired some 70,000 rounds of S.A.A. and had fired all its rifle grenades: the casualties inflicted on the Germans were severe: the work done by the Lewis gunners beyond all praise.

During the night, the line was re-adjusted, the battalion being helped to dig the new line by a Field Coy. RE. Four fresh officers were sent up to take the places of some of the losses - namely Lieutenants LYON and BURT and Captain MINCHIN to companies, and Lieut. MURRAY LAWES to Battalion Headquarters.

The new battalion frontage was 1800 yards in a line of absolutely flat country with no hedges, etc, to take advantage of to conceal the trenches. This was held by companies in isolated posts, the strength of the battalion being nine officers and about 180 other ranks - one man per ten yards of front.

The Commanding Officer, on going round, found the men cheerful, but, of course, tired. Rations and water were sent up, and as much S.A.A as possible as all the men had practically fired all their ammunition and grenades.

Battalion Headquarters was moved to Ferme BEAULIEU, E.28.d.5.2.

On visiting No. 2 Company (Left Coy), who had some thirty men left under Captain PRYCE, who was occupying a line of trench just in front of a water-meadow in E.20.c; 5 boxes of S.A.A were got up to him. On this company of thirty from 9/15.a.m the next morning until 6/15.p.m at night the bulk of the German fire, and heavy Infantry attacks fell. At about 9/15.a.m the next morning, 13th. the Commanding Officer learnt that strong German attacks were developing all along the front, also that his left flank was entirely in the air. He sent orders round to all companies that they must hold their line at all costs, and stay there and fight to the end. This message was acknowledges by all companies. The orderlies that had to take this message were obliged to go through the heaviest machine gun fire.

At about 10/30.a.m, the Brigade Major visited Battalion Headquarters and stated that the centre of the line at OARS BRUGGHE, between the 3rd Battalion COLDSTREAM Guards and the Battalion's front had been penetrated by the Germans. The Commanding Officer and Brigade Major went up and saw the men were in their trenches and line intact. A platoon of the 3rd Battalion COLDSTREAM Guards was ordered to fill in any gaps which existed but this was impossible for it to do.

On returning to Battalion Headquarters about 1/15.p.m the Commanding Officer received a message from Captain PRYCE, No. 2 Company, stating that since 9/15.a.m Germans had been in VIEUX BERQUIN and at La COURONNE, and a column estimated at two battalions, was advancing from BLEU. He had also been attacked twice on his immediate front, but had driven off the Germans, who left a number of dead just in front of his trenches. He also stated that, after the failure of the second attack, the enemy had brought up two field guns to a hedge some 300 yards to his front, and were flattening out his trench; there were no reinforcements available, so the Commanding Officer had no alternative but to tell him to hold his ground with his few available men, some 18 then. The orderly to come and go to his headquarters worked up a drain some three feet deep. One last message was received from Captain PRYCE from here about 3.p.m saying he was surrounded on two sides, and was fighting both ways shooting at the Germans; what subsequently happened is related by a Corporal who was with him, and who subsequently escaped through the German lines. At about 6/15.p.m Captain PRYCE, who realised that the situation was hopeless, as the Germans were already at VERTE RUE, and could be seen advancing behind to BOIS D'AVAL, called on his men to charge a party of Germans some 80 yards away, to his immediate front, at the same time exhorting them to fight to the end. The men cheered and followed him, and drove this party back: the enemy were unable to fire, as their own troops were behind. The party then returned to the trench. The men now had no ammunition left, having fired their 5 boxes S.A.A sent up at night.

The Germans started working up closer again, Captain PRYCE called for a final charge and the remaining men, some 14 in number charged with fixed bayonets. The Corporal and one man were stopped by a large ditch, from where they saw Captain PRYCE struggling with a large party of

Germans. He lay in the ditch till midnight, when he worked his way through the German line, and joined the Australians in BOIS D'AVAL.

Nos. 1 & 4 Coys., who had been enfiladed all day long, with machine gun and light gun fire, had lost all their officers; Captain H.H.SLOANE STANLEY,MC, commanding No. 1 Company had been killed, and Captain T.W. MINCHIN,DSO. severely wounded. Captain MINCHIN stated that of his company, only 6 men were not casualties; all the rest were killed and wounded. He was shot in three places by different bullets before leaving his trench. No. 1 Company had also suffered almost equally, both subalterns being wounded. No. 3 Company, who were on the right of No. 2, had also suffered severely, losing their company commander, who was believed to have been killed. This company was seen to be surrounded, and the Germans on both sides, and about twenty men were taken away as prisoners, so the rest must be presumed to be killed or wounded.

The survivors of Nos. 1 & 4 Coys. held on till night, though by 6/15.p.m the Germans had already occupied VERTE RUE, directly behind them. Some of them subsequently got through at night and attached themselves to the Australians, with whom they stayed in their front line for 24 hours.

At about 5/30.p.m, when the Germans were at VERTE RUE, some 300 yards away, Battalion Headquarters moved to 2nd. Battalion IRISH Guards Headquarters at CAUDESCURE, as the whole of the left flank had been turned, and the battalion surrounded.

Summary.

The Battalion had been three days and nights without rest, and fighting and digging trenches almost continuously.
Of the 19 officers who went into action, only two were not casualties: ie. the Commanding Officer and Adjutant.
The total casualties among the rest of the battalion was 504, some 90%, of which 50% were incurred on the first day.
I consider the heroic conduct of Captain PRYCE and No. 2 Company to be beyond all praise, and think that the action of this Officer, who, with a small body of men, held the Germans for no less than 12 hours, on the 13th. April - from about 8/15.a.m when his left flank had been turned, to 6/15.p.m, when he made his final charge, to be difficult to surpass. More especially, as his company had carried out a determined attack the day before, and its left flank continuously since it came into the line had been in the air. How the great influence of this company's action on the general battle front has been remains to be seen; it may well have been the determining factor of the whole British line being completely driven in.
The Officer who had commanded this company had already been awarded the Military Cross and Bar for gallantry, and had taken part in 7 attacks and raids upon the German trenches during the last three years.

Lt.Colonel,

16th.April,1918. <u>Commanding 4th. Battalion Grenadier Guards.</u>

XV Corps No. SGS/12/7
dated 27-4-1918.
31D/211 A.

War Diary

Second Army.
─────────────

I forward the attached narrative of the action of the
4th Guards Brigade during the operations of the 11th to 14th April
1918, for the information of the Army Commander.

An account of the operations of the Corps as a whole is
being prepared, but this record of the glorious stand against
overwhelming odds made by the 4th Guards Brigade is of exceptional
interest.

The history of the British Army can record nothing finer
than the story of the action of the 4th Guards Brigade on the
12th and 13th April, 1918.

The troops of the 29th and 31st Divisions by their stout
defence covered the detrainment of the 1st Australian Division
and saved HAZEBROUCK.

XV Corps.   sd/ Beauvoir de Lisle,
27-4-18.   Lieutenant-General,
                                               Commanding XV Corps.

"Copy to 31st Division".

- 2 -

─────────────────────────────

─────────────────────────────

Forwarded for your information.

                                               sd/ W.H.ANNESLEY, Lieut-Colonel,
28-4-18.   A.A.& Q.M.G., 31st Division.
─────────────────────────────

Apl 154

4th. Battalion Grenadier Guards.

Distribution of Officers, 1/5/18.

Lt. Colonel W. S. Pilcher, DSO..........Commanding.
Major C. F. A. Walker, MC..............2nd. in Command.
Captain C. R. Gerard, DSO..............Adjutant.
Captain I. H. Ingleby..................a/Quartermaster.
Lieut. R. L. Murray Lawes..............Intelligence Offr.
Lieut. G. W. Selby Lowndes.............Transport Officer.

No. 1 Company.	No. 2 Company.
Captain Hon. F. E. Needham.	Captain G. C. Sloane Stanley.
Lt. Hon. A. H. L. Hardinge, MC.	Lieut. C. E. Irby, MC.
Lieut. E. H. Tuckwell, MC.	Lieut. A. A. Morris.
2/Lt. Hon. S. E. Marsham.	2/Lt. P. G. S. Gregson Ellis.
	2/Lt. A. F. Alington.

Detached.

Lieut. a/Capt. C. G. Keith, MC...attd. Gds. Dvn.
Lieut. M. P. B. Wrixon, MC...Gds. Base x Hptl.
2/Lt. D. J. Knight..........4th. Gds. Bde. HQ.

4 Btn Grenadier G
April 1918

App 185 to
War Diary
1226/2

THIS ACCOUNT WAS SUBMITTED BY
Lt.-Col W.S. PILCHER D.S.O.
IN CONNECTION WITH LYS OPERATIONS.

ACTION OF 4th BATTALION GRENADIER GUARDS

12th to 14th APRIL 1918.

4th Guards Brigade.

31st Division.

The attached account was submitted by
Russian Major L. A. Schneur D.S.O. in connection with
L.H. operations - April 1918.

J.A. Schneur
Major
April 1918

4th Battalion de La Couronne
Position on April 13 1918

SKETCH I

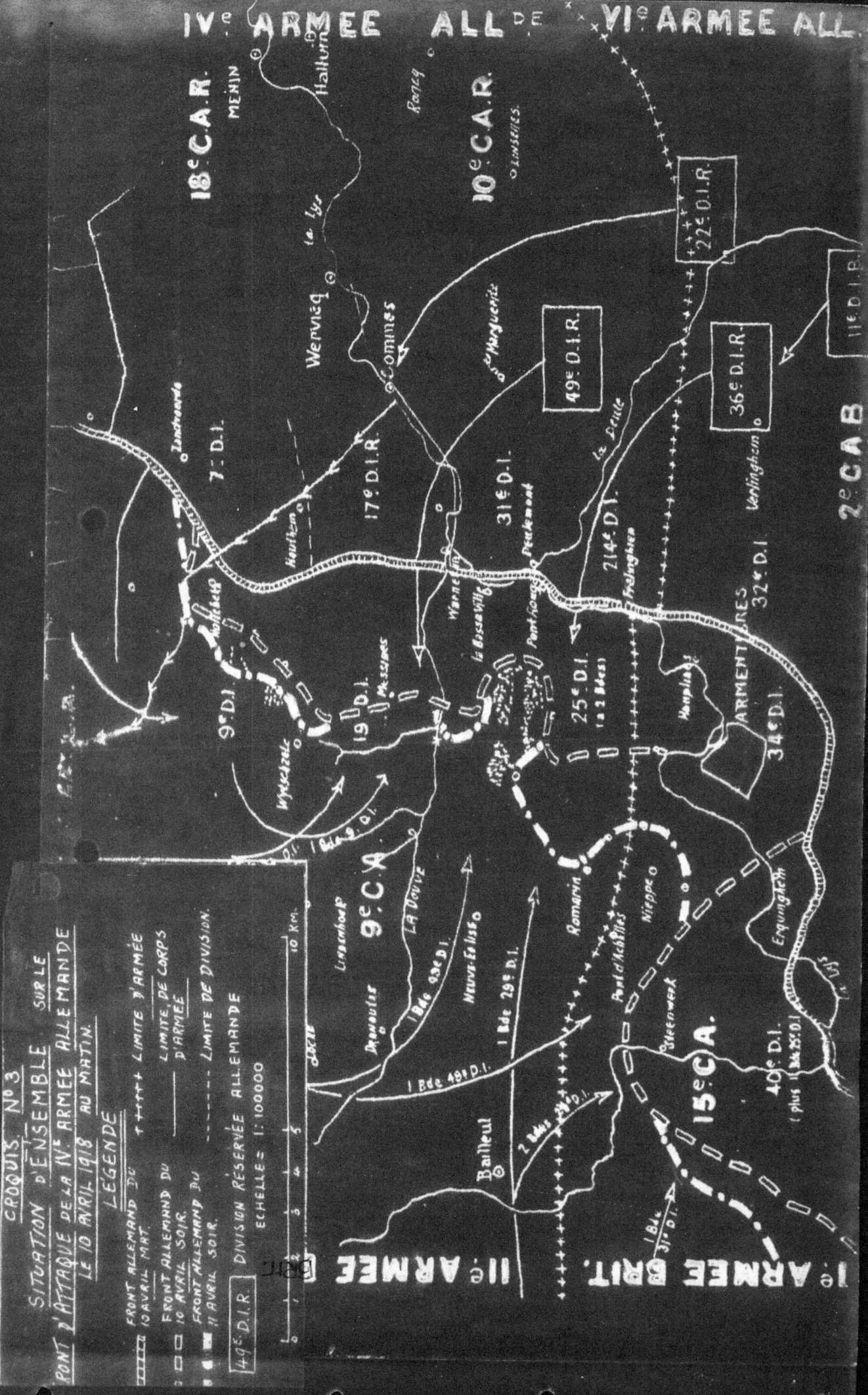

STAFF RIDE IN FRANCE

ACTION OF THE 4TH BATTALION GRENADIER GUARDS AT THE BATTLE OF HAZEBROUCK, 12TH TO 14TH APRIL, 1918.

- - - - - - - - - - - -

Reference Map: HAZEBROUCK. 1/100,000.
               Sheet 36A.N.E. 1/40,000.

OPENING SITUATION

      The great German attack on the British Third and Fifth Armies had commenced on the 21st March and had had a very considerable success, especially against the latter. The 31st Division, to which the 4th Guards Brigade belonged, were in G.H.Q. Reserve on the 21st March. The Brigade, which was composed of the 4th Battalion Grenadier Guards, the 3rd Battalion Coldstream Guards and the 2nd Battalion Irish Guards, was moved that day in buses to Blairville and took part in ten days active operations, more or less of open warfare. They were just on the right of the Guards Division, which was fortunate for both, and succeeded in easily repulsing the German attacks, though adjustments of the line held had continually to be made owing to the troops on the right having to retire.
The 4th Battalion had the following casualties - 4 officers and 75 men - a great many of these were caused by our own heavy artillery.

      The Battalion had come out of the battle with their morale very high and quite convinced that they could repel any German attacks. The Division once more returned to G.H.Q.Reserve, and were billetted at Villers Brulin. On the 9th April Ludendorff inaugurated his Northern Offensive with a concentrated attack of nine divisions under Von Quast on the line north of La Bassee. This attack had very considerable success against the Portuguese and the XV. Corps, and, reinforced by several Corps under Von Arnim, he pressed his attacks in the direction of Hazebrouck - Cassel - Mt.Kemmel, and endeavoured to take the Ypres salient, perhaps in the hope of capturing the Channel ports, or at least cutting the British communications. In any event, the capture of Hazebrouck, Cassel and Mt. Kemmel would have created a very difficult situation for the British troops in the north. Marshal Foch, in his diary, states that on the 12th he started to take a serious view of the situation.

      On the night of the 8th April, the Commanding Officer and the Adjutant (Capt.C.R.Gerard) had been invited to dine with Lord Horne, Commander of the First Army, at his headquarters some 16 miles behind the front line. As they were leaving, at about 2300 hours, a few shells from German long range guns pitched close to the village; the Army Commander, who was seeing his guests into their car, remarked that he thought that they forbode something and how glad he was that he had ordered the relief of the Portuguese, and that it would be completed in two or three days time. But it was not to be, for the attack started next morning.

At about midnight on the 9th April the Commanding
Officer received a Warning Order that the Battalion would
move by bus the next day. The next morning, the 10th,
this was confirmed, giving a rendezvous to meet the buses
on the main road at Tincques, near Villers Brulin, at 2345
hours.

The Battalion arrived there about an hour before the
time, and were told off into parties ready to "embus".
However, the buses never arrived until 11.30 hours the
next morning, the 11th. It was a very cold night, and, by
bad staff work, the Battalion was kept out all night, unable
to sleep and unable to cook any breakfast. Luckily, the
morale of the troops was so high that it had little effect
on their spirits, though a night without sleep is bound
to adversely effect the fighting qualities of troops.

For ten hours, very cramped and crowded, the battalion
was jolted along in very badly sprung lorries over the pave
roads. Sleep was impossible. As we drew closer to the
battlefield one could observe signs that all was not well.
Men walking down the road without arms or equipment -
Portuguese soldiers going west. It was reported that they
had actually taken off their boots to facilitate their
retreat. A Corps H.Q. was seen packing up in great haste,
and beds and pianos were being loaded into lorries. The
signs of a retreat are bad for advancing troops, and, during
the frequent halts, the Commanding Officer forbade any
conversation with men who were obviously retreating from
the battle field. The brigade finally arrived at
Strazeele at 2100 hours and started debusing. The Coldstream
Guards had arrived at 2000 hours.

The Brigade Commander held a conference at Le Paradis
(E.11?A) where it was stated that the situation in front
was obscure, but it was believed that the 50th Division
were holding a line about Pures Becques - Pont Rondin. The
Brigade was to occupy a position from L'Epinette (K.11.a.3.4)
to Kew Cross (K.6.E.) on the right of the 29th Division.
The 3rd Battalion Coldstream Guards on the right, the 4th
Battalion Grenadier Guards on the left, and the 2nd Battalion
Irish Guards in reserve. No definite boundaries were given.
There were supposed elements of other divisions on our right
and left, but the Brigadier was able to give very little
further information.

Battalions moved off at about 0230 hours and reached
their positions at about dawn. Great difficulty confronted
Commanders in settling their company localities. It was a
pitch black night and the men had had no hot meal for 28
hours and rations had not arrived.

Some problems to be considered during the description of the Battle which show the difficulties which confront a Commander in War and, in consequence, affect the operations and morale of the troops and point to the absolute necessity of commanders endeavouring to think ahead and anticipate problems with which they may be faced.

- - - - - - - - -

Many problems call for practically instant decisions and it is only by constant practice and repetition of the lessons taught in our Regulations for War can a Commander be certain of coming to a right conclusion. You must remember that he is nearly always tired, for war consumes his nervous energy. He has to think of a multitude of problems and is personally affected by the immediate course of events on his front. His responsibility is great, for on his decisions rests the fate of the men whom he commands.

Quotations. Foch.   "My study has been arduous for years.
                    "It gave me the knowledge to know that
                    "what I did was right and the confidence
                    "to stick to it."

           Wellington. "Habit second nature. Habit is ten
                       "times nature."

1. There was no personal reconnaissance by the Brigade Commander and the Commanding officers that was coupled with completely false information. A violation of our F.S.R. Would it not have been better had the brigade been moved to a position of readiness in areas Verte Rue and Vieux Berquin with protective posts in front. Then a reconnaissance to be carried out at dawn.

2. There was a lack of entrenching tools, wire, etc, and facilities for giving the men a hot meal, which they had not had for 28 hours. (Note: The Commanding Officer had managed to buy some bread in Strazeele - about a quarter of a loaf per man). This was a very serious matter and the brigade should have been fed before moving. The Staff Captain should have motored forward to Strazeele and arranged this. He knew where the brigade was going to debus. It was obviously going to be a defensive battle.

3. The effect of the bus ride through the area of retreating and dispirited troops. Could it have been avoided, since it must have had an adverse effect on the morale of the troops.

4. The officers and men had had no sleep or rest for 36 hour If the reconnaissance had been held at dawn, before launching the brigade, the troops would have had 5 hours sleep. This would have been invaluable.
Note: What a magnificent morale the brigade must have had to carry out the operation it did during the next three days.

5. The fact that the whole of the brigade was only covered by one battery of artillery (18-pdrs.) which did very good work.

6. An order issued by General de Lysle, commanding the XV.Corps, that no retirement should be made on the line readjusted, except by order of a responsible officer prepared to justify his decision before Court Martial. Did this

affect the decisions of the brigade commander ?
Undoubtedly the line should have been readjusted.
No definite orders were issued to Battalion Commanders and
there was no commander to ensure co-operation.

7. The Brigade Headquarters on the 12th were some 3 to 4
miles behind the front lines. This made proper control
almost impossible. Divisional Headquarters were no less
than 10 miles behind the lines. It is true that the
commander was relieved of his command. He failed
completely to have any influence on the attack.

8. Was Battn. H.Q. at Gars Brugg Brocche too far forward.
It was practically in the front line. It undoubtedly had
a good effect on the morale of the companies in front.
Would it have had an adverse effect had it been moved back
during the day of the 12th ? On the other hand, it lost
some 60 per cent of its effectives. A difficult decision to
make to change it. Faulty information at the brigade
conference had caused the choice of so forward a position.

9. The great difficulty of the supply of rations, ammunition etc., during a battle of this kind.

10. The difficulties of communication between companies
and battalion headquarters owing to the casualties among
the runners. Visual signalling was impossible.

LIST OF OFFICERS WHO TOOK PART IN THE OPERATIONS
12th and 14th APRIL.

Battalion Headquarters.

Lieut.-Colonel W.S.Pilcher DSO.	
Captain and Adjutant C.R.Gerard.	
Captain M.Chapman	(Killed)
Lieut.R.N.Abbey	(Killed)
2/Lieut.R.L.Murray-Lawes.	

No.1 Company.

Captain H.H.Sloane Stanley	(Killed)
2/Lieut.F.Stratford.	(Killed)
2/Lieut.R.S.Osborne	(Wounded on night of the 12th)
2/Lieut.G.C.Burt.	(Slightly wounded and captured).

No.2 Company.

Captain T.T.Pryce VC.MC.	(Killed)
Lieut.Hon.S.C.C.Rodney.	(Wounded and Prisoner)
2/Lieut.G.P.Phillips.	(Wounded and Prisoner)

No.3 Company.

Lieut.G.C.Nash M.C.	(Wounded)
Lieut.F.C.Lyon.	(Killed - came up on night of 12th).
Lieut.M.D.Thomas.	(Wounded and Prisoner)
2/Lieut.P.H.Cox.	(Wounded and Prisoner)

No.4 Company.

Lieut.G.R.Green	(Wounded)
Captain G.W.Minchin	(Wounded)
2/Lieut.J.E.Greenwood.	(Wounded - came up on night of 12th).
2/Lieut.G.W.Sich.	(Wounded and Prisoner)

Medical Officer.

Captain N.Grellier.MC. R.A.M.C.

STANDS FOR DESCRIPTION OF THE BATTLE.

1st STAND:

Halt at Strazeele for five minutes to get a view of the surrounding country.

2nd STAND:

Cars Brugghe. Description of the fighting of Nos. 1, 4 and 3 Companies and at Battalion Headquarters, and a short account of the attacks delivered on the 3rd Battalion Coldstream Guards.

3rd STAND:

Cross roads at La Couronne. Description of the action of No. 2 Company (Captain Pryce) during the fighting of the 12th and 13th April.

DESCRIPTION OF THE BATTLE - 12th APRIL.

Under cover of No.2 Company, 2/Irish Guards, who were sent down the road towards Merville, and who met some German transport about Pont Rondin, the battalion got into position from (incl.) Le Cornet Perdue to (incl.) Kew Cross with the Coldstreams on the right and the Irish Guards in reserve (See Sketch). The 12/K.O.Y.L.I. were at La Couronne.

The Companies of the 4th Battn. Grenadier Guards were disposed as follows:-
    No.1 Company on the right.
    No.2 " on the left
    No.4 " in the centre
    Bn.H.Q. at Gars Brugghe.
    No.3 Company in reserve about E/.30 A & D.

Dawn arrived after a very dark night and found the companies not properly dug in owing to lack of tools and the company commanders having had great difficulty in allotting the platoon areas. The transport had not been sent up - it had arrived later than the battalion. This was another breakdown on the part of the "Q" Staff. The whole front, when visibility became possible, was swept by M.G.fire and the enemy had many light mortars firing. The men of the 50th Div. had come through out line at dawn, followed by the Germans. At 0800 hours, the Germans attacked and were repulsed. At 0930 hours the brigadier visited Battn. H.Q. and ordered the Battn. with the 3/Coldstream on the right, to advance at 1100 hours. Patrols were to be sent down the road to Les Pures Becques - Sinbad Farm (K.17.b.) - Gent House (K.12.c.) - Neuf Berquin and any success exploited. Special stress was laid on the capture of Les Pures Becques - Vierhouck - and Pont Rondin. The object was to prevent any enemy movement along the road Merville - Neuf Berquin. The open flanks were not considered. The C.O. 4/Grenadier, at this conference, definitely told the brigadier that the enemy was holding a line in strength in front of the battalion. He had received messages that the Germans were occupying positions in front, and had endeavoured to advance. They had attacked at 0500 (?) hours and the attack was seen by Bn.H.Q.

Read Pryce's messages.

However, the brigadier determined to carry out the Divnl.orders - remember that they were situated about 10 miles in rear - and the attack took place unsupported by artillery or even M.G's, and with both flanks in the air. At 1115 hours, as per sketch map, the 3/Coldstream and the 4/Grenadier, and the companies of the Irish Guards echelonned in rear, started the attack. Some slight progress was made. Vierhouck and Les Pures Becques being very strongly held. The 3/Coldstream advanced some 400 yards, but could get no further. Nos.1 & 4 Coys. Grenadier Guards were held up in the line of La Plate Becques - whilst No.2 Coy. took Pont Rondin.

We will now turn to the fighting of Nos. 1 and 4 Coys. during the days of the 12th and 13th April from this stand, and also refer to the action of the Coldstream and Irish Guards.

After the holding up of the attack and the impossibility of crossing the Plate Becque, the front of Nos. 1 and 4 Coys. remained the same throughout the day.

At about 1530 hours the Germans made a determined attack on the front held by the Coldstream and Nos. 1 and 4 Coys. after a short bombardment by trench mortars and light artillery. They endeavoured to outflank the Coldstream and penetrate between the right and centre companies. The right company was handled with great skill by a Sergeant as all the officers had become casualties. An immediate counter-attack was launched by a Company of the Coldstream and a Company of the Irish Guards, which was completely successful in restoring the line. Another Irish Guards company filled a dangerous gap between the Coldstream and the Grenadiers. The attack was not pressed on the Grenadier front. Again at 1620 hours, the Germans renewed the attack, which was again repulsed with severe losses. About 1730 hours, the 5th Div. had come up on the right of the Coldstream and secured that flank. The Irish Guard Coys. had again withdrawn into reserve. Both Nos.1 and 4 Coys., by the evening of the 12th, had lost over 60 per cent of their effectives, the Coldstreams had lost about the same.

The battalion had fired 20,000 rounds of ammunition and all the rifle grenades. A disaster had overcome No.1 Co. for the rations had been destroyed by shell fire before they could be distributed. At this time, the front had been covered by one battery of artillery. The F.O.O. Lieut. Lewis, was wonderful. His O.P. at Gars Brugghe was heavily shelled all day, his wires broken, but in spite of it all he caused heavy casualties on the Germans, his personal bravery and that of his linesmen being beyond all praise.

No.3 Company. To turn to No.3 Company, which was in reserve, with its right 300 yards N.E. of Gombert Farm (E.29.c.) and its left on the road Verte Rue - La Couronne. The company throughout the day, several times without orders and on the initiative of its officers, restored the situation on the left of No.2 Coy., owing to the troops on their left, the K.O.Y.L.I., retiring and leaving an exposed flank. Lieut.Nash, the Company Commander, had his hand shot off by a direct hit from a whiz-bang at 1030 hours, the command of the company then falling upon Lieut.Thomas and 2/Lieut.Cox, who, with Sgt Palethorpe and two platoons, from 1230 hours until 1800 hours continually by counter-attacks and by fire, helped the left of No.2 Coy. The initiative shown by the above was beyond praise. A great many Germans were killed. As mentioned later, the line was readjusted during the night of the 12th, and No.3 Coy., as per sketch map No.2, came up into the front line.

To return to Nos. 1 & 4 Coys. The line during the night of the 12th and 13th had to be readjusted owing to the uncertain situation. The 3/Coldstream to hold from (incl.) L'Epinnette to (excl.) Le Cornet Perdue - 4/Grenadier, thence to (incl.) La Couronne, in touch with the 12/K.O.Y.L.I., on the left. (This was never established) The Irish Guards in reserve about Caudescure and Arrawage. This order lengthened the line to be held by the brigade by about 1000 yards. The Grenadier front to be held extending for no less than 1800 yards. This in spite of the fact that the battalion had had some 250 casualties.

The commanding officer, to hold this line of 1800 yds, moved up No.3 Coy. from reserve, and hence had all four companies in the line. The strength of the battalion could not have been more than 250 other ranks, and hence this was about one man per seven yards of front. In spite of the great difficulties and thanks to the great efforts of their Company etc. Commanders, the companies were able to dig themselves in in slits to hold four to five men along the new front.

This entailed considerable hardship and determination on behalf of the Officers and N.C.O's, for the men were dog tired. It was also again a very dark night - Captain Minchin had come up from the Transport and taken command of No.4 Coy. No.1 Coy. had a considerable gap between its right and the Coldstream left. A picquet was posted there by the Grenadier. Another difficulty was to fetch the ammunition which had been dumped at La Couronne in error, under orders of the Staff Captain and the Battalion Transport Officer.

Battalion Headquarters at Gars Brugghe.

During the day, from 0900 hours until dusk, Battn. H.Q. which had been observed by the Germans owing to the number of runners, and also the transport, with rations, who had come up at 0800 hours. had been fired at by two field guns in the open from L.7.a.3.3. and by a trench mortar and M.G's. The farm was set on fire, and Capt.Chapman, the I.O., and Lieut.Abbey were killed. The animals, cows, etc., were released from the burning buildings. The Battn. H.Q. lost some 50 per cent. The remainder were forced to take up a position behind the wall by the pond. At about 2100 hours, the Battn. H.Q. were moved to Fme Beaulieu (E.28.d.)

At dawn on the 13th the brigade was dug in, in slits, the 4/Grenadier as per sketch Map No.2.

The morning of the 13th was very foggy. At 0630 hours L'Epinette was captured and a German armoured car crossed the Becque, but retired owing to the fire of the Coldstream. Guardsman Jacotin, of the Coldstream Guards, though alone, held up the advance for 20 minutes until killed by a bomb. The Germans shouted out in English that they were the King's Company, Grenadier Guards, Nos.1.3 & 4 Companies were heavily engaged all day, the Germans working between the widely separated groups of the Coldstream, Grenadier, and Irish Guards on the left. At 0915 hours, the C.O. had sent orders that the line must be maintained at all costs. The officers had practically all become casualties - Capt. Sloane Stanley, No.1 Coy, and Lieut.Lyon, No.3 Coy, killed, Capt.Minchin, No.4 Coy. severely wounded, and nearly all the subalterns killed or wounded, and so the battle went on, the Germans continually breaking through the gaps on the Coldstream and Grenadier front, handling their M.G's with great skill. The Battn. H.Q. who were with the Coldstream H.Q. at Deaulieu Fme from 1500 hours, was severely engaged by Germans attacking from Verte Rue and north of it, owing to there being no one on the left of No.2 Coy. At dusk the survivors of the Companies were over-run, but the German attacks were at an end. The 1st Royal Australian Division had established its defended localities just in rear, along the eastern edge of the Nieppe Forest. The Battn. H.Q. and oddments, plus the same from the Coldstream and Irish Guards, held the line on the right of the Australians until the 14th, when they then were relieved.

We will now move to La Couronne and describe the battle on the left of the Brigade front.

No.2 Company. This company was under the command of Captain Pryce, who had been in the Gloucestershire Regt., where he had gained a Military Cross and Bar for gallantry in the face of the enemy. I think that by the end of my description of the action of this company, it will be proved what can be done with troops led by so gallant and cool a commander, who was gifted with natural military instinct. No.2 Coy. made a most skilful advance into Pont Rondin. Led by Captain Pryce, they worked down the road from house to house, which were strongly held by Germans with light automatic guns. Many Germans were killed. Capt.Pryce, armed with a rifle, killed several himself, and, from one of the survivors who went with him, I learnt that he led the way personally from house to house, and was always first. Two M.G's and two prisoners were captured, one a senior N.C.O. who had the Iron Cross and who spoke English, and these were sent to Battalion H.Q. The skill of this operation was beyond praise, as they were heavily shot at, a battery of enemy field guns 300 yards south of Pont Rondin firing down the road over open sights.

Read Captain Pryce's Messages.

Captain Pryce then determined that as he was not in touch with the company on his right and that there also seemed to be no British troops on his left, that it was useless to hold this forward position, and sent a message to that effect to Bn.H.Q. The C.O. concurred, so the line was withdrawn to its original position. The whole of the attack could be seen through glasses from Battn. H.Q.

This company, from now on, was under continual fire from trench mortars, light artillery, machine guns and snipers in the houses. Any movement was fired at. The Germans, during the afternoon made several attempts to advance, but their attacks were broken down under the fire of No.2 Company. The situation was reported as critical, at 1500 hours a message coming from Pryce that the enemy were in the buildings at Roosters Farm (F.25.d) and that the K.O.Y.L.I. seemed to be no longer holding any position and a strong German force could be seen in Bleu. The K.O.Y.LI had apparently joined in the general retirement, which seemed to be taking place on the left. Capt.Pryce adjusted the left of his line on his own initiative to meet the new tactical situation. At one period during the morning there had been a few of the West Yorks there, but they also had gone.

The company had lost some 60 per cent of their strength during the day. During the night, as has already been explained, the brigadier consented to the line being adjusted - the left flank of the company to be some 300 yards south of La Couronne.

The Commanding Officer visited Pryce during the night, and found him occupying a line of trench just in front of a water meadow at E.30 c - 400 yards S.W. of La Couronne. He had some 40 to 50 men left, dug in in slits along his front. Five boxes of S.A.A. and some rations were got up to him. During the day the 12/K.O.Y.L.I. (Pioneers who had been driven out of La Couronne) had retired to Fantasy, and Lug Farm (E.23.d & c) and a few men under the Adjutant returned that night. The attack which had driven the K.O.Y.L.I. out of their position, had started from Bleu and consisted of two battalions. No.2 Coy. then had to dig themselves in afresh and it was only by superhuman efforts that they were occupying trenches at dawn, dug in in slits, which held four to five men.

During the day of the 12th the company had fired 20,000 rounds of ammunition, resisted many attacks, had carried out one attack, and had their left flank exposed to enfilade fire, and had been heavily fired at by light artillery and trench mortars. Lessons may be learnt from the initiative shown by Captain Pryce and No. 3 Coy. (who were in reserve) in meeting the danger from the flank so quickly and that a defensive position, even on difficult ground to hold, is very hard to capture when held by determined men who refuse to yield an inch of ground.

The dawn of the 13th broke for No. 2 Coy. dug in in slits with a thickish fog shrouding the country and it was found that the Germans had worked closer to our lines with their machine guns. Captain Pryce had received orders from the commanding officer that the present line must be held at all costs. This message was acknowledged. The Germans were in the houses at La Couronne and had brought up a field gun to some 300 yards from the left of the company, where Lieutenant Phillips was with some six men. The latter moved a Lewis gun to a mould behind where they thought they could fire on the guns crew, but unfortunately Lieutenant Phillips and two men were wounded in this operation. Enemy could also be seen in Vieux Berquin. At 10.30 hours, the Brigade Major (Lyttleton) and the Commanding officer went up to within 50 yards of La Couronne, where they met Guardsman Bagshawe, the runner of No. 4 Company who reported that the centre was still intact. But by 1400 hours, the enemy were holding a line in Lug Farm along the line of the stream from La Becque (E.23.d.) to E.30.a.

[margin note: At 0915 hours, strong German attacks developed all along the line]

Colonel Alexander realised the situation from personal observation and he ordered a company of the Irish Guards, under Settrington to counter-attack. A desperate fight ensued with Germans advancing from La Becque and only six men got back that night. All of the others were casualties, but they had done splendid work and had held up the advance of the Germans, but its failure to drive back the Germans meant that the remainder of No. 2 Coy. would inevent-ably be destroyed. The Germans from La Becque, strength about 2 battalions, then hotly engaged Battn. Hqrs. and those of the 3rd Battn. Coldstream Guards, who were still together and who held up the advance. There only remains to tell the final scenes and end of No. 2 Company.

A final message was received by the commanding officer from Pryce, by a runner who crept along a ditch, to say that No. 2 Coy. was practically surrounded and the rest of the story was told by a Corporal who escaped and hid in Vieux Berquin and rejoined some 24 hours afterwards.

The Company was reduced to some 30 men by the afternoon and to some 18 men by 1815 hours, by which time the Germans were in Verte Rue and could be seen advancing towards Bois D'Aval. A short time later, the Germans determined to mop up the remainder of No. 2 Company, and advanced from the road, but Pryce charged with the bayonet, as his ammunition was exhausted, and the Germans retired. However, shortly afterwards, the Germans again charged, and the survivors were overwhelmed, fighting to the last. Two battalions had been held up by those few determined men led by an officer who, by his courage, proved himself a heroic leader of men. As one can judge from his epic messages, never once did the thought, though surrounded for several hours, occur to him to yield a single inch. His grave was never discovered. He was awarded a posthumous V.C. and no man has ever deserved it more. Only 14 men of this company of over 120 strong were heard of again, these being mostly wounded prisoners in Germany.

The battle was over, but the 4/Guards Brigade had accomplished its object. The 1st Royal Australian Division had detrained and were now holding along the Bois D'Aval and North of it.

The remaining companies of the 4th Battn. Grenadier Guards, who had lost all their officers, were surrounded and the unwounded survivors, some 60 in number, taken prisoner. Lieut. Burt, who was wounded in the arm, was shown a large number of German dead in front of the German trenches by an enemy officer. The total casualties of the Battn. were 504 Other Ranks, or 90% of their strength. That of the Coldstream Guards was practically as heavy and that of the Irish Guards was about 300. Total Brigade casualties were 39 Officers and 1,244 other ranks.

. . . .

MESSAGE FROM GENERAL DE LISLE (G.O.C. XV Corps.)

"The record of the glorious stand against overwhelming odds made by the 4/Guards Brigade is of exceptional interest. The History of the British Army can record nothing finer than the action of the 4/Guards Brigade on the 12th and 13th April."

From Lord Haig's Despatch.

"The performance of all the troops engaged in this most gallant stand, especially that of the 4/Guards Brigade, on whose front of some 4,000 yards the heaviest attacks fell, is worthy of the highest praise. No more brilliant exploit has taken place since the opening of the enemy's offensive, though gallant actions have been without number."

Lieutenant Kerr of the 8th Battn. Australian Infantry, reported that Sergeant Shaw, 4th Battn. Grenadier Guards, collected some men and remained with him in the line when told to go back to Battn. Hqrs., and remained there three days longer. He stated:-

"The men of my company and battalion are full of admiration for the way in which the Guards' fought. The morale effect on our troops by their resistance was excellent."

The 3rd Battn. Coldstream Guards and the 4th Battn. Grenadier Guards were amalgamated into a composite battalion with Major Gilbilan as second-in-command. In all the history of the regiments this has never been done before. They held the line until the 27th and had a certain amount of casualties owing to shelling, two Grenadier Officers, Rolfe and Richardson, being killed.

The A.P.M. sent a message to the 4th Guards Brigade that not a single straggler from the 4th Guards Brigade had been found on the roads during the 12th and 13th April.

APPENDIX II.

LESSONS TO BE LEARNT.

Colonel Beckwith-Smith will kindly give an appreciation of the situation of how he considers the Brigade front should now be held with our present arms, etc.

Opinions have differed considerably about this, and, during the London District Staff Ride which took place some years ago, no definite decisions were made. It will be interesting to hear an unprejudiced opinion from someone who was not there. Subaltern officers will then give out their company orders, etc.

There are, however, certain lessons which must be emphasised, as the action taken during the battle violates completely the teachings of our own F.S.R. and I.T.

1. The line held was a linear one, and not held in depth.

2. The Reserve Battalion was used to reinforce threatened points, and not to counter-attack.

   Note:- Colonel Alexander's decision on the 13th, without reference to the Brigade. An instantaneous decision which was a very difficult one to make. It had very important results.

3. The moving of the Brigade
   (i) Without dinners.
   (ii) Without any reconnaissance.
   (iii) With very faulty information.

4. The taking up of the defensive position. The Brigade front had open flanks, was held in the worst possible ground - low lying - open to observation - difficult to dig in. No use was made of the houses along the road Caudescure - La Couronne. Suggest that line for the forward line of defended localities should have been the road with outposts in front.

5. The attack on the 12th, at 1100 hours, without artillery or machine gun support and both flanks in the air. What was the object. The Brigadier should have refused.

6. The break down of administration. Look ahead - no wire, tools or arrangements for rations.

7. Lack of co-ordination and control. Brigade Headquarters some miles behind. Divisional Headquarters still many more miles behind.

8. Suggestion. Ought not battalion commanders, when they realised that there was no commander, to have met and readjusted the front held by the brigade on their own initiative. The Brigadier was more anxious about his right flank than his left. This was perfectly secure - the obstacle was the Foret de Nieppe, which secured it.

9. Attached is an appreciation of the situation written by the Lt.-Colonel with exactly the same information as the Brigadier, 4th Guards Brigade, had.

. . . .

INFORMATION AVAILABLE TO BRIGADIER WHEN MAKING HIS APPRECIATION.

(a) 50 Div. outskirts Merville.

(b) Elements 29th Div. about Vieux Berquin and some troops believed to be at Arrawage.

(a) and (b) above both lack confirmation.

(c) Orders from Div. to restore situation on right of 29 Div.

. . . .

SECRET.

SUGGESTED APPRECIATION.

By Brigadier-General Leslie Butler ..... hrs 11th April 1918.

Ref. Map 36 A. N.E.

OBJECT.

TO RESTORE SITUATION ON RIGHT FLANK 29 DIV. AND TO PREVENT ANY FURTHER ADVANCES OF THE ENEMY.

FACTORS.

1. Own Troops.

   (a) Elements 29 Div. believed to be Vieux Berquin (E.24) and to East but this is not confirmed.
   (b) 50 Div. is reported fighting northern outskirts Merville (K.29.) but no confirmation as to positions held tonight.
   (c) Troops reported about Arrawage (K.10.) - no confirmation.

2. Enemy.

   (a) Has been attacking successfully and he has made a further appreciable advance today. It is to be anticipated that the attack will be renewed. His artillery is deficient except in lighter natures owing, presumably, to difficulty in moving it forward.
   (b) West of Lille - Hazebrouck road, there is not much activity and the flanks of his attack at present seems to rest to East of Nieppe Forest.

3. Topography.

   (a) Waterways.
   R.Lawe and Merville - Estaires canal are formidable obstacles with few crossings. Before he can get heavier natures of artillery across, he will have to gain more room in the North.

   (b) Roads.
   (i) The roads are few which are of value for use by M.T., and the constant wear imposed by H.T. They radiate from Merville and Estaires.
   (ii) The road Merville - La Motte au Bois - Hazebrouck leads N.W. through Nieppe Forest. This route runs away from his general trend of attack, passes through the difficult attack area of the Forest, and can be quickly defended at La Motte au Bois bottle neck, which cannot be engaged by artillery with ground observation.
   (iii) The other routes from Merville and Estaires lead through Neuf Berquin (L.14.) or La Couronne (E.30.) to Mont de Merris (E.5.). All roads in the area are bad to line Mont de Merris - Merris (F.1.) - Outtersteene (N.9.)

   (c) Countryside.
   The area is very flat, much intersected by ditches and waterways: it does not lend itself to digging, nor indeed does it facilitate cross-country movement in attack. There are numerous villages and farms which form a strong defence if utilized; the enemy is deficient at present in heavier natures of artillery and he must be faced with difficulties about O.P's, unless he relies on very long comns - unreliable.

COURSES OPEN.

(a) ENEMY.

A renewal of the attack is certain. This can be directed:-
   (i) Towards Hazebrouck.
   (ii) North through Vieux Berquin towards Mont de Merris.

The Hazebrouck attack is eccentric to his direction of advance so far, and, for the topographical reasons previously stated, is far from attractive.
It may confidently be anticipated that an attack through Vieux Berquin will be made.

(b) **SELF**.

    (i) To counter-attack.
    (ii) To occupy a defensive position.

A counter-attack, with no information as to the present position of the enemy or of our own troops, is out of the question. The available artillery (one Field Battery) to support it is meagre, and, at present, there are no located targets to engage with precision. Anyway, the first duty is to restore the position on the right flank of 29 Div., to stop the enemy by fire, and then later an opportunity for counter-attack may present itself.

<u>To consider the defensive position.</u>

This must be in depth and full use made of buildings, so as to get cover as quickly as possible, and to make full use of surprise effect. The Nieppe Forest will prove a fine bastion if used to protect the right flank. It is all important amply to safeguard the road Neuf Berquin - Mont de Merris and the defence must be amply wide to either flank fit to frustrate local attempts at outflanking. 29 Div. right elements in Vieux Berquin, and some other troops believed to be ? Arrewage or ? Caubescure.
As the roads from Merville pass either through Verte Rue (E.29) or Neuf Berquin, and finally join up at La Couronne, this is a point of tactical importance. The present enemy positions are unknown, but it is important to establish the foremost line of defended localities on a position which can be consolidated and to use the Nieppe Forest to the best advantage. The line indicated would appear to be - S.E. corner of Nieppe Forest (E.28.c.) - Verte Rue - La Couronne - Bleu, with outposts at Arrewage, Le Cornet Perdue (K.5.), Kew Cross (K.6.), Rooster Farm (F.25.)

PLAN.

1. Forward Battns. 3/Coldstream Guards right, 4/Grenadier Guards left.

2. <u>Inter Bn. boundary.</u> (All incl. 3/Coldstream Guards) Vierhouck (K.12.) - Le Cornet Perdue (K.5.) - Verte Rue (E.29.) - La Becque (E.23.) - Ankle Fm. (E.17.) - Moleghein (E.10.)

3. <u>Foremost line of defended localities</u>, to include Houses, S.E. corner Nieppe Forest (E.28.), Verte Rue (E.29.), La Couronne (E.30.), Bleu (F.19.)

4. <u>Outposts.</u>
General line Arrewage (K.10.) - Le Cornet Perdue (K.5.) - Kew Cross (K.6.) - Rooster Farm (F.25.). To be withdrawn under Bn. arrangements when definitely known an attack is imminent.
<u>Patrolling</u>, in advance of the outpost line to be actively conducted with a view of ascertaining the positions occupied by the enemy.

5. <u>Reserve Coys. Forward Bns.</u>

    3/Coldstream Guards.   To have patrols in Aval Wood with a view to opposing any attempts of the Germans to penetrate into the forest. Liaison post with troops in La Motte au Bois to be established.

    4/Grenadier Guards.   In addition to any counter-attack role allotted by battn. commdr., to recce., with a view to occupation, to protect the left flank of the Bde., a position about Lessage Farm (F.13.) - Labbis Fm. (F.13.) - Lynde Fm. (F.13.).

6. <u>Bn. H.Q. Forward Battns.</u>

    (a) 3/Coldstream Guards.   Ankle Fm. (A.17.)
    (b) 4/Grenadier Guards.   Vieux Berquin.

7. <u>Reserve Bn.</u>

    2/I.Guards.   Grand Sec Bois.

8. <u>Fd. Batty.</u>

    To be in support 4/Grenadier Guards.
    Targets to be selected after recce.

9. <u>Bde. H.Q.</u>

    Mont de Merris.

                            (sgd) L. Butler.
                                        Br.-Gen.,
                                Bdr. 4/Guards Brigade.

. . . .

<u>APPENDIX III.</u>   (<u>Also study Sketch 3.</u>)

    Some translations made from the secret archives of the IV German Army (Von Arnim) and messages and orders issued by General Von Lessberg, Chief of Staff, IV Army.

    It is hoped by these to show a little of what was going on on the enemy's side.

1. As far as can be ascertained, the XV Corps were the attacking troops.
    The Brigade was attacked by the 35th German Div. plus one Bde. 25th Div. on the 12th and 13th. The 8th Division had taken Merville - see Sketch No.3.

2. General Ludendorff exercised a complete control over all the operations.

3. Not the commanders, but the General Staff, during the battles played the predominant role. It made the decisions and ran the battle. Not once during Ludendroff's conversations with Von Lossberg did he mention Hindenburg's name, nor did Von Lossberg ever refer to his commander, Von Arnim. Von Kuhl never referred anything to the Crown Prince Rupprecht.

4. The Germans were too cautious and did not exploit their successes.

5. The orders issued by the Staff were very clear and precise, and contained nothing extraneous.

6. Object.
To give the knock-out blow to the British by seizing Hazebrouck - Cassel and the hills of Flanders, Kemmel, etc., and then to seize Poperinghe, and the cutting off of the 2nd British Army (Plumer).

7. Orders to the IV Army to attack between Armentieres and the La Bassee Canal with the right Corps to seize Bailleul as soon as possible.

8. Reports on the roads. The roads are very bad and prevent the movement forward of the artillery.

9. Message. At 1045 hours, the river Lys is crossed at Sailly with one company and at Estaires with two battalions,

10. Translations of many messages from the Chief of Staff point to the fact that his mind was bent on the capture of the line Wulverghem - Neuve Eglise - Bailleul first and then Poperinghe. On the 11th he is issuing instructions in case the British evacuate the Ypres salient, so as to turn the defeat of the British into a disaster.

11. Another of his orders was that divisional and Bde. Hqrs. must be well forward to take control when difficulties arise.

12. Continuous blocks on the roads were caused by the transport.

13. The VI Army did not make its principal effort against Hazebrouck, as Sir Douglas Haig had conceived, but further north.

14. The premature movements of the British reserves in daylight, showed the Germans what use we were going to make of the reserves.

15. The Germans had the impression that the British had a great many machine guns but little artillery.

16. On the 13th, the axis of the attack of the VI Army should be directed on Monts des Cats (Godewaersvelde.).

17. Orders for the VI Army on the morning of the 13th 3 Divisions (II Corps) to capture Bailleul. Failure - Ludendorff arranges artillery.

18. On the 12th the Germans endeavoured to advance from Vieux Berquin but their attacks were repulsed.

19. The Chief of Staff contributes the lack of success of the Germans on the 13th, to the "scandalous" preparation of the artillery. Batteries who remained far too far behind the front troops. Probably difficulty about O.P's and communications.

20. On the afternoon of the 14th, the IV Army reported to Ludendorff that their advance was completly stopped.

21. Marshal Foch refused to relieve troops during the course of the battle as it renders uneffective both relieving and relieved troops for a considerable period. The loss of Kemmel was caused owing to the attack taking place at dawn on the morning the French had relieved the British.

22. From Von Lossberg's diary:-

> "The British, without doubt, are an extraordinary tenacious enemy who defend their ground foot by foot. Our greatest danger lies in the number of their machine guns, well sited and used. The English artillery does not trouble us a bit."

23. Germans listened in to one of our Corps wireless messages and learnt that the French were arriving.

. . . .

WO95

1226/2

4th Bttn Grenadier Guards
War Diary May 1918

WAR DIARY
or
INTELLIGENCE SUMMARY.

(Erase heading not required.)

Army Form C. 2118.

4th Bn Grenadier Guards

Vol 37

Place	Date	Hour	Summary of Events and Information	Remarks and references to Appendices
HONDEGHEM	1 May		Battalion found fatigue party of 200 men + 3 officers to work on the HALLEBAST Road. Defences. Captain C. Sloan & Captain Stanley returned to the Batt'n from XIII Corps Emp Coy. Remainder of Battalion trained under Lieut Tuckwell in L.G. Lewis Gun fatigue Party. Firing attacked at A.P.B. Orders from II Army Transferred received for XV Corps 231st Divn.	7/10/96 Alst 8/6
HONDEGHEM	2 May		Fatigue party of 3 Offrs - 200 o.r. Remainder of Batt's trained in Lewis Gun under Lt. Tuckwell. Subaltern Officers taken in Tactical Scheme by 2nd in Command.	Weather fine. as above. Weather fine.
HONDEGHEM	3 May		Batt's found bathing from 7AM to 10.30 PM. Coy Officers + Pelton-Sgt Instructor of XV Corps School Bardenberghem at work.	Weather fine. Heavy Bombardment at night.

WAR DIARY
or
INTELLIGENCE SUMMARY.

Army Form C. 2118.

Place	Date	Hour	Summary of Events and Information	Remarks and references to Appendices
HONDEGHEM	4th May		Fatigue party found B 200 men to work on HAZEBROUCK defences. Lewis Gun Training. Weather fine. Cricket match v Irish Guards Batt. won.	
HONDEGHEM	5th May Sunday	10 am	Fatigue party found B 200 men to work on HAZEBROUCK defences. Voluntary Divine Service. C.O.'s Inspection of Billets. Weather fine.	
HONDEGHEM	6th May Monday		Coy Training. Lewis Gun Training. Training of Officers in Tactical Schemes. Weather fine – Rain at night. Marned Mares and Fifes of Bde & C∘ B∘Sade [C o h 1 ar qd b gd] to Hazebrouck for Ceremonies. Gone 5 offrs 20 o.r. of Batt.	
HONDEGHEY	7th May Tuesday		Much Rain in morning. Coys trained in Billets. Instruction of young offrs by C.O. 31st Div Heavy bombardment around METEREN. o/c 31st Div promoted to rank over Comenel 83rd Div. Captain G C Sloane – Stanley been appointed A.D.C. to G.O.C. Div.	

Army Form C. 2118.

WAR DIARY
or
INTELLIGENCE SUMMARY.
(Erase heading not required.)

Place	Date	Hour	Summary of Events and Information	Remarks and references to Appendices
HONDEGHEM	8th Wed		Fatigue party of 175 men found to work as before.	
HONDEGHEM	9th Thur		Company training. 26500 A/Cpl. R. RICHMOND } awarded D.C.M. 28181 L/Cpl. R. BURT MASSEY }	
ditto	10th Frid		Company training and baths. C.O. started on leave.	
ditto	11th Sat		Fatigue party of 175 men found to work on "B" line. Instruction of young officers by 2nd in Command. Brigadier inspected transport	
ditto	12th Sun		Fatigue party as above. Lewis gunners and snipers shot on 30" range. Voluntary C. of E. Service at 6 p.m.	
ditto	13th Mon		No 1 Coy. fired on 30" range. No 2 Coy. trained and performed fatigue (bringing hay). G.O.C. 3rd 2nd Div. approved the Lieut the A.H.6. Fraseringe W.C. Vickwell M.C. Shirley Lafere Kasley, Batayle Eastein ...	

Army Form C. 2118.

WAR DIARY
or
INTELLIGENCE SUMMARY.
(Erase heading not required.)

Place	Date	Hour	Summary of Events and Information	Remarks and references to Appendices
HONDEGHEM	14th Tues		Brigade practised Ceremonial Parade for presentation of medal ribbons by Corps Commander. Order attached as App.	App 197
HONDEGHEM	15th Wed		The Army Commander (Gen. PLUMER) inspected the Brigade and presented Medal Ribbons. Orders & names of recipients attached.	App 198
HONDEGHEM	16th Thurs		Fatigue party of 175 men found to work on "B" line. No 2 Coy and Lewis gunners fired rifle practice on the range. Orders for Bn: to relieve Res. Bn: of Front Line Bde received. Attached as App. C.O. went up to Res. Line and arranged relief. A very hot day.	App 199.
HONDEGHEM	17th Fri		Orders for relief cancelled at 10 a.m. C.O. returned from leave. Battalion paraded for Till.	
HONDEGHEM	18th Sat		Befts found fatigue party 180 O.R. to work at HALLEBROCK Defences. Remainder under Coy Funeral under Capt Tuckwell O.C.	

Army Form C. 2118.

WAR DIARY
or
INTELLIGENCE SUMMARY.

(Erase heading not required.)

Instructions regarding War Diaries and Intelligence Summaries are contained in F. S. Regs, Part II. and the Staff Manual respectively. Title pages will be prepared in manuscript.

Place	Date	Hour	Summary of Events and Information	Remarks and references to Appendices
HONDEGHEM	19th Sunday	9.30 am	Church Parade attended by Major General Comg 31st Division and the Brigadier 4th Guards Brigade. The following J. Officers is made for living M.M.L Hodnye M.C. took over command Captain Hon M. A. A. Norm transferred from No 2 Co to No 2 Co Lt. A.A. Norm transferred from No 2 Co G No 1.5.C. Weather fine & very hot.	
HONDEGHEM SAULTY	20th Monday	11 am	left Hondeghem by march route. The Batt. left at P.H. Q reserve at SAULTY Administered by Brussels Division	
		5 pm	left STOMER DOCKEN to proceed via CHOCQUES to LABUISSIERE to HANDICOURT the Battalion's weather began	
SAULTY	21st Tuesday	2 am	Arrived HANDICOURT. Marched to SAULTY in camp by	
		4 pm	very hot Camp in SAULTY CHATEAU grounds. Weather very hot. Battn. bivouacked. Camp in afternoon. Battn. Brigade Orders for Move attached as	Apps 200

A5834 Wt.W4973/M687 750,000 8/16 D.D.&L. Ltd. Forms/C.2118/13.

WAR DIARY
or
INTELLIGENCE SUMMARY.
(Erase heading not required.)

Army Form C. 2118.

Place	Date	Hour	Summary of Events and Information	Remarks and references to Appendices
SAULTY	22nd Wednesday		Adjutants parade. Companies trained under Company Commanders. C.O. inspected defences of to be held with the Brigade. Weather fine.	
SAULTY	23rd Thursday		Training Adjutants Parade. Coy Training under Company Commanders. Classes of Instruction. Weather fine. The following appointments are promulgated:- No 13511 C.S.M. R.S. Bly L.R. to be Coy Sgt Major & O. Emoy of the Bn. No 11544 Sgt H. Adams to be Coy Br Sgt to No 4 Coy. No 14088 a/C.Q.M.S. E.J. Ross. To be Coy Sgt & Vice C.Q.M.S. Gamball &c &c	
PACITY	24th Friday		Adjutants Parade. Coy Training. His Majesty the King has awarded the VICTORIA CROSS to Captain T.T. Pryce. M.C. The act of gallantry in which he	Cop Dot

Army Form C. 2118.

WAR DIARY
or
INTELLIGENCE SUMMARY.
(Erase heading not required.)

Instructions regarding War Diaries and Intelligence Summaries are contained in F.S. Regs., Part II. and the Staff Manual respectively. Title pages will be prepared in manuscript.

Place	Date	Hour	Summary of Events and Information	Remarks and references to Appendices
SAUCY	25th Saturday		Coy training. Lieut P.H.B. Knox 2m. M.C. rejoined the Battalion & posted to No 1 Coy. Lieut H. h. Gillott joined the Battalion & 2 Lieut H.H.M. Portal to No 2 Co. posted to No 2 Co.	
SAUCY	26th Sunday		Divine Service. Inspection of Camp by C.O. Lieut J.F. Greenwood rejoined the Battalion and is posted to No 1 Co. — The following have been entered in the Chiefs dispatch of April 7th — Commander in Chief. Major C.P.H. WALKER D.S.O. Captain E.R. GENERAL D.S.O. 2 Lt ENGLEBY M.C. T.T. Ry. Co. M.C. R.S.M. R. FRANCIS A draft of 4 n.c.o.(subft) and 24 men joined the Battn.

12241 Irwin Major

Army Form C. 2118.

WAR DIARY
or
INTELLIGENCE SUMMARY.
(Erase heading not required.)

Instructions regarding War Diaries and Intelligence Summaries are contained in F. S. Regs., Part II. and the Staff Manual respectively. Title pages will be prepared in manuscript.

Place	Date	Hour	Summary of Events and Information	Remarks and references to Appendices
SAULTY	Monday 27th		Coy route marched. Distance 8 miles via Bavincourt and BARLY. Reptn 8 Battn went to Balls heater the football Match Officers v Sergeants Officers Won 2 - 1.	
SAULTY	Tuesday 28th		Coy Training and Adjutants Parade. High School Gun Shelled SAULTY. heather fine.	
SAULTY	Wednesday 29th		Coy Training and Adjutant Parade. No 2 Coy shot on the range at 5 p.m.	
SAULTY	Thursday 30th		Coy Training and Bath at BAVINCOURT. No 2 Coy held a concert in the Y.M.C.A. Hut.	

Army Form C. 2118.

WAR DIARY
or
INTELLIGENCE SUMMARY.

(Erase heading not required.)

Instructions regarding War Diaries and Intelligence Summaries are contained in F. S. Regs., Part II. and the Staff Manual respectively. Title pages will be prepared in manuscript.

Place	Date	Hour	Summary of Events and Information	Remarks and references to Appendices
SAULTY	July 31st		No 1 Coy. route marched. Posts. - BARLY - SOMBRIN - PAULTY.	
			No 2 Coy - Coy. training.	
			C.O. and Adjt. attended a lecture with the Brigadier.	
			Lt. R. de POER TRENCH joined the Battn. and posted to No 1 Coy. Army to-day.	
			High velocity gun shelled SAULTY and outskirts of the Camp during the night.	
	31st		List of officers serving with the Battn. attached as appendix.	App 20.2
			Strength of Battn. attached as appendix.	App 20.3

[signature] R. Pilcher
Lt. Col.
Cmdg. 4th Battalion
Grenadier Guards

SECRET.   Copy No. War Diary

4th Battalion Grenadier Guards Order No. 185.

Reference Map Sheet 27. 1/40,000.   19th May 1918.

1. (a) The Battalion will be transferred to the 3rd Army Area tomorrow May 20th.
   (b) The move will be carried out by march route, bus and rail.

2. (a) The Battalion will march to embussing point (C.22.a.8.0.) on the EBBLINGHEM - HAZEBROUCK road, and will embus at 1 p.m.
   (b) The head of the Battalion will pass the starting point (V.2.c.3.2.) at 11 a.m.
   (c) Order of March:-   B.H.Q.
                                Drums
                                No 1 Coy.
                                No 2 Coy.
   (d) Dress:- Service Dress Marching Order; Steel Helmets on packs; Water bottles filled.

3. Officers' kits, Mess Boxes &c will be collected at 7.30 a.m. from Company H.Qrs.

4. A Billetting party under Captain Tuckwell. M.C. consisting of
                                1 N.C.O. per Company
                                1 for B.H.Q.
                                1 for Transport
   will report to Captain E.H. Tuckwell, at 7 a.m. at No 1 Coy's H.Qrs. They will proceed to embussing point with the 2nd Bn Irish Guards and will proceed by train leaving ST OMER at 1 p.m.

5. Separate orders for the move of the transport have been issued. The Transport leaves the transport field at 8.30 a.m.

6. (a) Reveille tomorrow will be at 5 a.m.
       Breakfast tomorrow will be at 6 a.m.
   (b) Haversack rations will be carried.
       Teas will probably be provided at ST OMER.
   (c) There is a Canteen at ST OMER Station. If there is time, 2 men per section will be marched there to buy food if required.

7. On arrival at ST OMER, the Battalion will entrain and will detrain at MONDICOURT PAS. (Map Sheet LENS 11. 1/100,000). Train leaves at 6 p.m.

8. Battalion Headquarters will close at LINGHEM at 10.30 a.m. and re-open in the new area on completion of the move.

                                                    [signature]
                                                    Captain.
                                            Adjutant, 4th Battalion Grenadier Guards.

Copies to:-   1. No 1 Coy.   2. No 2 Coy.
               3. 2nd in Command.   4. Quartermaster.
               5. Captain Tuckwell. MC.   6. Transport Officer.
               7. 4th Guards Brigade.   8. 2nd Bn. Irish Guards.
               9. Sgt Major J. Little.   10. War Diary.

Extract of Divisional Routine Order 940/4063 d/ May 24/1918.
HONOURS & AWARDS.

Notification has been received that His Majesty the King has awarded the VICTORIA CROSS to Lieut.(a/Captain) T.T.PRYCE.MC 4th. Battalion Grenadier Guards:-

The following recommendation was submitted in favour of this officer:-

"During the German attacks about VIEUX BERQUIN, 11th.April, this Officer was in command of the Company on the left of the 4th. Battalion Grenadier Guards.

He was ordered to attack the village of PONT RONDIN on the morning of the 12th. April. He personally led forward two platoons, working from house to house, killing some thirty Germans, seven of whom he killed himself.

On the 13th, he was occupying a position near La COURONNE with some thirty to forty men, the remainder of his company having become casualties. As early as 8/15.a.m his left flank was surrounded, and the enemy was enfilading him.

He was attacked no less than four times during the day, and each time beat off the hostile attack, killing many Germans.

Meanwhile, the enemy brought up three field guns to within 300 yards of his line, and were firing over open sights and knocking his trench in. At 6/15.p.m the enemy had worked to within 60 yards of his trench - he then called on his men, telling them to cheer and charge the Germans and fight to the last. Led by Captain PRYCE, they left their trench and drove back the Germans with the bayonet some 100 yards. Half an hour later the Germans had again approached in stronger force. By this time Captain PRYCE had only 17 men left and every round of his ammunition had been fired. Determined that there should be no surrender, he once again led his men forward in a bayonet charge, and was last seen engaged in a fierce hand-to-hand struggle with overwhelming numbers of Germans.

This was witnessed by a Corporal who subsequently escaped through the German lines.

I consider this officer worthy of the highest honour, and his action and bravery unsurpassable. With some forty men he had held back at least a Battalion of Germans for over ten hours, with no troops on his left flank.

His company undoubtedly stopped the Germans advancing right through the British Line, and thus had great influence on the battle.

His company was practically destroyed in the Battle on the 12th. and 13th. April.

4th. Battn: Grenadier Guards.

Officers present with the Bn.
May 31/1918.

Lt. Colonel W. S. Pilcher, D.S.O.	Commanding.
Major C. F. A. Walker, MC.	2nd. in Command.
Captain Hon. F. E. Needham.	O.C., Coy.
Captain C. R. Gerard, D.S.O.	Adjutant.
Captain G.C.Sloane Stanley.	A.D.C., GOC.32nd.Dvn.
Captain I. H. Ingleby.	a/Quartermaster.
Captain Hon.A.H.L.Hardinge, MC.	O.C., Coy.
Captain E.H.Tuckwell, MC.	I/C. Lewis Guns.
Lieut. R.P.LeP. Trench, MC.	
Lieut. C.G.Keith, MC.(a/Capt).	Staff learner.Gds.Dvn
Lieut. C.E.Irby, MC.	
Lieut. G.W.Selby Lowndes.	Transport Officer.
Lieut. M.P.B.Wrixon, MC.	
Lieut. J.E.Greenwood.	
Lieut. R.L.Murray Lawes.	Intellgce. Officer.
2/Lieut. D.J.Knight.	attd.4th.Gds.Bde.H.Q.
2/Lieut. A.F.Alington.	
2/Lieut. Hon.S.E.Marsham.	Hospital(Sick).
2/Lieut. P.G.S.Gregson Ellis.	
2/Lieut. H.V.Gillett.	

WO 95

1226/2

4 Btth Grenadier Guards

June 1918

4th Bn Grenadier Guards.

WAR DIARY
or
INTELLIGENCE SUMMARY.

Army Form C. 2118.

June 1918

Place	Date	Hour	Summary of Events and Information	Remarks and references to Appendices
SAULTY	Saturday 1st June		Adjutants Parade. Kickets fuse. Coy Training. 2Lt R.H.P. Trench M.C. joined the Battalion and is posted to No 1 Co. R.S.M. LITTLE R.I.C.M. and Sgt PITT D.C.M. proceeded to England on 6 days duty with the 5th Batt.	Apx 52 Append.
"	Sunday 2nd June		Batn Rath R.C. Service. C.O. inspected Camp, lines & all rooms. Wet canteens attached. Batt. Sports list attached	Apx 52 Append.
"	Monday 3rd June		Battalion found fatigue party of 250 men to work at BARLINCOURT. N.C.Os Class Lewis Gun Class Class of Signalers, Chain of NCOs for a scheme. C.O. took officers.	
"	Tuesday 4th June		Coy Training — Programme Lieut E. L. Vaux joined the Battalion this day and is posted to No 2 Co.	Apx 52 (not attached).
"	Wednesday 5th June		Batt fatigue party of 125 men formed to put in posts in 52nd Div Heaven. Training continued. Brigadier Inspected the Camp and expressed himself well pleased with its state	

Army Form C. 2118.

WAR DIARY
or
INTELLIGENCE SUMMARY.
(Erase heading not required.)

Place	Date	Hour	Summary of Events and Information	Remarks and references to Appendices
SAUCHY	Thursday 6th June		Work and Training as in previous day. Battalion bathed at Sauchy Baths. Birthday Honours. The undermentioned were awarded the MILITARY CROSS — Lieutenant G.R. Green — Sgt Major J. Littler D.C.M. 8380	
"	Friday 7th June		Both — Training as in previous day. C.O took officers on a route march & bath. weather a hope.	
"	Saturday 8th June		Both — Training as in previous day. Weather fine.	
"	Sunday 9th June		C.O. inspected Camp. Divine Service 9 A.M. Birthday Honours. The undermentioned awarded the D.C.M. No 11086 Trib. Sgt F.W. Nay.	
"	Monday 10th June		Fatigue Party of 160 men formed for training. C.O took officers instructional Class. Orders to move to No 2 H.Q. CHQ CHIE for Officers School	

WAR DIARY
or
INTELLIGENCE SUMMARY.

(Erase heading not required.)

Army Form C. 2118.

Instructions regarding War Diaries and Intelligence Summaries are contained in F.S. Regs., Part II. and the Staff Manual respectively. Title pages will be prepared in manuscript.

Place	Date	Hour	Summary of Events and Information	Remarks and references to Appendices
La CAUCHIE	Tuesday 11th June		Battalion moved to LA CAUCHIE. Transport personnel at SAULTY - New Class 'A' billets for much. Order for much - days Rats is. Billetted in orchard. Made Camp.	A.F/3 209
La CAUCHIE	Wednesday 12th June		Battalion improved Camp. Weather fine.	
La CAUCHIE	Thursday 13th June		Battalion found fatigue party to work on POW BERLES AU BOIS Shitch. Every man available work. Weather fine.	
"	Friday 14th June		Battalion worked as above from 8 A.M - 2 P.M. Drums sent out Recreation fine. Battalion marched off from billets 6.45 P.M.	
"	Saturday 15th June		Work as above. Weather fine.	
"	Sunday 16th June	9.0 A.M	Drums & Bugles. 10 A.M C.O. bats general Camp. S.M. Oakley joined the Battn on as Battleyeant Major - Sergeant Dixon to xxx a draft of 14 men to Battn on furlough before leaving for England for week.	
"	Monday 17th June		The draw fell for lants as a previous week. 25 keber of 11th Battalion averaged 10 England as Instructors. Security. Weather fine	

War Diary

SECRET.

Copy No....7...

4th Battalion Grenadier Guards Operation Order No.167.

Ref. Map Sheet 51c. 1/40,000.   10th June 1918.

1. The Battalion (less Details and Transport) will move to LA CAUCHIE tomorrow 11th. for work on the BERLES-AU-BOIS – GOUY Switch.

2. The Battalion will parade in Camp at 3 p.m.
    Dress:- Service Dress Marching Order.
    Route:- Road junction V.8.d.8.8. – LA HERLIERE – LA CAUCHIE.
    Order of March:-   Drums
                                B.H.Q.
                                  1
                                  2
                                Transport.
    Distance:- 100 yards between Companies.

3. No 2 Company will furnish a party of 20 men for pitching the new camp. Parade 7 a.m. under Lieut C.E.IRBY. MC.

4. Kits, Lewis Guns and 21 Magazines per gun will be loaded on the limbers at 2 p.m.

5. Separate orders have been issued to the Transport Officer.

6. Details left behind will come under the orders of Capt HON. A.H.L. HARDINGE.MC.

7. Advanced Battn. H.Qrs will open at LA CAUCHIE on completion of the move.

                                                Captain.
                        Adjutant, 4th Battalion Grenadier Guards.

Copies issued to:-

1. No 1 Company.   2. No 2 Company.
3. Quartermaster.   4. Transport Officer.
5. Lieut C.E.IRBY. MC.   6. Capt HON. A.H.L.HARDINGE.MC.
7. Drill Sgt E.DAY. DCM. 8. 4th Guards Brigade.
    9 & 10. War Diary.

Army Form C. 2118.

WAR DIARY
or
INTELLIGENCE SUMMARY.
(Erase heading not required.)

Place	Date	Hour	Summary of Events and Information	Remarks and references to Appendices
Le Cauchy	Tuesday 18th June		Fatigue party as on previous days - Weather fine.	
"	Wednesday 19th June		Fatigue party as on previous day. The following awards have appeared in Companies list Battalion Honours List Meritorious Service Medal. No 11594 Sgt J. Burrows " 20691 " H. Perchin	
"	Thursday 20th June		Fatigue Party as above.	
"	Friday 21st June		Fatigue Party as above. Some rain.	
"	Saturday 22nd June		Fatigue Party as above. General Divisional Horsplr Battalion quit in the Batn. Cost Competition and Coleman. Competition.	
"	Sunday 23rd June		9.30 Divine Service. 10.30 Camp Inspection by Camp 2nd Brace Battalion Sports.	

A5534 Wt.W4973/M687 750,000 8/16 D. D. & L. Ltd. Forms/C.2118/13.

WAR DIARY
or
INTELLIGENCE SUMMARY.

Army Form C. 2118.

Place	Date	Hour	Summary of Events and Information	Remarks and references to Appendices
LA COUCHIE	Monday 24th June		Battalion Fatigue Party as on previous week. Captain J.H.E. Simpson joined the Battalion and is posted to No. 2 Co.	
	Tuesday 25th June		Fatigue party as on previous day. Lt. H.G. Higgins M.C. joined the Battalion and is posted to No. 2 Co	
	Wednesday 26th June		Fatigue Party as on previous day. A demonstration of Lewis Gun tactics given by 2nd So Wales Bde an attack by Lewis gun party.	
	Thursday 27th June		Same Fatigue Party.	
	Friday 28th June		Same Fatigue Party. XI Corps issued the following Award MILITARY MEDAL No. 13210 A/Sgt. B. SHARP for attack on No. 12 2nd April	
	Saturday 29th June		Same Fatigue Party. Weather very hot.	

Army Form C. 2118.

WAR DIARY
or
INTELLIGENCE SUMMARY.
(Erase heading not required.)

Place	Date	Hour	Summary of Events and Information	Remarks and references to Appendices
LA CAUCHIE	Sunday 9AM Church 30th June	10 AM	Parade Coy inspection & Billets. H.R.H the Duke of Connaught & Colonel of the Regiment inspected the billets and Cookers & watched Coy of the Battalion the Command Officer in their appearance. Programme of his visit attached. List of Officers serving with the Battalion. Strength of Batt.ⁿ	* App 207 App 208 App 209
			A party of 50 other ranks under Capt.ⁿ F. H. TUCKWELL M.C. proceeded by bus to ORIEL PLACE for the purpose of erecting a camp for the Battalion before attacked as app...	App. 210

B.S.Allen Lt Colonel
Comdg 4th Bn. Gren. Guards.

* Not attached.

4th. Battalion Grenadier Guards.

PROGRAMME
of
SPORTS
to be held
SUNDAY, June 2nd, 1918,
by kind permission of,
Lt-Colonel W.S. PILCHER, D.S.O., Commanding 4th Bn: Grenadier Guards.

---

1. 2- 0.p.m. — Battalion 100 yards. — 1st. Prize, 30 francs.
   2nd. " 20 "
   3rd. " 10 "

2. 2-15.p.m. — Long Jump. — 1st. Prize, 20 francs.
   2nd. " 10 "

3. 2-45.p.m. — Corporals' Race. 220 yards. — 1st. Prize, 20 francs,
   2nd. " 10 "
   3rd. " 5 "

4. 3- 0.p.m. — High Jump. — 1st. Prize, 20 francs.
   2nd. " 10 "

5. 3-30.p.m. — Battalion 220 yards.
   (If less than 8 runners,
   2 prizes only.) — 1st. Prize, 20 francs.
   2nd. " 10 "
   3rd. " 5 "

6. 3-45.p.m. — Final:Tug-of-War.Catch weight — 1st. Prize, 50 francs
   (6 teams:1.2.3.4.BHq.Tspt.) — 2nd. " 20 "

7. 4- 0.p.m. — Old Soldiers' Race.(Handicap) — 1st. Prize, 15 francs.
   (Entries:10 years' service & — 2nd. " 10 "
   over; 1 yd start for every — 3rd. " 5 "
   year over 10 yrs' service.
   Time on reserve to count.)

8. 4-15.p.m. — Reveille Race - 6 teams.1 NCO — 1st. Prize, 20 francs.
   & 6 men each. 1.2.3.4.BHq.Tspt — 2nd. " 10 "
   Conditions. Boots & Putties off:
   lying in tents; tents to be
   fastened;Reveille sounds,strike
   tents,get dressed in F.S.M.O. &
   do 1 lap as a team(only coat in
   pack);teams timed & inspected
   afterwards.

9. 4-45.p.m. — 1 Mile. (Open to all). — 1st. Prize, 30 francs,
   Flat. — 2nd. " "
   3rd. " "

*********** T E A ***********

10. 5-15.p.m. — Comical Relay. 440 yards. — 1st. Prize, 20 francs,
    7 teams:1.2.3.4.BHq.Drs.Tspt — 2nd. " 10 "
    4 in each team.
    Conditions. 1 man runs 120 yards on
    hands & feet;2nd.man jumping
    120 yards with feet tied; 3rd.
    man runs backwards 120 yards;
    4th. man 40 yards sack race.

11. 5-30.p.m. — Serjeants' Race. 1 mile. — 1st. Prize, 20 francs,
    220 yards. — 2nd. " 10 "
    3rd. " 5 "

-2-

12.	5-45.p.m.	Fast Bicycle Race. 1 Mile. 12 competitors;Battn.Bicycles.	1st. Prize, 20 francs 2nd. " 10 " 3rd. " 5 "
13.	6- 0.p.m.	Officers' Race: 100 yards. 1 yd. start for every year: under 2 years, Scratch. Last to have a very special prize.	
14.	6-15.p.m.	Battalion ¼ Mile. (If less than 6 runners, only 2 prizes.)	1st. Prize, 20 francs, 2nd. " 10 " 3rd. " 5 "
15.	6-30.p.m.	Relay Race.(7 teams:1.2.3.4.BHQ. Drs.Tspt.all to do 220 yards).	1st. Prize, 30 francs, 2nd. " 15 " 3rd. " 5 "
16.	6-45.p.m.	Obstacle Race.(Post entries).	1st. Prize, 20 francs, 2nd. " 15 " 3rd. " 10 " 4th. " 5 "
17.	7- 0.p.m.	Wrestling on Horses.	1st. Prize, 10 francs, 2nd. " 5 "
18.	7-15.p.m.	Consolation Race. Post entries: Open to all competitors who have not taken a prize in any event.	1st. Prize, 20 francs, 2nd. " 10 " 3rd. " 5 "

JUDGES.

Capt. the Hon.F.E.Needham,
Capt. the Hon.A.H.L.Hardinge,MC.
Capt. E.H.Tickell, MC.
Capt. J.K.Best, MC. CF.

COMMITTEE.

D/Sgt. E.W.Day.
D/Sgt. J.Norton.
C.S.M. C.A.Marriott,MM.
C.S.M. H.Burch.
C.S.M. W. Weeks.
C.Q.M.S. G.H.Masterman,DCM.MM.

STARTER.

Lieutenant J. E. GREENWOOD.

TIMEKEEPER.

Captain I. R. INGLEBY.

Selections will be played by
the Battalion Orchestral Band.

4th Battn Grenadier Guards

Programme of Sports

Drums	B.H.Q	Transport	No 1 Coy	No 2 Coy	No 3 Coy	No 4 Coy
Battalion 100 Yards						
Dmr. Jolly T. " Blake R. " Bartoll A	Pte. Hoare " Carr " Lowe " Hickey		Cpl. Asher Pte. Beckett " Barton " Greenfield	Cpl. Bud Massey Pte. Brown H. " Hill " Roberts	Cpl. Dyson Pte. Rockley " Shiagg " Goodman	Pte. Sparr " Corcoran Cpl. Fromont Pte. Bromlow
Long Jump						
	Pte. Carr " Hickey " Lowe " Dale " Moore	Pte. Birtwhistle " Shingler " Simpson " Ledgerton	Pte. Hackworth " Hills " Palmer " Stuart " Smith Cpl. Starbuck Pte. Hirst " Howarth " O'Byrne		Pte. Goodman Bird J.	Sgt. Walker Pte. Corcoran
Corporals' Race 220 Yards						
Cpl. Snellings	Cpl. Lillieshakes		Cpl. Starbuck " Burton " Cooper " Archer	Cpl. Tyndal " Robinson " Bud Massey " Otloway " Hamlet	Cpl. Dyson " Clavers " McKim " Oliver " Cobb " Cunnell " Unger " Beesley " Slade	Cpl. Booth " Piggott " Nantle " Fromont " Hanes
High Jump						
	Pte. Carr " Hickey " Lowe " Dale	Pte. McCaffrey " Smith P. " Lesterton	Pte. Straw " Fitzjoy " Hirst Cpl. Starbuck Pte. Tilting " Johnson	Cpl. Chambers " Richards Pte. Churchyard		Pte. Threadgold
Battalion 220 Yards						
Dr. Blake " Truman	Pte. Hoare " Wilson " Lowe	Pte. Simpson " Preece " Stayfe	Pte. Course " Beckett " Barton Cpl. Durtin Pte. O'Byrne " Prentice	Pte. Easy " Drake " Robert	Cpl. Dyson Pte. Rockley " Goodman " Laurie Sgt. Williams Pte. Smithen	Pte. Sago " Bridgewater " Corcoran
Final Tug-of-War						
	Team	Team	Team	Team	Team	Team
Old Soldiers' Race						
			Cpl. Shaw 17 " Thomson 11 " Caswell 10 Dr. Stuart 11 Pte. King 12 J.B. Sinland 14 Pte. Hinds 11	C.S.M. Birch 14 Sgt. Tupp 11 " Hilder 12 Pte. Simm 9 " Hanyold 8	Pte. Palach " Kerber " Brock	C.S.M. Halsall 14 Pte. Sherith 15 " Harris 11	C.S.M. Meekes Sgt. Walker " Bridges
Reveille Race						
Team	Team	Team	Team	Team	Team	Team

4th Battn. Grenadier Guards

Programme of Sports

Drums	B.H.Q	Transport	No 1 Coy.	No 2 Coy.	No 3 Coy.	No 4 Coy.
\multicolumn{7}{c}{**Battalion 100 Yards**}					
Dmr Jolly T. " Blake A. " Bartoff A.	Pte. Hoare. " Carr " Lowe. " Hickey.		Cpl. Archer. Pte. Beckett. " Barrons. " Greenfield.	Cpl. Burr Massey Pte. Brown H. " Hill " Roberts.	Cpl. Dyson. Pte. Rockley " Spragg " Goodman	Pte. Sparr. " Corcoran. Cpl. Fromant Pte. Bromilow.
\multicolumn{7}{c}{**Long Jump**}					
	Pte. Carr. " Hickey. " Lowe. " Dale. " Moore	Pte. Birtwhistle " Shingler " Simpson " Lesterton	Pte. Wakworth " Allis " Palmer. " Shaw " Smith Cpl. Starbuck. Pte. Hirst. " Howarth " O'Byrne.		Pte. Goodman. " Rockley	Sgt. Walker Pte. Corcoran.
\multicolumn{7}{c}{**Corporals' Race. 220 Yards**}					
Cpl. Spellings.	Cpl. Littleshales.		Cpl. Starbuck. " Burton. " Cooper. " Archer.	Cpl. Tyndall. " Richardson. " Co t. " Burr Massey " Ottaway " Barker.	Cpl. Dyson. " Clowes " Holden " Moss. " Coles. " Cramwell. " Inger. " Beasley. " Slade.	Cpl. Booth. " Pragett. " Mantle. " Fromant. " Hanes.
\multicolumn{7}{c}{**High Jump**}					
	Pte. Carr. " Hickey. " Lowe. " Dale.	Pte. McCaffrey " Smith R. " Lesterton.	Pte. Shaw. " Frailey. " Hill. Cpl. Starbuck. Pte. Tilling. " Jemison.	Cpl. Chambers. " Richards. Pte. Churchyard		Pte. Threadgold.
\multicolumn{7}{c}{**Battalion 220 Yards**}					
Dr. Blake. " Truman.	Pte. Hoare. " Wilson. " Lowe.	Pte. Simpson " Preece. " Scarfe.	Pte. Course. " Beckett " Barron. Cpl. Burton. Pte. O'Byrne. " Prentice	Pte. Easy " Drake. " Roberts	Cpl. Dyson Pte. Rockley. " Goodman " Loburn Sgt. Williams Pte. Sullivan	Pte. Spargo. " Bridgewater " Corcoran
\multicolumn{7}{c}{**Final Tug-of-War.**}					
	Team.	Team.	Team.	Team.	Team.	Team.
\multicolumn{7}{c}{**Old Soldiers' Race**}					
			Cpl. Shaw 14 " Simpson 11 " Barrons Dr. Smart. 14 Pte. Knig 12 L/S. Stirland 14 Pte. Hinds. 10	C.S.M. Birch 14 Sgt. Topp 11 " Gay. 12 Pte. Shaw. 4 " Wakefield 11.	Pte. Isted " Kimber " Booth	C.S.M. Horriott 14 Pte. Jarrold 14 " Murray 15	C.S.M. Weekes Sgt. Walker " Bridges.
\multicolumn{7}{c}{**Reveille Race**}					
Team.	Team.	Team.	Team.	Team.	Team.	Team.

4th Battalion Grenadier Guards

List of Prizewinners in Sports held at Saulty
June 2nd 1918

Battn. 100 Yds.	No.	Prize (Frcs)	Long Jump	No.	Prize (Frcs)	Cpls. 220 Yds.	No.	Prize (Frcs)	High Jump	No.	Prize (Frcs)	Battn. 220 Yds.	No.	Prize (Frcs)	Final Tug-of-War	No.	Prize (Frcs)
Pte. Goodman (3)	1	30	Pte. Goodman (3)	1	20	Cpl. Dyson (3)	1	20	Pte. Goodman (3)	1	20	Pte. Goodman (3)	1	20	Bn. H.Q. (D/Sgt Norton)	1	50
" Roxley (3)	2	20	" Hoare (B.H.Q.)	2	10	" Richards (2)	2	10	" Frogley (1)	2	10	L/Cpl. Dyson (3)	2	10	Transport.	2	20
L/Cpl. Dyson (3)	3	10	17'5½" & 15'11"			" Chambers (2)	3	5	4'10" & 4'9"	3	5	Dmr. Blake.	3	5			
Time 11 Secs.						Time 32 Secs.			Sgt Mansell Gren. Gds. Exhibition Jump 5'4"			Time 28 Secs.					

Old Soldiers' Race	No.	Prize (Frcs)	Reveille Race	No.	Prize (Frcs)	1 Mile (Open)	No.	Prize (Frcs)	Comical Relay	No.	Prize (Frcs)	Sgts' Race 220 Yds	No.	Prize (Frcs)	Bicycle Race	No.	Prize (Frcs)
Cpl. Shaw (Tspt)	1	15	No. 1 Coy.	1	20	Sgt Constable (P.&C.)	1	30	Transport.	1	30	CSM. Marriott (3)	1	20	Pte. Parry (D.H.Q.)	1	20
CSM. Marriott (3)	2	10	No. 4 Coy.	2	10	Capt. Lancine (I Gds)	2	-	No. 4 Coy.	2	20	L/Cpl. Masterman (3)	2	10	Cpl. Stevens (1)	2	10
" Burgh (1)	3	5				Pte. Timmey (I Gds)	3	20				Sgt Evans (3)	3	5	Pte. Palmer (1)	3	5
						Pte. Moffatt (2 G.G.)	4	10				Time 34 Secs.					

Officers' Race	No.	Prize (Frcs)	Battn ¼ Mile	No.	Prize (Frcs)	Relay Race	No.	Prize (Frcs)	Obstacle Race	No.	Prize (Frcs)	Wrestling on Horses	No.	Prize (Frcs)	Consolation Race	No.	Prize (Frcs)
Capt. Needham	1	20	Cpl. Dyson (3)	1	20	No. 3 Coy.	1	30	Pte. Bardsley (4)	1	20	Cpl. Shaw	1	10	Pte. Carr (B.H.Q.)	1	20
Lt.-Col. Pilcher	2	10	Pte. Wilson (B.H.Q.)	2	10	Bn. H. Qrs.	2	15	Smith G. (1)	2	15	Sgt Stirland	2	5	Sgt Peacock (2)	2	10
Capt. Gerrard	3	5	" Spragg (3)	3	5	Drums	3	5	Noakes (3)	3	10	Mountain the Mule			Pte. Tilling (1)	3	5
									Sgt Stirland (Tpt)	4	5	Pte. Toner (4)		5			

4th. Battalion Grenadier Guards.

Officers present with Battalion
June 30/1918.

Lt.Colonel W. S. Pilcher, DSO.
    Major C.F.A.Walker, MC.
    Captain Hon.F.E.Needham.
Capt. & Adjt.C.R.Gerard,DSO.
    Captain J.H.C.Simpson.
    Captain I. H. Ingleby.
    Captain Hon.A.H.L.Hardinge,MC.
    Captain E.H.Tuckwell,MC.

Lieutenant R.P.Le P.Trench,MC.
Lieutenant E.W.Nairn.
Lieutenant H.G.Wiggins,MC.
Lieutenant C.E.Irby,MC.
Lieutenant M.P.B.Wrixon,MC.
Lieutenant J.E.Greenwood.
Lieutenant G.W.Selby Lowndes.
Lieutenant R.L.Murray Lawes.

2/Lieutenant A.F.Alington.
2/Lieutenant Hon.S.E.Marsham.
2/Lieutenant P.G.S.Gregson Ellis.
2/Lieutenant H. V. Gillett.

****

Captain G.C.Sloane Stanley........Hospital.
Lt.(a/Capt) G.G.Keith,MC.......... attd. 4/Gds.Bde.
Lieutenant D. J. Knight................... do ......

****

4th. Battalion Grenadier Guards.
Details of variation in strength for June, 1918.

Reinforcements. (Officers.   Lt.E.W.Nairn, Capt.J.H.C.Simpson,
                (Other ranks..... 32 O.R.   (Lt.H.G.Wiggins MC.
Rejoined x Hptl.(Officers.   2/Lt Hon.S.E.Marsham.
                (Other ranks..... 3 O.R.
Sick Wastage.   (Officers.   Capt.G.C.Sloane Stanley. to Hospital.
                (Other ranks..... 10 O.R.
Other Decreases. Other ranks..... 24 O.R. to Eng. for instructional
                                                           (duties.

****

Strength of Bn June 30th   O. O.R.
                              23 561

"A" Form.
MESSAGES AND SIGNALS.

Army Form C. 2121.
(In pads of 100.)

TO: No 1 Coy   Quartermaster
No 2 Coy.

Sender's Number	Day of Month	In reply to Number	
S.D.6	29		AAA

Each Company will find an advance party for CRIEL, leaving camp tomorrow 30th by bus at a time to be notified later AAA Numbers from each Company will be 1 Sgt 2 Cpls 24 men AAA. Sgt Jones (Pioneer) and 4 pioneers will accompany the party AAA Further orders follow.

From: Adjutant, H.C.I.
Place:
Time:

(Sd) C. Gerard Capt

"A" Form
MESSAGES AND SIGNALS.

Army Form C. 2121.
(In pads of 100.)

| TO | No 1 Coy |
| | No 2 Coy |

Sender's Number: S.D.4
Day of Month: 29
AAA

Reference S.D.6 AAA Sgt Peacock as A/C.S.M Sgt Toscone as A/CQMS a cook to be detailed by No 1 Coy Pte Carr (signaller) will proceed with the party AAA Numbers to be found by Companies will now be 1 Sgt 2 Cpls 22 men from No 1 Coy, 1 Sgt 2 Cpls 21 men from No 2 Coy AAA Parade in camp at 8 A.M under Capt TOLKWELL with the days rations + rations for the 1st prox AAA. Two dixies will be taken from B.H.Q.

From: Adjutant

(Sgd) Gerard Capt

1226/2

War Diary
4 Bttn Grenadier Guards
July 1918

CONFIDENTIAL.

WAR DIARY

OF

4th Bn. Grenadier Guards

Vol. VII, 1918.

FROM: 1st July, 1918
TO: 31st July, 1918.

4th Bn Grenadier Guards

Army Form C. 2118.

WAR DIARY
or
INTELLIGENCE SUMMARY
(Erase heading not required.)

Place	Date	Hour	Summary of Events and Information	Remarks and references to Appendices
LA CAUCHIE	1st July Monday		Fatigue Party found by Bn. Rest of Bn. BERLES AU BOIS. Weather fine	
"	2nd July Tuesday		The same fatigue Party as above 1st Guards Brigade Symphoma. Weather fine	
"	3rd July Wednesday		Fatigue Party as above - 6 batts. of officers + N.C.O's attended a lecture in scouting etc by Canadian Division	
"	4th July Thursday		Fatigue Party as in previous day - Also demonstration by Canadians. Weather fine	
"	5th July Friday		Fatigue Party as in previous day - Also demonstration by Canadians - Weather fine	
"	6th July Saturday		Adjutants' Parade. Coy found Physical Exercises & Bayonet Exercises. Bng. ordered to proceed to CRIEF PLACE tomorrow.	
"	7th July Sunday		Church Parade - C.O.'s Inspection of Billets. C.O. proceeded to H.Q. 1st Cavalry Division for three days.	

Army Form C. 2118.

WAR DIARY
or
INTELLIGENCE SUMMARY.
(Erase heading not required.)

Instructions regarding War Diaries and Intelligence Summaries are contained in F. S. Regs., Part II. and the Staff Manual respectively. Title pages will be prepared in manuscript.

Place	Date	Hour	Summary of Events and Information	Remarks and references to Appendices
La Cauchie	8th July		Adjutants Parade. Packing up of Camp etc. Weather fine.	
ORIEL PLAGE	9th July Tuesday		Battalion arrived EU 7 P.M. & reached Camp at 10 P.M. Camp well situated on hill overlooking the sea. Party of 116 men's then under Major Walker sent missing & Nixon proceeded to Paris to take part in 14th July Celebration. Battn in clean.	App 2.11
"	10th July Wednesday		Battalion Employed on Fatigues on Camp. Weather fine.	
"	11th July Thursday		Adjutants parade for Officers. Men Employed under R.E. on Fatigues. C.O. saw all officers. Weather fine.	
"	12th July Friday		Adjutants Parade Coy Training. 100 men emp loyed on Fatigues under R.E.	

A5834 Wt. W4973/M687 750,000 8/16 D. D. & L. Ltd. Forms/C.2118/3.

Army Form C. 2118.

WAR DIARY
or
INTELLIGENCE SUMMARY.
(Erase heading not required.)

Instructions regarding War Diaries and Intelligence Summaries are contained in F. S. Regs., Part II. and the Staff Manual respectively. Title pages will be prepared in manuscript.

Place	Date	Hour	Summary of Events and Information	Remarks and references to Appendices
CRIEL PLAGE	13th July Saturday		Fatigue Parts found by Improvement of Camp. Coy Training. The following Promotions have been made C.Q.M. Sgt No 15175 C.H. Macferran to be Coy. Sgt. Major 3rd Battn. D.C.R.M.M. Sgt No 11594 F. Brown - C.Q.M.S 1st Battn. Sgt No 12558 H. Foxon - C.Q.M.S 2nd Battn. Sgt No 16390 A. Pitt N.B - C.Q.M.S. 4th Battn.	
"	14th July Sunday		Brigade Parade Service in morning. The Army Commander General Sir H. Rawlinson attended & afterwards inspected the Battn. Camp, heard few	
"	15th July Monday		Fatigue Party found for work on Camp Training as per Scheme	App 212
"	16th July Tuesday		Fatigue Party found for Camp. Training as per Scheme	
"	17th July Wednesday		Fatigue Party found for Camp. Training as per Scheme. Paris Party Returned. Major Walker in charge. Unable to refreshments clearly.	W. H. Owen M.

Army Form C. 2118.

WAR DIARY
or
INTELLIGENCE SUMMARY.
(Erase heading not required.)

Instructions regarding War Diaries and Intelligence Summaries are contained in F.S. Regs., Part II. and the Staff Manual respectively. Title pages will be prepared in manuscript.

Place	Date	Hour	Summary of Events and Information	Remarks and references to Appendices
ORIEL PLAGE	Thursday 18th July		Fatigue Party found for battery & Camp Coy Trainers in the Bivouac area	
"	Friday 19th July		Fatigue Party found to Canp Coy Training as in his scheme	
"	Saturday 20th July		The Celebration of the 3rd Anniversary of the Battalion was held. Football Match Right Half Battalion v Left Half Battalion. Won by the Right Half Battalion. Concert in the evening. the Brigadier & Sergeants Concert in the evening. the Brigadier & Officer Commanding 6/Yorks attended. the Officers of the Battalion walked to previous days Bivouac inspected Camp.	
"	Sunday 21st July	9.30 am	Church Parade. Fatigue Party found.	
"	Monday 22nd July		Coy Training as by Bg scheme. Fatigue Party found for a Camp.	
"	Tuesday 23rd July		Training and Fatigues Path as a previous day. Captain Tuckwell gave a Lecture to Officers in Lewis Gun	

Army Form C. 2118.

WAR DIARY
or
INTELLIGENCE SUMMARY.
(Erase heading not required.)

Place	Date	Hour	Summary of Events and Information	Remarks and references to Appendices
CRIEL PLAGE	Wednesday 24th July		Fatigue Party & Coy Training as on previous day. Some rain.	
"	Thursday 25/7/14		As in previous day	
"	Friday 26th July		Training as per scheme. Small fatigue Party found. Some rain	
"	Saturday 27/7/14		As in previous day	
"	Sunday 28th July		Church parade 8.30 AM C.O.'s inspection of Camp at 10.30. 60 young officers joined the Battalion for 2 months Course in Trenches appointed to be an Sr Officer. 14 Officers commanded the Coy present exclusive of the officers of the Battalion. Regimental ?? Young Officer to be attached. Total number of young officers 243.	

Army Form C. 2118.

WAR DIARY
or
INTELLIGENCE SUMMARY.
(Erase heading not required.)

Instructions regarding War Diaries and Intelligence Summaries are contained in F.S. Regs., Part II. and the Staff Manual respectively. Title pages will be prepared in manuscript.

Place	Date	Hour	Summary of Events and Information	Remarks and references to Appendices
ERIE PLACE	Monday 29th Sept.		Fatigue Party detailed to camp. Company Training to be Scheme. Young Officers addressed by Brigadier in Casino. Lieut E.W. Nairn took over temporary Command of No.1 Co in place of Captain Needham. Command of Young Officers Company detailed.	
"	Tuesday 30th Sept.		Train to fatigue party as on previous day. Young Officers drill & instruction.	
"	Wednesday 31st Sept.		Training as per programme. Part of Officers and N.co of Battalion attached.	

B. Pilcher
LIEUT-COL.
COMMANDING 4th BATTN. GRENADIER GUARDS.

SECRET. War Diary   App 2/1   COPY NO...6...

4th Battalion Grenadier Guards Order No 162.

Ref. Map Sheets:- LENS 11 & ABBEVILLE. 1/100,000.   8th July 1918.

1. The 4th Guards Brigade will move to CRIEL PLAGE for training tomorrow July 9th.

2. (a) The Battalion (less party detailed for PARIS) will march to MONDI-COURT Station where it will entrain for CRIEL PLAGE.
   (b) The head of the Battalion will pass the starting point (road junction V.17.d.6.7.) at 6.40 a.m.
   (c) Order of march:-   B.H.Q.
                           No 2 Company.
                           No 1 Company.
   (d) Route:- Road junction V.17.d.9.9. - road junction V.10.d.4.2. - X roads V.10.a.8.4. - X roads V.9.b.6.3. - X roads V.9.b.9.8. - X roads V.9 a.7.4.
   (e) Distance:- 100 yards between Companies. B.H.Q. will march with No 2 Company.
   (f) Dress:- S.D.M.O. 1 day's rations will be carried.
   (g) Transport at SAULTY will move independently so as to reach MONDICOURT Station at 9.10 a.m.
       Transport at LA CAUCHIE will move with the Battalion.

3. (a) Lewis Gun limbers at LA CAUCHIE will be at the Orderly Room at 6 a.m. where they will be loaded.
       Lewis Guns at SAULTY will be collected under arangements to be made by Transport Officer.
   (b) Kits, stores, washbowls, rifle racks etc. will be dumped on the road outside the guard tent by 6.30 a.m. No 1 Company will find a guard of 1 man.
   (c) Tents, watertanks etc. will be dumped in Camp outside the guard tent by 6.30 a.m. No 2 Company will find a guard of 1 man.
   (d) All Officers' servants will report to Lt R.L.MURRAY LAWES at 7 a.m. for loading.
   (e) Lt R.L.MURRAY LAWES will be responsible for handing to representative of VI Corps at LA CAUCHIE and will proceed to MONDICOURT Station with guards and loading party as soon as handing over is completed. The Qmr. Sgt will be responsible for handing over at SAULTY and obtaining receipts.

4. Drums and Details (less party detailed for PARIS) will march under Battalion Sgt Major to MONDICOURT Station and report to Capt Hon. F.E. NEEDHAM by 10.40 a.m.

5. (a) Party proceeding to PARIS from LA CAUCHIE will parade under Lt H.G.WIGGINS. MC., and will march to MONDICOURT Station where they will report to O.C. 1st Bn IRISH GUARDS by 10 a.m.
   (b) Following party detailed for PARIS from SAULTY will march to MONDICOURT Station under Qmr. Sgt. and report to Lt. H.G.WIGGINS.MC. by 9.50 a.m.
               13246. Pte Wakefield   T.
               21049. " Burton   T.
               Major Walker's servant.
               Major Walker's groom.
               1 Drummer detailed by Major Walker.
   (c) Dress:- S.D.M.O. 1 day's rations will be carried and rations for 10th issued at the station.

                           (Sgd)   A. HARDINGE.   Captain.
                    A/Adjutant, 4th Battalion Grenadier Guards.

Copies issued to:-
    1. No 1 Company.   2. No 2 Company.
    3. O.C.Details.   4. Transport Officer.
    5. Qmr. Sgt Richmond.   6 & 7. Retained.

4th Battalion Grenadier Guards.

TRAINING PROGRAMME - 14th JULY to 21st JULY, 1918.

Training on Monday, Wednesday, Thursday and Saturday.

8.30 a.m. - 9.30 a.m.	Adjutant's Parade.
9.45 a.m. - 12 noon.	N.C.Os' Class. Lewis Gun Class. Bayonet Fighting. Physical Training. Musketry - Fire Orders etc. Section Training. Extended Order Drill. Scout Training. Simple Schemes for N.C.Os.
12 noon.	Young Officers instruction by Commanding Officer.
Afternoon.	Bathing and Games.

Training on Tuesday and Friday.

Company Training on ground above Camp and on MONT JOLIBOIS.

Section Training.   Platoon Training.
Extensions - Attack and Consolidation.
Defence and Retirement.
Training of Platoons to keep direction.
Use of Compass by Section Commanders.

                        (Sgd)   A. HARDINGE.   Captain.
14/7/18.   A/Adjutant, 4th Battalion Grenadier Guards.

4th. Battalion Grenadier Guards
O. O.R.

```
Strength July 1st.                  23  561
    Decrease WE. 6th... 12.
    Increase WE. 6th...  7. 23  556
    Decrease WE.13th...  3.
    Increase WE.13th... Nil 23  553
    Decrease WE.20th...  3.
    Increase WE.20th...  4. 23  554
    Decrease WE.27th...  4. XX
    Increase WE.27th... 14. 22* 564* (Cpt. Sloane Stanley off
                                                    strength)
```

App 213

4th Battalion Grenadier Guards.

LIST OF OFFICERS BY SENIORITY - 1/8/18.

App. 314.

```
Lt-Colonel W.S.Pilcher. DSO.              Commanding.
Major C.F.A.Walker. MC.                   2nd in Command.
Captain Hon. F.E.Needham.                 O.C.Training Coy.
Captain C.R.Gerard. DSO.                  Adjutant.
* Captain I.M.Ingleby.                    A/Quartermaster.
Captain Hon. A.H.L.Hardinge. MC.          O.C.Coy.
* Captain E.H.Tuckwell. MC.               Lewis Gun Officer.
Captain H.G.Simpson.                      Training Coy.
Lieut R.P.De P.French. MC.                Cadet Company.
Lieut E.F.Heim.                           O.C.Company.
Lieut J.C.Wiggins. MC.
(Lieut (A/Capt) G.C.Knight. MC.)          attd. 4th Guards Bde.
Lieut C.E.Irby. MC.
Lieut G.W.Selby Lowndes.                  Transport Officer.
Lieut A.P.J.Brixon. MC.
Lieut J.E.Greenwood.
* Lieut R.L.Murray Lewes.                 Special Duties.
(Lieut D.J.Knight.)                       attd. 4th Gds. Bde.
2/Lieut A.F.Alington.
2/Lieut Hon S.E.Marsham.
* 2/Lieut P.L.Gregson Ellis.              Special Duties.
* 2/Lieut H.V.Gillett.                    Special Duties.
```

* Will be available for duty with their companies etc. when not employed with Cadet Company.

WO 95
1226/2

Aug 1918
4 Bth Grenadier Guards

SECRET.

WAR DIARY.

4TH. BN. GRENADIER GUARDS.

VOLUME VIII.
(1918).

Period :-

AUGUST 1ST. to 31ST. 1918.

Army Form C. 2118.

WAR DIARY
or
INTELLIGENCE SUMMARY.
(Erase heading not required.)

Instructions regarding War Diaries and Intelligence Summaries are contained in F. S. Regs., Part II. and the Staff Manual respectively. Title pages will be prepared in manuscript.

Place	Date	Hour	Summary of Events and Information	Remarks and references to Appendices
CRIEL PLAGE	1st Aug Thursday		Training. Programme for Young Officers. Fatigue party found. Coy Training as per Training Scheme.	1 - 27th August Scheme. App 2/15 attached
"	2nd Aug Friday		Fatigue Party found for Camp – Coy Training as per scheme – weather fine.	
"	3rd Aug Saturday		Fatigue Party found. Coy Training as per scheme. Brigade Sports results attached.	App 2/6
"	4th Aug Sunday		Brigade Divine Service held at 10.30 a.m. to Commemorate 5th Anniversary of the War.	
"	5th Aug Monday		Fatigue Party found. Coy Training as per Scheme etc attached.	App 2/17
"	6th Aug Tuesday		Fatigue Party found. Coy Training as per scheme.	
"	7th Aug Wednesday		Fatigue Party found. Coy Training as per Scheme. B.F. School gave a Lecture to the Brigade. Colonel Campbell on Bayonet fighting.	
"	8th Aug Thursday		Fatigue Party found. Training as per Scheme. Major Dalbe was President of a 25 C.M.	

A5834 Wt. W4973/M687 730,000 8/16 D. D. & L. Ltd. Forms/C.2118/13.

Army Form C. 2118.

WAR DIARY
or
INTELLIGENCE SUMMARY.
(Erase heading not required.)

Instructions regarding War Diaries and Intelligence
Summaries are contained in F. S. Regs., Part II.
and the Staff Manual respectively. Title pages
will be prepared in manuscript.

Place	Date	Hour	Summary of Events and Information	Remarks and references to Appendices
CRIEL PLAGE	9th Aug Friday		Battalion Route march. Sent fatigue Party to find	
"	10 Aug Saturday		Coy Training as per scheme. Fatigue party 250 O.R.	
"	11th Aug Sunday		Divine Service 8 A.M. C.O's inspected of Camp 10 A.M.	
"	12th Aug Monday		Training as per scheme. Steins for bath	App 2R
"	13th Aug Tuesday		Training as per scheme. Weather very hot. Corps had batting parade	
"	14th Aug Wednesday		Training as per scheme Coy Battery parade. weather fine & warm.	
"	15th Aug Thursday		Training as per scheme. Weather fine & warm. Corps Battery Parades. Lieut Greenwood passed fever at D.H.Q P. B.T Training School	
"	16th Aug Friday		The Batt'n fired on the Polygon Range in the afternoon. A very hot day. Batth bathed in the evening.	

Army Form C. 2118.

WAR DIARY
or
INTELLIGENCE SUMMARY.
(Erase heading not required.)

Place	Date	Hour	Summary of Events and Information	Remarks and references to Appendices
CRIEL PLAGE	17th Aug Saturday		The Battn. fired on the POLYGON range in the morning. Fatigue parties found. The Commanding Officer proceeded on leave to ENGLAND. Weather changed to colder and very stormy.	
-ditto-	18th Aug Sunday		Divine Service 9 A.M. A cold morning but warm in the afternoon. Inspection of Camp 10 A.M.	
-ditto-	19th Aug Monday		Training as per scheme. Scheme for march attacked. Cold and windy all day. Fatigue parties found.	App 219
-ditto-	20th Aug Tuesday		Fatigues found. Training as per scheme. Weather changed to intense heat. Battn. Football match v. Young Officers. Result 1 goal all.	
-ditto-	21st Aug Wednesday		Training as per scheme. Novices Boxing Competition held in the afternoon. Programme & Diagram attached. Very hot all day.	App 220
-ditto-	22nd Aug Thursday		Training as per scheme. The whole Battn. had bathes. All officers attended a lecture by Col. CAMPBELL on Recreational Training. Fatigues found. A very hot day.	

Army Form C. 2118.

WAR DIARY
or
INTELLIGENCE SUMMARY.
(Erase heading not required.)

Instructions regarding War Diaries and Intelligence Summaries are contained in F. S. Regs., Part II. and the Staff Manual respectively. Title pages will be prepared in manuscript.

Place	Date	Hour	Summary of Events and Information	Remarks and references to Appendices
RIFLE RANGE	23rd Aug. Friday		The Bn: fired their practice of the 13th Course on the POLYGON RANGE in the afternoon. A cool day.	
ditto	24th Aug. Saturday		The Bn: fired on the POLYGON RANGE commencing at 8 a.m. (Continuation of 13th Course) Rain in the morning and light head.	
ditto	25th Aug. Sunday		Divine Service at 9 a.m. Inspection of Camp at 10 a.m. A very hot day.	
ditto	26th Aug. Monday		Training on Mt. TOLIBOSS as per scheme. Training scheme for week attached. Preliminary rounds of 13th Noring Brown Competition at 5 p.m. Cool and windy.	App 22.
ditto	27th Aug. Tuesday		Training as per scheme. Finals 2 rounds of 13th Brown attached. A draft of 70 other ranks marked for 1st Battn. — List of draft attached.	App 222 App 223
ditto	28th Aug. Wednesday		Young Officers proceeded to join their regiments. Officers attached as instructors to Y. O. Coy:— Capt. Hn: F.B. NEEDHAM. Capt. H.C. SIMPSON. Lt. CONTREMEN. 2 Lt. P.G.R. BACON ELLIS. 120 young officers were attached to the Battn. the morning Rain and mud all day. Training for per scheme.	

Army Form C. 2118.

WAR DIARY
or
INTELLIGENCE SUMMARY.
(Erase heading not required.)

Instructions regarding War Diaries and Intelligence Summaries are contained in F. S. Regs., Part II. and the Staff Manual respectively. Title pages will be prepared in manuscript.

Place	Date	Hour	Summary of Events and Information	Remarks and references to Appendices
C RIEL PLAGE	29th Aug. Thursday		Company training on MT. JOLIBOIS. Lecture on Gas by 3rd Army Chemical Adviser in the afternoon. Lieut. C.C. Cubitt M.C. joined the Bn. Posted to No. 1 Coy.	
– do –	30th Aug. Friday		A fine day. A draft of 5 Officers 197 other ranks joined to proceed to Base on 31st. Officers for the draft — Capt. H.F.SIMPSON, Lt. C.E. CUBITT, 2/Lt. F. ALINGTON, 2/Lt. H.A. S.E. MARSHAM. — Range in afternoon cancelled.	App. 224.
– do –	31st Aug. Saturday		The draft left LE TREPORT at 10 A.M. list of draft attached. A windy day.	App. 225.
			List of Officers and strengths of Battn. attached	

M. Walker Major
O.C. Comdg. 4th Battn.
Grenadier Guards

App 16

**** P R O G R A M M E ****

OF

4TH GUARDS BRIGADE SPORTS

To be held at 2.0 p.m. on Saturday, August 3rd, 1918,
on high ground above Camp at ORIEL PLAGE,
by permission of
Brigadier-General the Hon. L. Butler, C.M.G., D.S.O.,
Commanding 4th Guards Brigade.

****

*** BRIGADE CHAMPIONSHIP. ***

Points will be allotted towards the Brigade Championship as follows :-

5 points for 1st, 2 for 2nd, 1 for 3rd - In Events 2, 3, 5 & 7.
5 points for 1st, 2 for 2nd - In Events 1, 4 & 6.
5 points for Winning Team - In Events 12 & 13.

*** SPORTS OFFICIALS. ***

REFEREE

Lt.-Col. R.B.J. Crawfurd, D.S.O., 3rd. Bn. Coldstream Guards.

JUDGES

Capt. R.S. Lambert, M.C.,   Brigade Major.
Capt. L.E.O. Everard, M.C., 3rd Bn. Coldstream Guards.
Lieut. J.E. Greenwood,   4th Bn. Grenadier Guards.
Lieut. C.B. Hamilton,   2nd Bn. Irish Guards.
Capt. E.R.D. Hoare,   4th Guards T.M. Battery.

STARTER

Lieut. E.W. Evans,   3rd Bn. Coldstream Guards.

RECORDER

Capt. E.D. Mackenzie, D.S.O.,   Staff Captain.

TIMEKEEPER : Bett. Sergt-Major, 4th Bn. Grenadier Guards.
MARSHAL : Drill-Sergt. Pettit, 3rd Bn. Coldstream Guards.
CLERK OF COURSE: Bn.Sergt-Major, 2nd Bn. Irish Guards.

****

EVENTS & TIMES.

1. HIGH JUMP. ... ... 2.0 p.m.
   1st .... 2nd .... 3rd ....

2. 100 YARDS. ... ... 2.15 p.m.
   1st .... 2nd .... 3rd ....

3. MILE. ... ... 2.20 p.m.
   1st .... 2nd .... 3rd ....

4. LONG JUMP. ... ... 2.30 p.m.
   1st .... 2nd .... 3rd ....

5. QUARTER MILE. ... ... 2.45 p.m.
   1st .... 2nd .... 3rd ....

6. THROWING THE CRICKET BALL. 2.50 p.m.
   1st .... 2nd .... 3rd ....

7. HALF MILE. ... ... 3.5 p.m.
   1st .... 2nd .... 3rd ....

8. TUG OF WAR. (Heats). 3.10 p.m.
   Qualified for Final :-

9. BOAT RACE. ... ... 3.25 p.m.
   Winners :-

10. HALF MILE (Open). ... 3.30 p.m.
    1st .... 2nd .... 3rd ....

11. WRESTLING ON HORSEBACK. 3.40 p.m.
    Winners:-

12. RELAY RACE. ... ... 4.0 p.m.
    Winners :-

13. TUG OF WAR. (Final). ... 4.5 p.m.
    Winners :-

14. OFFICERS' RACE. ... ... 4.20 p.m.
    (Open to officers of 4th Guards Bde. Only).
    1 yd. start for every yr of age over 20.
    1st .... 2nd .... 3rd ....

15. YOUNG OFFICERS' RELAY RACE. 4.25 p.m.
    (1 Team from each Battn's attached Officers).
    Winners :-

16. Q.M.A.A.O's RACE. ... 4.50 p.m.
    1st .... 2nd .... 3rd ....

17. CONSOLATION RACE.

* * * * * * * * * * * * * * * * * * * *
PRIZE GIVING.
* * * * * * * * * * * * * * * * * * * *

CONDITIONS.:— All Races are only open to 4th Guar. Brigade with the exception of Nos.10 & 15.
All Entries for Events Nos. 9,10,14,16 & 16 will be post entries.
Events 1 to 7 inclusive are limited to 3 entries per Battalion, Brigade H.Q., & T.M.Battery.

4th Battalion Grenadier Guards.

TRAINING PROGRAMME - AUGUST 5TH. to AUGUST 10TH. 1918.

Training on Monday and Thursday.

8.30 a.m.   Company training on MONT JOLIBOIS.

Training on Tuesday, Wednesday and Saturday.

8.30 a.m. - 9.30 a.m.	Adjutant's Parade.
9.45 a.m. - 12 noon.	N.C.Os' Class.
	Lewis Gun Class.
	Bayonet Fighting.
	Physical Training.
	Musketry - Fire Orders etc.
	Section Training.
	Extended Order Drill.
	Scout Training.
	Simple schemes for N.C.Os.
12 noon.	Young Officers instruction by Commanding Officer.
Afternoon.	Bathing and Games.

Training on Friday.

8.30 a.m.   Route March.

                                                              Captain.

4th August 1918.   Adjutant, 4th Battalion Grenadier Guards.

4th. Battalion Grenadier Guards.

TRAINING PROGRAMME August 12th. to August 17th. 1918.

Day of Week.	Time.	Nature of Training.
Monday.	8/30.a.m.	Company Training on MONT JOLIBOIS.
	8/30.am-9/30.am	NCOs' class - Bayonet Fighting under QMS.I.Elliott, AGS.
	9/0.a.m.	Lewis Gun firing on YAUVILLE Range. (12 men from each company).
Tuesday.	8/30.am-9/30.am	Adjutant's Parade.
	9/45.am-12 noon.	N.C.Os' class.
		Lewis Gun class.
		Bayonet Fighting.
		Physical Training.
		Musketry - Fire Orders, etc.
		Section Training.
		Extended Order Drill.
		Scout Training.
		Simple schemes for N.C.Os.
	12 noon.	Young Officers instruction by Commanding Officer
	Afternoon.	Bathing and Games.
Wednesday.	As for Tuesday.	
	8/30.am-9/30.am	NCOs' class - Bayonet Fighting under QMS.I.ELLIOTT, AGS.
	9/0.a.m.	Lewis Gun firing on YAUVILLE Range. (12 men from each company).
Thursday.	8/30.a.m.	Company Training on MONT JOLIBOIS.
Friday.		ROUTE MARCH.
Saturday.	As for Tuesday.	
	8/0.am - 9/0.a.m.	NCOs' class - Bayonet Fighting under QMS.I.ELLIOTT.AGS.

Firing rifle practices on POLYGON Range on days on which allotted.

Captain,

August 11/1918.   Adjutant, 4th. Battalion Grenadier Guards.

App 219

4th Battalion Grenadier Guards

TRAINING PROGRAMME - 19th August to 24th August 1918.

MONDAY. 19TH.

8.30 a.m.	Company Training on MONT JOLIBOIS.
9.0 a.m.	Lewis Gun Firing on YAUVILLE Range. (15 men from each Company)
10.30 - 11.30 a.m.	N.C.Os' Class under QMSI. ELLIOTT.
2.30 p.m.	All Officers will attend a lecture on 'Tanks' in No 2 Mess Tent (Young Officers').

TUESDAY. 20TH.

8.0 - 8.30 a.m.	No 1 Coy. P. & B.T. under QMSI. ELLIOTT.
8.30 - 9.0 a.m.	No 2 Coy. P. & B.T. under QMSI. ELLIOTT. (Companies will parade in time to arrive at the P. & B.T. Course at 8.0 and 8.30 a.m.)
9.15 a.m.	Lewis Gun Class. N.C.Os' Class. Musketry. Gas Drill.
Afternoon.	Games.

WEDNESDAY. 21ST.

8.30 a.m.	Route March.
9.0 a.m.	Lewis Gun Firing on YAUVILLE Range. (15 men from each Company).

THURSDAY. 22ND.

8.30 a.m.	N.C.Os' Class. Musketry. Extended Order Drill. Physical Exercise. Gas Drill.
9.30 - 10.30 a.m.	No 1 Coy. P. & B.T. under QMSI. ELLIOTT.
11.45 - 12.45 a.m.	No 2 Coy. P. & B.T. under QMSI. ELLIOTT.
Afternoon.	Games.

FRIDAY. 23RD.

8.30 a.m.	Adjutant's Parade.
9.45 a.m.	Musketry.
1.0 p.m.	Commence firing 1st three practices of Musketry Course.

SATURDAY. 24TH.

7.30 a.m.	Commence firing 2nd three practices of Musketry Course. (N.B. Reveille 5.30 a.m. on this date).

18/8/18.

Captain.
Adjutant, 4th Battalion Grenadier Guards.

B. H. R. two

App 220

4th Battalion.

Grenadier Guards.

NOVICES BOXING COMPETITION.

held on

21st August, 1918,

by kind permission of

Lt-Colonel. W.S.PILCHER, D.S.O.,

Commanding 4th Bn. Grenadier Guards.

REFEREE. Lieut.E.W.EVANS, 3rd Bn. Coldstream Guards.

JUDGES. Q.M.S.I.ELLIOTT, Army Gymnastic Staff.
Sergt. WOOD, 3rd Bn. Coldstream Guards.

TIMEKEEPER. Lieut.J.E.GREENWOOD, 4th Bn.Grenadier Guards.

M.C. Sergt.Major.F.OAKLEY, 4th Bn.Grenadier Guards.

Boxing to commence at 5 p.m.

PROGRAMME.

Light-Weights.

Final.	Winner.

Pte. BROWN (1). ⎫
                ⎬ .... Winner.
Pte. ALTON (1). ⎭

Welter Weights.

1st Round.   Semi Final.   Final.   Winner.

A. ⎧ Pte. E..H. (2)   ⎫
   ⎨   ⎬ Winner of A. ⎫
   ⎩ Pte. SINN.A. (1) ⎭   ⎬ ....
                                      ⎫
   ⎧ Pte. SMITH. (2)   ⎫   ⎬ .... Winner.
B. ⎨   ⎬ Winner of B. ⎭
   ⎩ Pte. COOKSON. (1) ⎭

      ⎧ Pte. BELCHER. (2)
Byes ⎨
      ⎩ Pte. COX. (1)

Middle Weights.

1st Round.   Semi Final.   Final.   Winner.

A. ⎧ Pte. SMITH. (1)   ⎫
   ⎨   ⎬ Winner of A. ⎫
   ⎩ Pte. SAUNDERS. (2) ⎭   ⎬ ....
                                        ⎫
   ⎧ Pte. PARKINSON (2) ⎫   ⎬ .... Winner.
B. ⎨   ⎬ Winner of B. ⎭
   ⎩ Pte. HARVEY. (1)   ⎭

      ⎧ Pte. JACKSON. (1)
Byes ⎨
      ⎩ Pte. LANCASHIRE (2).

Light Heavy Weights.

1st Round.   Semi Final.   Final.   Winner.

   ⎧ Pte. BROOKS (2)   ⎫
A. ⎨   ⎬ Winner of A. ⎫
   ⎩ Sgt. TAYLOR (1)   ⎭   ⎬ ....
                                      ⎫
   ⎧ Pte. PATEMAN (2) ⎫   ⎬ Pte. HUTCHINS (2) ⎫
B. ⎨   ⎬ Winner of B. ⎭   ⎬ ....
   ⎩ Pte. WELLS. (?)   ⎭   L/S STIRLAND. (2) ⎭

      ⎧ L/S STIRLAND. (2)
Byes ⎨
      ⎩ Pte. HUTCHINS. (2)

Catch Weights.

Semi Final.   Final.   Winner.

Cpl. DYSON. (2)   ⎫
                  ⎬ ....
Sgt. WALKER (2)   ⎭   ⎫
                                 ⎬ .... Winner.
Bye. Pte. ROUNDS. (1) ....⎭

G O D   S A V E   T H E   K I N G.

4th Battalion Grenadier Guards.

PRIZEWINNERS AT BATTALION BOXING COMPETITION.

Weight.		Rank & Name.	Coy.
LIGHT WEIGHT.	Winner.	Pte. Brown.	1.
	Runner-up.	" Alton.	1.
WELTER WEIGHT.	Winner.	Pte. Cookson.	1.
	Runner-up.	" Emm.	2.
MIDDLE WEIGHT.	Winner.	Pte Jackson.	1.
	Runner-up.	Lancashire.	2.
LIGHT HEAVY WEIGHT.	Winner.	Sgt Taylor.	1.
	Runner-up.	L/S Stirland.	2.
CATCH WEIGHT.	Winner.	Pte Rounds.	1.
	Runner-up.	Sgt Walker.	2.

21/8/18.

4th Battalion Grenadier Guards.

TRAINING PROGRAMME - 26TH. AUGUST - 31ST. AUGUST 1918.

Monday 26th August.

8.30 a.m.	Company Training on MONT JOLIBOIS.
8.30 a.m.	Lewis Gun firing on YAUVILLE RANGE. (15 men from each Company)
8 - 9 a.m.	N.C.Os' Class under QMSI. ELLIOTT.
9 - 10 a.m.	B.H.Q., Shops, Drums, Servants etc. under QMSI. ELLIOTT.

Tuesday 27th August.

8.30 a.m.	Adjutant's Parade.
9.45 a.m.	Musketry.
	Gas Drill.
	Lewis Gun Class.
	N.C.Os' Class.

Wednesday 28th August.

8.30 a.m.	Route March.
8.30 a.m.	Lewis Gun firing on YAUVILLE RANGE. (15 men from each Company)

Thursday 29th August.

8.30 a.m.	Company training on MONT JOLIBOIS.

Friday 30th August.

8.30 a.m.	Adjutant's Parade.
9.45 a.m.	Musketry.
1 p.m.	Commence firing on POLYGONE RANGE.

Saturday 31st August.

7.30 a.m.	Commence firing on POLYGONE RANGE.

Captain.

25th August 1918. Adjutant, 4th Battalion Grenadier Guards.

app 222

4th Guards Brigade.

NOVICES BOXING COMPETITION.
2nd Day.

Light Weights.

Semi-final.		Final.	Winner.
Cpl.Halsall. C.Gds.	} –	Pte Mc.Mullen.(I.G.)	
Pte.McMullen. I.Gds.			Pte. Beck.(I.G.)
L.Cpl.Fogerty. I.Gds.	} –	Pte Beck. (I.G.)	
Pte.Beck. I.Gds.			

Welter Weights.

Semi-final.		Final.	Winner.
Pte.Cox. G.Gds.	} –	Pte Gray. (I.G.)	
Pte.Gray. I.Gds.			Pte.Gray.(I.G.)
Pte.Brennan. I.Gds.	} –	Pte Brennan.(I.G.)	
Pte.Cookson. G.Gds.			

Middle Weights.

Semi-final.		Final.	Winner.
Pte.Lancashire. G.Gds.	} –	Pte Garvey. (I.G.)	
Pte.Garvey. I.Gds.			Pte Rice:(I.G.)
Pte.Aylward. I.Gds.	} –	Pte Rice. (I.G.)	
Pte.Rice. I.Gds.			

Light Heavy Weights.

Semi-final.		Final.	Winner.
Pte.Harwood. G.Gds.		Pte Harwood.(G.G.)	
Cpl.Howard. I.Gds.		Cpl Howard.(I.G.)	Pte Harwood.(G.G.)
Piper.Byrne. I.Gds.			

Catch Weights.

Final.		Winner.
Sgt.Walker, G.Gds.		Pte Rounds.(G.G.)
Pte.Rounds. G.Gds.		

GOD SAVE THE KING.

4th Guards Brigade.

NOVICES BOXING COMPETITION&

held on

Monday & Tuesday August 26th & 27th

by kind permission of

Brigadier-General Hon. L.J.P.Butler, C.M.G.,D.S.O,

Commanding 4th Guards Brigade.

---ooOoo---

Referee.	Major.C.Burn-Callander.
Judges.	(Lieut.E.W.Evans., 3rd Bn.Coldstream Gds. (Lieut.E.W.Nairn., 4th Bn.Grenadier Gds. (2/Lt.R.C.V.de Wessolow, 3rd Bn.Coldm.Gds. (Q.M.S.I.Elliott, Army Gymnastic Staff.
Timekeeper.	2/Lieut.T.Mathew, 2nd Bn. Irish Gds.
M.C.	R.S.M.F.Oakley, 4th Bn.Grenadier Gds.

Boxing to commence each day at 5 p.m.

---ooOoo---

1

Light-Weights.

1st Round.

A. { Cpl.Halsall.C.Gds.
     Pte.Brown. G.Gds.

B. { Pte.McMullen.I.Gds.
     Pte.Kettle. I.Gds.

C. { L.Cpl.Fogerty.I.Gds.
     Pte.Quinn. I.Gds.

Bye. Pte.Beck. I.Gds.

Semi-final.

Winner of A. ....
Winner of B.

Winner of C. ....
Pte.Beck.I.Gds.

Final.

.... Winner.

Welter Weights.

1st Round.

A. { Pte.Cookson. G.Gds.
     Pte.O'Connor.I.Gds.

Pte.Brennan. I.Gds.)
Pte.Gray. I.Gds.)
Pte.Young. I.Gds.)
Pte.Metters. C.Gds.) -Byes.
Pte.Cox. G.Gds.)
Pte.Hayes. G.Gds.)
Pte.Emm. G.Gds.)

2.

Middle-Weights.

Semi-final.

Winner of D. ....
Winner of E.

Winner of F. ....
Winner of G.

Final.

.... Winner.

Light Heavy Weights.

1st Round.

A. { Pte.Thornburn. Pte.Carter.
                   C.Gds.
     Cpl.Howard. Pte.Harwood.
     I.Gds.   G.Gds.

   { Sgt.Taylor.
     G.Gds.
     Pr.Byrne.
     I.Gds.

Byes. { Pte.Carter.
        C.Gds.
        Pte.Harwood.
        G.Gds.

Semi-final.

Winner of A. ....
Winner of B.

Final.

.... Winner.

Catch Weights.

Semi-final.

A. { Sgt.Walker. G.Gds.
     Cpl.Dyson. G.Gds.

Bye.Pte.Rounds. G.Gds.

Final.

Winner of A. ....
Pte.Rounds.G.Gds.

.... Winner.

GOD SAVE THE KING.

WELTER WEIGHTS.

2nd Round.

B. (Pte. Emm, (G.G.)
   (Pte. Cox, (G.G.) ....

C. (Pte. Gray, (I.G.)
   (Pte. Young, (I.G.) ....

D. (Pte. Brennan (I.G.)
   (Pte. Hayes (G.G.) ....

E. (Pte. Metters, (C.G.)
   (Winner of A. ....

SEMI-FINAL.	FINAL.	WINNER.
Winner of B.)		
Winner of C.)		
Winner of D.)		
Winner of E.)		

MIDDLE WEIGHTS.

First Round.

A. (Pte. Rice (I.G.)
   (Cpl. Eccleston (C.G.)

B. (Pte. Lancashire (G.G.)
   (
   (Pte. Mulcahy (I.G.)

C. (Pte. Aylward (I.G.)
   (
   (Pte. Harvey (G.G.)

Pte. Fagan, (C.G.))
Pte. Garvey (I.G.))
Dr. Scott, (G.G.)) A Bye.
Pte. Saunders (G.G.))
Pte. Wells, (G.G.))

Second Round.

D. (Pte. Wells (G.G.)
   (
   (Winner of B.

E. (Pte. Fagan (C.G.)
   (
   (Pte. Garvey (I.G.)

F. (Winner of C.
   (
   (Dr. Scott (G.G.)

G. (Pte. Saunders (G.G.)
   (
   (Winner of A.

4th. Battalion Grenadier Guards.

List of Draft proceeded 28/8/18 to join 1st. Bn: Grenadier Guards.

app 223

Reg.No.	Rk.	Name		Reg.No.	Rk.	Name	
17825	L/Sgt.	Ashworth	J.	17014	L/Sgt.	Bright	W.
22533	L/Cpl.	Blower	W.	27004	L/Cpl.	Povey	H.
25950	Cpl.	Page	E.	26482	"	Prosser	G.
23075	Pte.	English	G.	25117	Pte.	Anderson	A.
30122	"	Gartland	S.	26564	"	Dawson	E.
29720	"	Lynn	J.	29749	"	Fowler	A.
27537	"	Naylor	H.	27820	"	Huxley	J.
27906	"	Meek	F.	27453	"	Gifkins	C.
29806	"	Parker	F.	28518	"	James	J.
29792	"	Phillips	F.	20626	"	Jones	F.
3019?	"	Ransom	W.	13389	"	Murray	B.
29305	"	Watson	E.	29925	"	Mathers	F.
26970	"	Yearsley	J.	25726	"	Powell	W.
20639	"	Dale	R.	27365	"	Page	A.
27335	"	Breakspear	S.	23576	"	Parsons	J.
21206	"	Chambers	E.	27636	"	Scull	S.
29715	"	Camplin	G.	27286	"	Shepherd	W.
29780	"	Fallon	L.	21789	"	Shaw	W.
21786	"	Green	E.	26792	"	Westhead	G.
21915	"	Harris	H.	30587	"	Burney	T.
14352	"	Holton	E.	25987	"	Colton	A.
29685	"	Hill	B.	27647	"	Curme	A.
26481	"	Jones	J.	11938	"	Degg	W.
25650	"	Jagger	J.	30209	"	Hanlon	F.
29702	"	Jenkins	G.	24896	"	Medcalf	H.
30605	"	Kay	F.	27049	"	Orrell	C.
1932?	"	King	H.	30613	"	Parkinson	E.
27265	"	Richardson	W.	30142	"	Pickles	F.
30619	"	Smith	F.	30423	"	Smith	S.
29682	"	Taylor	L.	28506	"	Scrivener	E.
29778	"	Walker	L.	29431	"	Toner	R.
28633	"	Stocks	J.	29998	"	Webster	F.
25963	"	Harmer	G.	30625	"	Weaver	F.
28646	"	Keith	J.	27596	"	Weaver	T.
26727	"	Peach	J.	26246	"	Jackson	A.

4th Battalion Grenadier Guards.

DRAFT PROCEEDING TO GUARDS DIVISION – 31/8/18.

Captain J.H.G. Simpson   Lt. C.G. Cubitt
Lt. R.P. Le P. Trench MC   2/Lt. A.F. Alington   2/Lt Hon S.E. Marsham

Reg.No.	Rk.	Name		Specialist	Reg.No.	Rk.	Name		Specialist
					19726	Lt.	Fromant	J.H.	
12489	Sgt	Gray	A.		14505	Sgt	Knowles	W.	
13918	"	Wood	J.		11136	"	Bridges	O.	
20600	L/S	Browning	C.		20996	L/S	Hawker	A.	
25266	"	Clowes	A.	Gas NCO	19749	"	King	F.	
19510	Cpl	Dixon	O.		25119	Cpl	Cartwright	H.	L.G.
22156	L/C	Farrah	A.	Sig.	29877	L/C	Jackson	J.	
22137	"	Davies	S.		30598	"	Howatt	N.	
18690	"	Chambers	H.		21882	"	Clapton	F.	
19901	"	Good	G.		26302	"	Davison	G.	
28669	"	Wilson	J.		17144	"	Vaughan	A.	Bomber.
28307	"	Holden	A.	L.G.	30308	"	Wainwright	E.	
21793	"	Inger	W.	L.G.	29901	"	Beasley	J.	
19896	"	Wood	W.	L.G.	20151	"	Docking	R.	L.G.
26751	"	Thomas	J.	L.G. Bmbr	27574	"	Piggott	J.	
19408	"	Smith	T.		27276	Pte	Arthurs	J.	
26594	Pte	Brett	J.	L.G.	28670	"	Bell	E.	L.G.
25764	"	Barron	H.	L.G.	25336	"	Beckett	H.	Sig.
24908	"	Bond	C.		25889	"	Butchers	G.	
20783	"	Course	J.	L.G.	24845	"	Dennis	C.	L.G.
27375	"	Day	L.	L.G.	30592	"	Dixon	C.	Offs.Cook.
27132	"	Eley	N.	L.G.	27447	"	Firth	W.	
30595	"	Fullard	P.		27860	"	Gray	C.	S.B.
26918	"	Hughes	T.	L.G.	30140	"	Howell	B.	L.G.
20950	"	Hill	C.	L.G.	23857	"	Hirst	C.	L.G.
30599	"	Hambrook	F.		30588	"	Cox	W.	
23641	"	Humphreys	G.	Sig.	26888	"	Hilsley	L.	L.G. fell out at late
24373	"	Johnson	R.	L.G.	27114	"	Lamb	T.	S.B.
24487	"	McGarry	J.	Sig.	25908	"	Myddleton	W.	L.G.
23622	"	Mealey	B.		19195	"	Oxley	T.	Sig.
22566	"	O'Byrnne	F.	L.G.	30159	"	Prentice	G.	L.G.
21501	"	Powell	J.		26287	"	Richmond	W.	Sig.
29765	"	Skinner	A.		23882	"	Smith	G.	L.G.
12964	"	Straw	J.	L.G.	25644	"	Sloggett	R.	L.G.
28135	"	Stancliffe	G.		16405	"	Tilling	E.	
21764	"	Waterworth	T.	S.B.	13247	"	Wakefield	T.	Sig.
25070	"	Wadley	R.	L.G.	19444	"	Austin	G.	
28587	"	Arnold	R.		26208	"	Bryant	R.	
28437	"	Bell	W.		114027	"	Bailey	W.	
29676	"	Bashford	R.		30583	"	Brown	E.	
28408	"	Churchyard	H.		22089	"	Cooper	S.	
25679	"	Cork	A.	Sig.	28571	"	Dean	F.	L.G.
26471	"	Easey	W.	Svt.	25653	"	Dudder	E.	
21136	"	Hudson	W.		16361	"	Hardstaff	J.	L.G.
27623	"	Harvey	J.		11130	"	Hulse	G.	Svt.
26907	"	Maiden	J.	L.G. Bmbr	21547	"	Mayo	J.	
22339	"	Mullock	H.	Svt.	23620	"	Mason	W.	
21681	"	O'Neil	J.	S.B.	24432	"	Owen	A.	
28196	"	Price	H.		26730	"	Robertson	W.	
26541	"	Sheard	E.	L.G. Bmbr	20787	"	Smith	W.	L.G.Bmbr.
29670	"	Simner	J.	L.G.	27106	"	Stocks	H.	
29374	"	Turner	J.	L.G.	26702	"	Volckman	K.	L.G.
21151	"	Wood	A.	L.G. Bmbr	29669	"	Wright	T.	L.G.
14279	"	Whitehouse	H.	Sig.	28207	"	White	A.	
1743	"	Barratt	C.	S.B.	24475	"	Allen	F.	Svt.
28725	"	Ayliffe	C.	L.G.	29870	"	Andrew	A.	
29597	"	Buck	B.	L.G.	30240	"	Brooks	C.	
26357	"	Brooks	E.		29134	"	Cole	E.	
27641	"	Dent	G.	L.G.	25680	"	Frost	C.	Sig.
17085	"	Green	H.	L.G.	27248	"	Gibbons	J.	L.G.
19341	"	Hillier	H.		18778	"	Hewitt	A.	
29837	"	Hutchins	H.	L.G.	29776	"	Hinkley	H.	
28510	"	Johnson	A.	L.G.Bmbr	28110	"	Keyte	S.	

(contd)

Reg.No.	Rk.	Name.		Specialist.	Reg.No.	Rk.	Name.		Specialist.
22836.	Pte	Lancashire	E.		29602.	Pte	Labram	S.	
28897.	"	Maskell	A.	L.G.	27753.	"	Newman	W.	L.G.
28696.	"	Pender	J.		15891.	"	Plant	W.	L.G.
29068.	"	Poole	A.	L.G.	22569.	"	Robinson	J.	
15507.	"	Rockley	A.		20330.	"	Smith	H.	
28658.	"	Smith	A.	L.G.	26191.	"	Sullivan	J.	L.G.
20076.	"	Spragg	V.	L.G.	15309.	"	Sturman	A.	
28799.	"	Saunders	A.		29761.	"	Vince	B.	
26700.	"	White	J.	L.G.	~~xxxxx~~	"	~~xxxxx~~	~~xxxxx~~	
13883.	"	Aldridge	J.	S.B.	26112.	"	Bridgwater	J.	
26538.	"	Birch	G.	L.G.	28716.	"	Butterworth	S.	L.G.
16854.	"	Battle	R.		19453.	"	Bell	P.	
21753.	"	Corcoran	J.	Sig. ~~xxxxx~~	28497.	"	Cocker	W.	L.G.
29826.	"	Cox	S.		27876.	"	Dixon	A.	
22760.	"	Dingle	D.		22853.	"	Emm	H.	L.G.
15937.	"	Eade	C.		26053.	"	Fisher	J.	Sig.
22688.	"	Flanders	C.		29829.	"	Jackson	E.	
23674.	"	Lewin	W.	L.G.	25445.	"	Norris	O.	
22458.	"	Orviss	A.	L.G.	20640.	"	Pateman	B.	
16797.	"	Port	J.		24252.	"	Pulling	W.	
26244.	"	Price	E.		27209.	"	Packer	H.	
25686.	"	Port	G.		11857.	"	Roe	E.	
26394.	"	Spurr	J.	S.B.	25826.	"	Stratton	H.	
23482.	"	Smith	R.		29004.	"	Saunders	D.	L.G.
28558.	"	Tribe	L.		23931.	"	Threadgold	G.	
22389.	"	Wallis	W.		26626.	"	Wall	A.	L.G.
28567.	"	Wing	F.		27260.	"	Wells	P.	L.G.
26887.	"	Robinson	T.	S.B.	23331.	"	Baddock	W.	Sig.
30629.	"	Wilson	G.	Sig.	25871.	"	Newberry	A.	
19824.	"	Orange	R.		22759.	"	Bridgland	A.	
19638.	"	Gladwin	H.		19156.	"	Rider	C.	
26297.	"	Rabjohn	D.		26608.	"	Tilson	G.	
23063.	"	Peters	C.	L.G.	27631.	"	Rushworth	H.	
25262.	"	Stocks	G.		25457.	"	Harris	C.	
24892.	"	Masters	A.		21567.	"	Doughty	W.	
~~17420~~	"	~~Thomas~~	~~X~~		30604.	"	Jarvis	S.	
30333.	"	Clarke	T.	Svt.	20676.	Dmr	Barrett	A.	Drums.
11955.	"	Jeskins	W.		~~17490~~	Pte	~~Thomas~~	~~T~~	
~~17836~~		~~Flack~~	~~W~~		26408	·	FOSTER	G.	

4th. Battalion Grenadier Guards.

```
                                          O. OR.
Strength of Battalion August 1st.      22  567.
      Nett decrease WE. Aug. 10th.            1.
Strength W.E. August 10th.             22  566.
      nett increase WE. Aug. 17th.            2.
Strength W.E. August 17th.             22  568.
      nett increase WE. Aug. 24th.            3.
Strength W.E. August 24th.             22  571.
      nett decrease WE. Aug. 31st.           67.
Present Strength.                      22  504.
Draft proceeded to Gds. Dvn 31/8/8      5  196.
                                       17  308.(Strength 1/9/18.
```

4th. Battalion Grenadier Guards.

Distribution of Officers. 1/9/18.

Commanding.... Lt.Colonel W.S.Pilcher, DSO.
2nd.in Cmd.... Major C.F.A.Walker, MC.
Adjutant...... Captain C.R.Gerard, DSO.
a/Quartermaster Captain I.H.Ingleby.
Transport Offr. Lt. G.W.Selby Lowndes.
Intllgce Offr.. Lt. R.L.Murray Lawes.

Young Officers' Tng. Coy. Captain Hon.F.E.Needham.
                         2/Lt. P.G.S.Gregson Ellis.

Special Duties........... Captain I.H.Ingleby. (BHQ)Available
                          Captain E.H.Tuckwell,MC.(1)for duty
                          Lt.R.L.Murray Lawes. (BHQ)with Coys &c
                          2/Lieut.H.V.Gillett. (2).when not
                                  specially employed with Y.O.

No. 1(double) Coy.   No. 2(double) Coy.

Lieutenant E.W.Nairn.   Captain Hon.A.H.L.Hardinge,MC.
Lieutenant M.P.B.Wrixon,MC.   Lieutenant H.G.Wiggins,MC.
Lieutenant J.E.Greenwood.   Lieutena-nt C.E.Irby,MC.

    Captain C.G.Keith,MC. attd. 4th. Gds. Bde. H/Q.
    Captain R.WOLRIGE-GORDON,MC. Posted:not yet joined.

****

1226/2

4 Bttn Grenadier Gds

War Diary
SEP 1918

CONFIDENTIAL.

WAR DIARY

OF

4th Bn. Grenadier Guards.

Vol. IX, 1918.

Period:

From : 1st September, 1918
To: 30th September, 1918.

Army Form C. 2118.

WAR DIARY
or
INTELLIGENCE SUMMARY.
(Erase heading not required.)

Instructions regarding War Diaries and Intelligence Summaries are contained in F. S. Regs., Part II. and the Staff Manual respectively. Title pages will be prepared in manuscript.

Place	Date	Hour	Summary of Events and Information	Remarks and references to Appendices
CRIEL PLAGE	1st Sept. Sunday		Voluntary Service at 10 A.M. A cold and wet day.	
— ditto —	2nd Sept. Monday		Lewis gun firing on PAUVILLE RANGE.	
— ditto —	3rd Sept. Tuesday		C.O. returned from leave. Lewis gun Teaching N.C.Os Trenches	
"	4th Sept. Wednesday		Training Carried out	
"	5th Sept. Thursday		2/Lt Yard & 2/Lt Clive attached to the Battalion — Training scheme for 1/6 officers starting on officer Training of N.C.Os as per scheme.	Appx 2.6
"	6th Sept. Friday		Brigade Route March	

Army Form C. 2118.

WAR DIARY
or
INTELLIGENCE SUMMARY.
(Erase heading not required.)

Instructions regarding War Diaries and Intelligence Summaries are contained in F. S. Regs., Part II. and the Staff Manual respectively. Title pages will be prepared in manuscript.

Place	Date	Hour	Summary of Events and Information	Remarks and references to Appendices
CRIEL PLAGE	Saturday 7th Sept.		Battalion found on range	
"	Sunday 8th Sept.		Divine Service 9.45 a.m. C.O.'s Inspection of Camp.	
"	Monday 9th Sept.		Train instructed in for scheme. Scheme attached to —	Appx 22
"	Tuesday 10 Sept.		Training as per scheme	
"	Wednesday 11th Sept.		Training as per scheme	
"	Thursday 12th Sept.		Training as per scheme.	
"	Friday 13th Sept.		Brigade Route March	
"	Saturday 14th Sept.		Training as per scheme. Bath for the Battalion in afternoon.	

Army Form C. 2118.

WAR DIARY
or
INTELLIGENCE SUMMARY.
(Erase heading not required.)

Instructions regarding War Diaries and Intelligence Summaries are contained in F. S. Regs., Part II. and the Staff Manual respectively. Title pages will be prepared in manuscript.

Place	Date	Hour	Summary of Events and Information	Remarks and references to Appendices
CRIEFF PLACE	Sunday 15th Sept		Divine Service. Battalion Parade 9.45am. C.O.'s Inspection. Major Bottler R.A.O.C. reported to the Battalion. Captain R. join..... posted temporarily to the Young officers' the 13th Company.	4/5228
"	Monday 16th Sept		Training as per scheme. Field strength as appears to attend.... manoeuvres for 2 days. C.O. went to	
"	Tuesday 17th Sept		Training as per scheme.	
"	Wednesday 18th Sept		Training as per scheme. Lieut. Hallidan 2 draft of 16 have been ground to October but proceeded to....day a reinforcement to Seaside Bn.	
"	Thursday 19th Sept		Training as per scheme. The Major General Officer.... their best. S.h. Namy shield after the Lodge. The rank of Captain from the announcement in the London Gazette.	

Army Form C. 2118.

WAR DIARY
or
INTELLIGENCE SUMMARY.
(Erase heading not required.)

Instructions regarding War Diaries and Intelligence Summaries are contained in F. S. Regs., Part II. and the Staff Manual respectively. Title pages will be prepared in manuscript.

Place	Date	Hour	Summary of Events and Information	Remarks and references to Appendices
CRIEL PLAGE	Friday 20th Sept		Brigade Route March. Map Reading lecture to Officers.	by 2/Lt H Sillett to all
"	Saturday 21st Sept		Training as per Scheme.	
"	Sunday 22nd Sept		Voluntary Church Service Sergeants Shooting Competition won by C.S.M. Leek.	
"	Monday 23rd Sept		Coy Training. Lecture on Tanks by Officers from Tank Corps. Cleaning up of Camp. Training of young Officers handed over to 2nd B.E. Smith Evans	App 228 2nd Lt Ins 6 Evans
CRIEL PLAGE HIERMONT	Tuesday 24th Sept		Battn moved to new Area at CRIEL Guards remained at Battn Orders Brigade Orders and Battn Orders	App 228
HIERMONT	Wednesday 25th Sept		Battn arrived in Billets 5.6 A.M. No 1 & 2 Coys billeted HIERMONT No 3 & 4 Coys in CONTEVILLE.	

Army Form C. 2118.

WAR DIARY
or
INTELLIGENCE SUMMARY.
(Erase heading not required.)

Instructions regarding War Diaries and Intelligence Summaries are contained in F. S. Regs., Part II. and the Staff Manual respectively. Title pages will be prepared in manuscript.

Place	Date	Hour	Summary of Events and Information	Remarks and references to Appendices
FIENVENT	25 Sept		The Brigade came under orders to be moved the Cavalry Corps as a Mobile Infantry Brigade to be moved by Motor Transport.	
		6.30 P.M.	Batt. Transport moved to HEM and came under orders of Commandant Cavalry Reserve Park under Brigade orders.	App 230
"	Thursday 26th Sept		Coy Training. Under Coy Commanders. Weather fine. Brigade Conference for Commanding Officers to discuss information of new force formed under the Command of G-O-C Cavalry Corps.	
"	Friday 27th Sept		Batt. Training as per Reading - adopted practised Embussing.	App 231
		7 P.M.	Departure of Battalion for NOEUX = CERNEY area. Batt. orders Brigade.	App 232

WAR DIARY
INTELLIGENCE SUMMARY

Place	Date	Hour	Summary of Events and Information	Remarks and references to Appendices
HON COURT	Saturday 28th Sept	5 A.M.	Arrived 5 A.M. very wet morning. Battⁿ to Tents. Huguents. Battⁿs received orders to move to Bray S/R - Somme. Transport rejoined Battalion orders attached Buside	App 233 App 234
BRAY-SUR-SOMME	Sunday 29th Sept		Battⁿ billeted in old Battⁿ close to town. Brigade Conference at 11.0.12. to be launched. Plan of operation. Enemys Prisoners observed. Clear objective - General Plan of Photoroad	
"	Monday 30th Sept		Battⁿ Training. Bombers, Rockets, Rip Readings. Battalion at 3 hours Notice. Progress of 18 platoon kept up. Officers Captⁿ ?. Taylor and 160 o.rs Joined the Battalion. Draft of 3 officers 2nd Lt. P. Stirling 2nd Lt. W.R. Beatts	App 235 App 236

Lieut. Col.
COMMANDING 4th BATTN. GRENADIER GUARDS.

4th GUARDS BRIGADE.

TRAINING PROGRAMME FOR COMPANY OF YOUNG OFFICERS ATTACHED TO 4th BN. GRENADIER GUARDS.

From 7th Sept.
To 14th Sept.

DATE.	HOUR.	PLACE OF ASSEMBLY.	SUBJECT.
Sat: Sept. 7th. MORN.	9.0 a.m. - 10.0 a.m.	Bn. Parade Ground.	Drill.
	10.15-11.15.	CASINO.	Tactical Lecture No. 1 - Lt-Col. W.S. Pilcher, D.S.O.
	11.45-12.45.	Bn. Parade Ground.	P. and B.T.
Mon. Sept. 9th. MORN.	9.0 a.m. - 12.45 p.m.	Outside CASINO.	Tactical Scheme No. 1 - Lt-Col. W.S. Pilcher, D.S.O.
AFTN.	2.30 - 3.45 pm.	No. 1 Mess Tent.	Lewis Gun instruction - Lieut C.H.N. Bunbury.
Tues: Sept. 10th. MORN.	9 a.m. - 12.45 pm.	Bn. Parade Ground.	Platoon Training No. 1.
AFTN.	2.30 - 3.45 pm.	No. 1 Mess Tent.	Lewis Gun Instruction - Lieut. C.H.N. Bunbury.
Wed: Sept. 11th. MORN.	9-10 am	CASINO.	Lecture: "Organisation of a Battalion" - Major T.E.G. Nugent, M.C.
	10.15-11.15.	Bn. Parade Ground.	Drill.
	11.45 am - 12.45 pm.	CASINO.	Lecture: "Tactics of Lewis Gun" - Capt. E.H. Tuckwell, M.C
AFTN.	2.30 - 3.45 pm.	No. 1 Mess Tent.	Lewis Gun Instruction - Capt. E.H. Tuckwell, M.C.
Thurs: Sept. 12th. MORN.	9-10 am.	Bn. Parade Ground.	Drill.
	10.15-11.15.	CASINO.	Tactical Lecture No. 2 - Lt-Col. R.B.J. Crawfurd, D.S.O.
	11.45-12.45.	Bn. Parade Ground.	P. and B.T.
AFTN.	2.30 pm - 3.45 pm.	No. 1 Mess Tent	Lewis Gun Instruction - Capt. E.H. Tuckwell, M.C.
Fri: Sept. 13th. MORN.	9.0 a.m. - 12.45 pm.	Junction of track with main rd. just N. of 1st N of CHANTEREINE.	Tactical Scheme No. 2 - Lt-Col. R.B.J. Crawfurd, D.S.O.
AFTN.	2.30 - 3.45 pm.	No. 1 Mess Tent.	Lewis Gun Instruction - Capt. E.H. Tuckwell, M.C.
Sat: Sept. 14th. MORN.	9 a.m. - 12.45 pm.	CASINO.	Map Reading Lecture and Scheme No. 1 - 2/Lieut. H.V. Gillett.

4th Guards
Brigade H.Q.

Captain,
Brigade Major,
4th Guards Brigade.

4th GUARDS BRIGADE.

TRAINING PROGRAMME FOR COMPANY OF YOUNG OFFICERS ATTACHED TO

3rd BN. COLDSTREAM GUARDS.

From 7th Sept.
To 14th Sept.

DATE.	HOUR.	PLACE OF ASSEMBLY.	SUBJECT.
Sat: Sept. 7th. MORN.	9.0 a.m. - 12.45 pm.	Bn. Parade Ground.	Platoon Training No. 1.
Mon. Sept. 9th. MORN.	9-10 am.	Bn. Parade Ground.	Drill.
	10.15-11.15.	CASINO.	Tactical Lecture No. 2 - Lt-Col.R.B.J.Crawfurd,D.S.O.
	11.45-12.45.	Bn. Parade Ground.	P. and B.T.
AFTN.	2.30 pm. - 3.45 pm.	Bn. Parade Ground.	Drill & Revolver Practice.
Tues: Sept. 10th. MORN.	9.0 am - 12.45 pm.	Junction of track with main rd. just N. of 1st N in CHANTEREINE.	Tactical Scheme No. 2 - Lt-Col.R.B.J.Crawfurd,D.S.O.
AFTN.	2.30 - 3.45 pm.	Bn. Parade Ground.	P. and B.T., and Conference.
Wed: Sept. 11th. MORN.	9 am - 12.45 pm.	Bn. Parade Ground.	Platoon Training No. 2.
AFTN.	2.30 -3.30.	CASINO.	Lecture:"Organisation of a Bn."-Major T.E.G.Nugent,M.C.
Thurs: Sept. 12th. MORN.	9.0 am - 12.45 pm.	CASINO.	Map Reading Lecture & Scheme No. 1 - 2/Lieut.H.V. Gillett.
AFTN.	2.30-3.45.	Bn. Parade Ground.	Drill & Revolver Practice.
Fri: Sept. 13th. MORN.	9 - 10 am.	Bn. Parade Ground.	Drill.
	10.15-11.15.	CASINO.	Tactical Lecture No. 3 - Lt-Col.the Hon. H.R. Alexander, D.S.O,M.C.
	11.45-12.45.	Bn. Parade Ground.	P. and B.T.
AFTN.	2.30 - 3.45 pm.	Bn. Parade Ground.	P. and B.T., and Revolver Practice.
Sat. Sept. 14th. MORN.	9 a.m. - 12.45 pm.	ORIEL Church.	Tactical Scheme No. 3 - Lt-Col. the Hon. H.R. Alexander,D.S.O.,M.C.

4th Guards
Brigade H.Q.

Captain,
Brigade Major,
4th Guards Brigade.

4th GUARDS BRIGADE.

TRAINING PROGRAMME FOR COMPANY OF YOUNG OFFICERS ATTACHED TO 2nd BN. IRISH GUARDS.

From 7th Sept. To 14th Sept.

DATE.	HOUR.	PLACE OF ASSEMBLY.	SUBJECT.
Sat: Sept. 7th. MORN.	9.0 a.m. - 12.45 pm.	CASINO.	Map Reading Lecture and Scheme No. 1 - 2/Lieut. H.V.Gillett.
Mon. Sept. 9th. MORN.	9.0 am - 12.45 pm.	Bn. Parade Ground.	Platoon Training No. 1.
AFTN.	2.30-3.45.	Bn. Parade Ground.	P. & B.T., & Revolver Practice.
Tues: Sept. 10th. MORN.	9-10 a.m.	Bn. Parade Ground.	Drill.
	10.15-11.15.	CASINO.	Tactical Lecture No. 3 - Lt-Col. Hon.H.R.Alexander,D.S.O.,M.C.
	11.45-12.45.	Bn. Parade Ground.	P. and B.T.
AFTN.	2.30 - 3.45 pm.	Bn. Parade Ground.	Drill & Revolver Practice.
Wed: Sept. 11th. MORN.	9.0 am - 12.45 pm.	CRIEL Church.	Tactical Scheme No. 3. - Lt-Col Hon.H.R.Alexander,D.S.O.,M.C.
AFTN.	2.30-3.45.	Bn. Parade Ground.	Drill & Revolver Practice.
Thurs: Sept. 12th. MORN.	9 - 10 am.	Bn. Parade Ground.	Drill.
	10.15-11.15.	Bn. Parade Ground.	P. and B.T.
	11.45-12.45.	CASINO.	Lecture: "Organisation of a Battalion" - Major T.E.G.Nugent,M.C.
AFTN.	2.30-3.45.	Bn. Parade Ground.	P. and B.T. & Conference.
Fri: Sept. 13th. MORN.	9.0 am - 12.45 pm.	Bn. Parade Ground.	Platoon Training No. 2.
AFTN.	2.30-3.30.	CASINO.	Lecture:"Routine of Trench Warfare." - The Brigade Major.
Sat: Sept. 14th. MORN.	9 - 10 am.	Bn. Parade Ground.	Drill.
	10.15-11.15.	CASINO.	Tactical Lecture No. 1 - Lt-Col.W.S. Pilcher, D.S.O.
	11.45-12.45.	Bn. Parade Ground.	P. and B.T.

4th Guards Brigade H.Q.

Captain,
Brigade Major,
4th Guards Brigade.

4th GUARDS BRIGADE.

TRAINING PROGRAMME FOR COMPANY OF YOUNG OFFICERS ATTACHED TO

4th BN. GRENADIER GUARDS.

From 16th Sept.
To 21st Sept.

DATE.	HOUR.	PLACE OF ASSEMBLY.	SUBJECT.
Mon: Sept. 16th. MORN.	9 - 10 am.	Bn. Parade Ground.	Drill.
	10.15-11.15 am	CASINO.	Tactical Lecture No. 3 - Lt-Col.the Hon. H.R.Alexander,D.S.O.,M.C.
	11.45 am-12.45.	Bn. Parade Ground.	P. and B.T.
AFTN.	2.30-3.45 pm.	No. 1 Mess Tent.	Lewis Gun Instruction. - Capt.E.H.Tuckwell,M.C.
Tues: Sept. 17th. MORN.	9.0 am - 12.45 pm.	ORIEL Church.	Tactical Scheme No. 3 - Lt-Col.the Hon. H.R.Alexander,D.S.O.,M.C.
AFTN.	2.30 pm - 3.30 pm.	CASINO.	Lecture: "Routine of Trench Warfare" - The Brigade Major.
Wed: Sept. 18th. MORN.	9 a.m. - 12.45 pm.	Bn. L-G. Range.	Firing on Lewis Gun Range. - Capt.E.H.Tuckwell,M.C.
AFTN.	2.30-3.45 pm.	Bn. Parade Ground.	P. & B.T., & Conference.
Thurs: Sept. 19th. MORN.	9 a.m. - 12.45 pm.	Bn. Parade Ground.	Platoon Training - 2nd Day.
AFTN.	2.30-3.45.	Bn. Parade Ground.	Drill & Revolver Practice.
Fri: Sept. 20th. MORN.	9-10 am.	Bn. Parade Ground.	Drill.
	10.15-11.15.	CASINO.	Lecture:"Arrest & Summary Punishment" - The Staff Captain.
	11.45-12.45.	Bn. Parade Ground.	P. and B.T.
AFTN.	2.30-3.45 pm.	Bn. Parade Ground.	P. & B.T. & Revolver Practice.
Sat: Sept. 21st. MORN.	9 - 10 am.	Bn. Parade Ground.	Drill.
	10.15-11.15.	CASINO.	Tactical Lecture No. 4 - Lt-Col.W.S.Pilcher,D.S.O.
	11.45-12.45.	Bn. Parade Ground.	P. and B.T.

4th Guards
Brigade H.Q.

Captain,
Brigade Major,
4th Guards Brigade.

4th GUARDS BRIGADE.

TRAINING PROGRAMME FOR COMPANY OF YOUNG OFFICERS ATTACHED TO 3rd BN. COLDSTREAM GUARDS.

From 16th Sept.
To 21st Sept.

DATE.	HOUR.	PLACE OF ASSEMBLY.	SUBJECT.
Mon: Sept. 16th. MORN.	9.0 - 10.0 a.m.	CASINO.	Lecture: "Routine of Trench Warfare" - The Brigade Major.
	10.15-11.15.	Bn. Parade Ground.	Drill.
	11.45-12.45.	CASINO.	Lecture: "Tactics of Lewis Gun." - Capt. E.H.Tuckwell, M.C.
AFTN.	2.30-3.45.	Bn. Parade Ground.	Drill & Revolver Practice.
Tues: Sept. 17th. MORN.	9-10 am.	Bn. Parade Ground.	Drill.
	10.15-11.15.	CASINO.	Lecture: "Arrest & Summary Punishment." - The Staff Captain.
	11.45-12.45.	Bn. Parade Ground.	P. and B.T.
AFTN.	2.30-3.45 p.m.	No. 1 Mess Tent.	Lewis Gun Instruction - Capt. E.H.Tuckwell, M.C.
Wed: Sept. 18th. MORN.	9-10 am.	Bn. Parade Ground.	Drill.
	10.15-11.15.	CASINO.	Tactical Lecture No. 1 - Lt-Col. W.S.Pilcher, D.S.O.
	11.45-12.45.	Bn. Parade Ground.	P. and B.T.
AFTN.	2.30-3.45.	No. 1 Mess Tent.	Lewis Gun Instruction - Capt. E.H.Tuckwell, M.C.
Thurs: Sept. 19th. MORN.	9.0 a.m. - 12.45 p.m.	Outside CASINO.	Tactical Scheme No. 1 - Lt-Col. W.S. Pilcher, D.S.O.
AFTN.	2.30-3.45.	No. 1 Mess Tent.	Lewis Gun Instruction - Capt. E.H. Tuckwell, M.C. - and Conference.
Fri: Sept. 20th. MORN.	9.0 am - 12.45 pm.	Bn. Parade Ground.	Platoon Training, 3rd Day.
AFTN.	2.30-3.45.	No. 1 Mess Tent.	Lewis Gun Instruction - Capt. E.H.Tuckwell, M.C.
Sat. Sept. 21st. MORN.	9.0 a.m. - 12.45 pm.	CASINO.	Map Reading Lecture & Scheme No. 2 - 2/Lt. H.V. Gillett.

4th Guards
Brigade H.Q.

Captain,
Brigade Major,
4th Guards Brigade.

4th GUARDS BRIGADE.

TRAINING PROGRAMME FOR COMPANY OF YOUNG OFFICERS ATTACHED TO

2nd BN. IRISH GUARDS.

From 16th Sept.
To 21st Sept.

DATE.	HOUR.	PLACE OF ASSEMBLY.	SUBJECT.
Mon: Sept. 16th. MORN.	9.0 a.m. - 12.45 pm.	Outside CASINO.	Tactical Scheme No. 1 - Lt-Col.W.S.Pilcher,D.S.O.
AFTN.	2.30-3.45.	Bn. Parade Ground.	Drill & Revolver Practice.
Tues: Sept. 17th. MORN.	9.0 am - 12.45 pm.	CASINO.	Map Reading Lecture & Scheme No. 2. - 2/Lt. H.V. Gillett.
AFTN.	2.30-3.45.	Bn. Parade Ground.	P. and B.T., & Conference.
Wed: Sept. 18th. MORN.	9.0 am - 12.45 pm.	Bn. Parade Ground.	Platoon Training - 3rd Day.
AFTN.	2.30-3.30.	CASINO.	Lecture: "Arrest & Summary Punishment" - The Staff Captain.
Thurs: Sept. 19th. MORN.	9 - 10 am.	Bn. Parade Ground.	Drill.
	10.15-11.15.	CASINO.	Tactical Lecture No. 2 - Lt-Col.R.B.J.Crawfurd,D.S.O.
	11.45-12.45.	Bn. Parade Ground.	P. and B.T.
AFTN.	2.30-3.45.	Bn. Parade Ground.	P. & B.T. & Revolver Practice.
Fri: Sept. 20th. MORN.	9 a.m. - 12.45 pm.	Junction of track with main rd. just N. of 1st N in CHANTEREINE.	Tactical Scheme No. 2 - Lt-Col.R.B.J.Crawfurd, D.S.O.
AFTN.	2.30-3.45.	Bn. Parade Ground.	Drill & Revolver Practice.
Sat: Sept. 21st. MORN.	9 - 10 am.	Bn. Parade Ground.	Drill.
	10.15-11.15.	Bn. Parade Ground.	P. and B.T.
	11.45-12.45.	CASINO.	Lecture:"Clothing & Supplies &c" (Part I) - Capt. I.H.Ingleby.

Captain,
Brigade Major,
4th Guards Brigade.

4th Guards Brigade H.Q.

4th. Battalion Grenadier Guards.

Scheme for Training. Week ending 14th. Septr. 1918.

Day of Week & Date.	Time and Nature of Training.
Monday, 9th. September.	All N.C.Os' scheme - Tactical Exercise No 1 with Young Officers' class.
	Men - Drill 8/30.a.m to 9/30.a.m under Sergt. Major.
	Lewis Gun 9/30.a.m to 12/30.p.m - Firing on FAUVILLE Range under Lieut. C.E.Irby.MC.
Tuesday, 10th. September.	NCOs and men.
	8/30.a.m to 9/15.a.m Parade - Drill.
	9/30.a.m to 10/15a.m. P & C I A Instruction under Q.M.S.I.Elliott.
	10/30.a.m to 12 noon. Lewis Gun class. N.C.Os'. Musketry for men.
	2.p.m to 3.p.m. N.C.Os Instruction under Sergt. Major - Books, Discipline, etc.
Wednesday, 11th. September.	8/30.a.m to 9/15.a.m. Parade - Drill.
	9/30.a.m to 10/15.a.m. Instruction in Rifle Bombing, etc.
	10/30.a.m to 11/15.a.m. Lecture by 2/Lieut. TILLEY on Map Reading.
	11/30.a.m to 12/30.p.m. Instruction in Lewis Gun.
Thursday, 12th. September.	8/30.a.m to 10/30.a.m. Lewis Gun class and Lewis Gun firing on Range
	11.a.m to 12/15.p.m. Bombing & Musketry Instruction.
	2.p.m to 2/45.p.m. Lecture on Map Reading and Message writing by 2/Lieut. TILLEY.
Friday, 13th. September.	8/30.a.m - Brigade Route March.
Saturday, 14th. September.	9/30.a.m to 12/30.p.m. Firing on POLYGONE Rifle Range: Musketry Instruction for NCOs.

Small Box Respirators to be worn during Training twice a week for 30 minutes.
Fifteen minutes Physical exercise on Breakfast Parade daily.
Signalling Instruction daily.

K.Clauson - Captain,

A/Adjutant 4th. Battalion Grenadier Guards.

Apx 228

SECRET.   Copy No...9....

4th Battalion Grenadier Guards Order No. 169.

Ref. Maps:- ABBEVILLE 14.1/100,000.   LENS 11.1/100,000.

23rd September 1918.

1. (a) The Battalion will move to the Cavalry Corps Area tomorrow, September 24th.
   (b) The move will be carried out by march route, rail and bus.

2. (a) The Battalion will march to EU Station and will entrain at 9.40 p.m.
   (b) The head of the Battalion will pass the starting point (Central Entrance to Camp) at 5 p.m.
   (c) Order of March:-   B.H.Q.
                                 Drums.
                         No 1 (double) Coy.
                         No 2 (double) Coy.
   (d) Dress:- Service Dress Marching Order. Steel helmets on packs. Waterbottles filled.

3. Officers' kits, Mess Stores and blankets will be collected at the Central Entrance to Camp at ~~11 a.m.~~ 3pm.

4. TRANSPORT.
   (a) The head of the Transport will pass the Central Entrance of the Camp at ~~12 noon.~~ 4pm.
   (b) A loading party of 1 N.C.O. and 20 other ranks detailed by O.C. No 1 Company will report to the Transport Officer at the Central Entrance of the Camp at ~~11.50 a.m.~~ 3/4.5pm

5. (a) Dinners tomorrow will be at 12.30 p.m.
   (b) Haversack rations will be carried.
   (c) Teas will be ~~provided~~ eaten at EU. at 8/15pm.

6. On arrival at AUXI-LE-CHATEAU, the Battalion will detrain and will embus for HIERMONT and CONTEVILLE.

7. Battalion Headquarters will close at CRIEL PLAGE tomorrow at ~~12 Noon~~ 4pm and re-open at HIERMONT on completion of the move.

                                        R.Murray Lawes
                                                      Lieut.
              A/Adjutant, 4th Battalion Grenadier Guards.

Copies issued to:-

1. No 1 Company.   2. No 2 Company.
3. 2nd in Command.   4. Quartermaster.
5. Transport Officer.   6. 4th Guards Brigade.
7. Sgt Major F. Oakley.   8 & 9. War Diary.

SECRET.
Copy No... 12... 231

4th Battalion Grenadier Guards Order No. 170.

Ref. Maps LENS 11 and AMIENS 17.   27th September 1918.

1. The Battalion will move by lorry to the 4th Army Area on the night 27th/28th September, and on arrival will be billeted in the MONCOURT - CERISY area.

2. The allotment of lorries to the Battalion is temporarily as follows:-

Lorry.	Disposal.
1.	B.H.Q.Officers. 2 signallers plus 1 signalling lamp. 1 light Lewis Gun and 1 anti-aircraft Lewis Gun plus 2 Lewis Gunners to be detailed by Lieut C.E.IREY.MC.
2.) to 5.)	B.H.Q.Servants and proportion of signallers. Sgt Major. Drill Sgts. Drums and remainder of B.H.Q. Also B.H.Q. Officers' kits.
6.) 7.) 8.) 9.)	Q.M.Stores. Shops and all their personnel.
10.) to 17.)	No 1 (double) Company. (will include Coy. Offrs' kits, Coy. Mess kit and Coy. blankets etc.)
18.) to 25.)	No 2 (double) Company. - do. - - do. -
26.	Empty lorry in rear of column.

Each Company will take two bicycles.

3. Dress:- Service Dress Marching Order; waterbottles filled; haversack ration.

4. (a) The head of the column will pass the starting point (HIERMONT CHURCH) at 7 p.m.
   (b) No 2 Company will be formed up with all personnel and stores, with the head of the Company on the road outside their Company H.Qrs at CONTEVILLE by 7 p.m., where they will embus on arrival of the column.

5. Battalion Headquarters will close at HIERMONT at 6 p.m. and re-open in the new area on completion of the move.

27/9/18.   A/ Adjutant, 4th Battalion Grenadier Guards.
                                                     Captain.

Copies issued to:-
1. No 1 Company.   2. No 2 Company.
3. 2nd in Command.   4. Quartermaster.
5. Officer i/c M.T.Section.   6. 4th Guards Brigade.
7. Sgt Major.   8. Intelligence Officer.
              9 & 10. War Diary.

SECRET.   Copy No. 10

4th Battalion Grenadier Guards Order No. 171.

Ref. Map. AMIENS 1/100,000.   28th September 1918.

1. (a) The 4th Guards Brigade will vacate the present area today.
   (b) The new area will be in the vicinity of BRAY and ETINEHEM.

2. The allotment of lorries will be the same today as for yesterday. All lorries must be clearly marked with a large A on both sides of the body.

3. (a) The Battalion group will pass the starting point (MORCOURT CHURCH) at 2.30 p.m., and form up behind the H.A.C. on the MORCOURT - MERICOURT road.
   (b) Lorries are parked in the field behind the Church (S.W.)
   (c) Route:- via MERICOURT and FROISSY to BRAY.
   (d) Dress:- Service Dress Marching Order.

4. (a) Kits and all stores will be loaded by 1.45 p.m.
   (b) Tents issued today will be struck and taken to the new area.

5. A billeting party under Lieut C.E.IRBY.MC. has been detailed and separate orders issued to all concerned.

6. The transport will move at approximately 5 p.m., under orders to be issued by the Brigade Transport Officer.

7. Reports to the head of the Battalion group on the move.

8. Battalion Headquarters will close at MORCOURT at 2.30 p.m., and re-open in the new area on arrival.

                                                    Captain.
                        Adjutant, 4th Battalion Grenadier Guards.

Copies issued to:-

1. No 1 Company.   2. No 2 Company.
3. 2nd in Command.   4. 4th Guards Brigade.
5. Quartermaster.   6. Transport Officer.
7. Intelligence Officer.   8. Sgt Major.
         9 & 10. War Diary.

4th. Battalion Grenadier Guards.
Variations of Strength, September 1918.

```
                  O.   O.R.
W.E. 7/9/18.      22   504.
     Decrease.     5   198
W.E.14/9/18.      17   306
     Decrease.         8
W.E.21/9/18.      17   298
     Decrease.         2
W.E.28/9/18.      17   296.
```

Draft Lt.B.C.Layton, 2/Lts.W.R.Wearne & A.G.Snelling and 161 O.R. joined late 30/9/18.
                                    O.   O.R.
           Actual strength 30/9/18 20   457.

4th Bn. Grenadier Guards.

List of Officers by Seniority Sept 30th 1918

Lt. Colonel.	W. S. Pilcher D.S.O.	Commanding
Major.	C. F. A. Walker M.C	2nd In Command
Captain.	Hon. F. E. Needham	O.C. Coy.
Captain.	R. Wolrige-Gordon M.C.	O.C. Coy.
Captain.	C. R. Gerard D.S.O.	Adjutant
Captain.	J. H. Ingleby	A/Quartermaster
Captain.	Hon. A. H. L. Hardinge M.C.	O.C. Coy
Captain.	E. H. Tuckwell M.C.	4th Guards Bde.
Captain.	E. C. Nairn	O.C. Coy.
Lt.	H. G. Wiggins M.C	
Lt.	C. E. Irby M.C.	I/c Lewis Guns
Lt.	G. W. Selby Lowndes	Transport Officer
Lt.	M. P. B. Nixon M.C.	
Lt.	J. E. Greenwood	
Lt.	R. L. Murray Lawes	Intelligence Officer
2/Lt.	P. G. S. Gregson Ellis	
2/Lt.	H. V. Gillett	

WO 95

1226/2

War Diary

OCT 1918

4 Bttn Grenadier Guards

CONFIDENTIAL

WAR DIARY

of

4th Battalion, Grenadier Guards.

Vol. X, 1918.

PERIOD :

From   1st October

To   31st October, 1918.

WAR DIARY or INTELLIGENCE SUMMARY

Army Form C. 2118.

4th Bn. Grenadier Guards.

Place	Date	Hour	Summary of Events and Information	Remarks and references to Appendices
BR.Hy hut SOUTH	Tuesday 1st October		Coy Training under Coy Commanders. C.O. spoke to the Battalion about future operations. 6 C. Taylor on leaving 2/Lt A.S. Snelling joined the Battalion.	
"	Wednesday 2nd October		Coy Training. Battalion embussed & proceeded to BRIE. Head of Battalion was halted at MILLERS-CARBONNEL owing to the non-employment of the Cavalry. Coys Battalion returned to BRAY.	App 237. App 238
			Brigade Orders. Battn.	
			Captain Nairne appointed Liaison Officer. Major C.F.A. Walker M.C. proceeded to 2nd Battn to take on Command.	App 23.
FRISE	Thursday 3rd October		Battalion embussed & proceeded to VILLERS-CARBONNEL at 7.30.a.m and here received instructions to proceed to FRISE. Battalion reached destination at 11.30.P.M. & Battalion billeted in huts. Battn. Brigade orders	App 239

Army Form C. 2118.

WAR DIARY
or
INTELLIGENCE SUMMARY.
(Erase heading not required.)

Instructions regarding War Diaries and Intelligence Summaries are contained in F.S. Regs., Part II. and the Staff Manual respectively. Title pages will be prepared in manuscript.

Place	Date	Hour	Summary of Events and Information	Remarks and references to Appendices
FRISE	Friday 4th Oct 16		Company Training. Weather continues showery.	
FRISE	Saturday 5th Oct 16		Company Training. Inter Company Football Match. Co. "B" attached Royal Regt. 2 Battery R.F.A. 1 Officer & 1 Battalion from S.O. Organisation of Battalion at present 2 Companies of 3 Platoons each.	
"	Sunday 6th Oct 16		Church Parade 09.30 a.m. Several men, gun fire, by aeroplane. Warning note received that the Battalion would probably move soon.	
"	Monday 7th Oct 16		Company Training in morning. Rain in afternoon. C.O. lectured Details. Some shoot at same army.	

Army Form C. 2118.

WAR DIARY
or
INTELLIGENCE SUMMARY.
(Erase heading not required.)

Place	Date	Hour	Summary of Events and Information	Remarks and references to Appendices
FRISE POESILLY BELLENGLISE	Tuesday 8th Oct		Aleft FRISE 3.50 A.M. The Column arrived at POESILLY at 8.15 A.M. No lorries took down both the Battalion small shower during the morning. Men breakfasted from Bn G.S. supplied by H.Q. C.H. but left POESILLY at abt 11.15 A.M. and arrived at BELLENGLISE 12.15 P.M. Battalion had dinner by roadside. News arrived that attack by 3rd and 4th armies was progressing satisfactorily but that it had not been able to be launched to Casualty Cpt. H.E. Reinville club has been of the enemy. The country thought of the tank fought on it when the Germans here Great preventing by when the Germans here arrived out of HINDENBURG LINE and the G.A.N at Cond. Battalion stayed in Colonie by the 5th Ly the Road. Enemy Aircraft bombed the Column which resulted in no casualties B.3 Lewis Battn - Brigade orders attached to the b-.th Battalion. T. June 30 casualties A.C.R. 2.40	

WAR DIARY or INTELLIGENCE SUMMARY

Army Form C. 2118.

Place	Date	Hour	Summary of Events and Information	Remarks and references to Appendices
BRANCOURT	Tuesday 9th		The Column moved off at 10.15 A.M. Considerable signs of recent fighting on roads. Many German dead seen & equipment & machine guns abandoned by the enemy. The Battalion formed up through MONTBREHAIN Captured at BRANCOURT about noon by 12th American Corps. It killed at Eastern edge of village there on line went to Eastern c.ge of village. flank advancing of Infantry Could be seen & then to relieve towards BOHAIN the Boers to RIQUERVAL and also Germans Could be seen & then to relieve gun fire heard village was shelled shot at the day by one Eln at very long range. Whilst awaiting were formed in the Cottages Battalion escaped the German Evacuation That hurled in the Cellars Eld released fire on troops	

Place	Date	Hour	Summary of Events and Information	Remarks and references to Appendices
BRANCOURT	9th Wednesday (Ctd)		They been delighted Even Received to Chicken that were bought. They had never seen the French Convoy in to have a seen NCO's Flight Lewis During morning 2nd Major J.S. Hughes R.E. joined the Battalion as 2nd in Command from 5th (Res) Battalion August R.S. Welsh	App 241
MONTIGNY	10 Oct Thursday		Battalion left BRANCOURT at 5.20 A.M. passing through PREMONT where the main road had been completely blocked by the Germans blowing down the Church. The Column halted somewhere by a field opposite The Queens had evident by wire in a hurry, as they left Good a tabletles in not honor, as if abandoned in the middle of their dinners. Battalion had dinners in the field here untouched. More evidence of recent fighting was seen by the road - a German Machine Gun had been charged by the	

WAR DIARY
or
INTELLIGENCE SUMMARY.

Army Form C. 2118.

Place	Date	Hour	Summary of Events and Information	Remarks and references to Appendices
	Thursday 10th Sept		Cavalry, though at Acident (on to horses) have been rested. The billets in MONTIGNY have been good, was passed. The village untouched with many civilians still in. The church had been used but it had been discovered that the church had been saved. News that de CHATEAU had been entered by our troops had been received. It has now been 4 years since the 4th Guards Brigade had put out outposts since leaving the Retreat. A fine day. One Brigade Batt'n other attached as Reserve Batt'n.	MR 242
GOUY	Friday 11th Oct		Battalion left MONTIGNY at 1 PM for GOUY. The roads have been very slippery in consequence of the rain & progress slow in consequence. Arrived at Gouy at 5:30 PM and Batt'n billeted in Lewes—Cellars, the town being totally destroyed by recent heavy fighting. Blankets still being received from the details

Army Form C. 2118.

WAR DIARY
or
INTELLIGENCE SUMMARY.
(Erase heading not required.)

Instructions regarding War Diaries and Intelligence Summaries are contained in F. S. Regs., Part II. and the Staff Manual respectively. Title pages will be prepared in manuscript.

Place	Date	Hour	Summary of Events and Information	Remarks and references to Appendices
Port	Saturday 12th Oct		Stayed at Port. Battalion and Company Training in morning. Polo played in the afternoon at intervals during morning.	
"	Sunday 13th Oct		A half day. Voluntary Church Service. Major Hughes came up for the attack.	
"	Monday 14th Oct		Coy Training in morning. Companies marched to Canal in the afternoon in parties to Constantinople by which there 5 miles long. A series of dug-outs 8 Regiments on the Transport reported Battalion by 6pm along.	
"	Tuesday 15th Oct		Coy Training in morning. Details reported Battalion.	

Army Form C. 2118.

WAR DIARY
or
INTELLIGENCE SUMMARY.
(Erase heading not required.)

Instructions regarding War Diaries and Intelligence Summaries are contained in F. S. Regs., Part II. and the Staff Manual respectively. Title pages will be prepared in manuscript.

Place	Date	Hour	Summary of Events and Information	Remarks and references to Appendices
BURLES	Wednesday 16th Nov.		Batt. left Bours at 10.15 A.M and arrived at CORBIE 2.15 P.M. Billetted in huts made & left by the Germans. Comforts were the Battalion as those occupied by the Battalion in the winter 1916-1917. A funeral ar- Batt. magazine worker	App 243.
"	Thursday 17th Oct		Company Training - cleaning up Billets Fine day.	
"	Friday 18th		Brigade Field Day. Batt. started in reserve and proceeded to PRESSOIRE, & then proceeded to Country attack as far as DETRANLOY. Marched home via TROUVETS & MORVAL, places taken by Guards Division in September 1916	Opn 243A.

Army Form C. 2118.

WAR DIARY
or
INTELLIGENCE SUMMARY.
(Erase heading not required.)

Instructions regarding War Diaries and Intelligence Summaries are contained in F. S. Regs., Part II. and the Staff Manual respectively. Title pages will be prepared in manuscript.

Place	Date	Hour	Summary of Events and Information	Remarks and references to Appendices
COMBLES	Saturday 19th Oct		Company Training in morning. Two dupps 2/Lts Rogers & Co. visited Grenade Instruction at LTMB also Graves of the which has formed interest also Graves of the of six officers who fell on 25th Sept 16.	
"	Sunday 20th		Very wet day. Voluntary Divine Service Battalion salvaged.	
"	Monday 21st		Company Training - wet day. 2/Lt M.C. Stephen Hornby joined the Battalion and posted to No 2 Company.	
"	Tuesday 22nd		Company Training. A draft of 42 including 17 N.C.O's sent home in pay for two hundred supposed arrived the leather fine	

WAR DIARY or INTELLIGENCE SUMMARY

Army Form C. 2118.

Place	Date	Hour	Summary of Events and Information	Remarks and references to Appendices
GABLES	Wednesday 23rd		No 1 Co. did Scheme set by C.O. No 2 Co. trained under Company Commander. The following is an extract from the Coy awards in Chief Despatch of Operation during March & April - "a General Determined attacks in which a German Armoured Car came into action against the 4th Guards Brigade here repulsed with great loss to its enemy --- The enemy's advance was held up all day by desperate fighting, in which our advanced posts displayed the greatest Gallantry, maintaining their Ground when entirely surrounded, and standing back to back in the trenches shooting to front and rear. The Enemy had a further determined effort by throwing on the Enemy weight of numbers forced our troops through the gaps in our depleted line, the Germans pushing where the troops of the 2nd Battalion with bullet & bayonet."	

Army Form C. 2118.

WAR DIARY
or
INTELLIGENCE SUMMARY.
(Erase heading not required.)

Place	Date	Hour	Summary of Events and Information	Remarks and references to Appendices
CARLES	Wednesday 23rd		The heavy resistance of two Troops however had given the leading Brigade of the 13th Australian Div. to halt their efforts of positions. The fighting as HAZE B Rock was definitely closed. The performance of all the troops engaged in this hot gallant stand, and especially that of the 9th Sherwood Brigade on whose front some 400 yards the heaviest attacks fell is beyond praise. No more brilliant exploit has taken place since the opening of the offensive, though gallant actions have been without record.	
"	Thursday 24th		No. 26 did a scheme set by C.O. No. 1 C. Training under Company arrangements. Scheme order issued that the Battalion would move to the CRIEL area.	

A5834 Wt. W4973/M687 750,000 8/16 D.D. & L. Ltd. Forms/C.2118/13.

Army Form C. 2118.

WAR DIARY
or
INTELLIGENCE SUMMARY.
(Erase heading not required.)

Place	Date	Hour	Summary of Events and Information	Remarks and references to Appendices
CAMBLET	Friday 25th		Battalion moved in Train departed 1.30 hours & arrived at EU at 0600 hours the next morning. Batt: Brigade order attached. Instructions & orders issued by Battalion when employed with the Cavalry Corps.	Apps 24. Apps 25.
CRIEL	Saturday 26th		Brigade left the Command of the Cavalry Corps. Battalion marched Eleur. Battalion occupied same Camp Billets as in previous stay at CRIEL.	
	Sunday 27th		C.O. took over Command of the Brigade in the Brigadier proceeding on leave. Major Hughes took Command of Batt: Voluntary Divine Service	

Army Form C. 2118.

WAR DIARY
or
INTELLIGENCE SUMMARY.
(Erase heading not required.)

Instructions regarding War Diaries and Intelligence Summaries are contained in F. S. Regs., Part II. and the Staff Manual respectively. Title pages will be prepared in manuscript.

Place	Date	Hour	Summary of Events and Information	Remarks and references to Appendices
CRIEL	Weds 28th		A draft of 121 O.R. proceeded to join the Guards Division. List of names attached. Coy Training under Company arrangement.	App 246
"	Tuesday 29th		Coy Training. Battalion inter Brigade Belts Platoon Football Match Competition started. Rules & rather training Scheme.	App 247 App 248
"	Wednesday 30th		Training as per scheme. Cont of Inter Coy Proceeding. Capt'n Hardwick. leather Furs.	
"	Thursday 31st		Coy Training as per scheme. Football match v Grenadier Guards. Result 1-1.	App 245

Strength of Battalion — Officers 37

B.F. Fisher
Lieut Col
Comdg 1st Battn Scots Guards

SECRET.   App 238   Copy No...

4th. Battalion Grenadier Guards' Order No. 172.

Ref. Maps.-(AMIENS 1/100.000
         (ST.QUENTIN ......   October 2nd1918.
         (62 b & c.

---

1. 4th. Guards Brigade (following 1st. Bn. H.W.G.Bn) will move to a position of readiness with head of column at BELLENGLISE Bridge today.

2(a). The Battalion will be in busses ready to move off at 7.a.m.
 (b). <u>Route</u>:-
        CAPPY - ESTREES - BRIE - VERMAND - BELLENGLISE.
 (c). <u>Dress</u>:-
        Fighting Order with greatcoats & light packs(No haversacks)

3. Details, under Captain I.H.POWLEY, will join 3rd. Cavalry Division M.T.Coy. (N.14.d) after the Brigade has departed, under separate orders from Captain Hon. E.BOSCAWEN, 3rd. Coldstream Guards.

4. Officers' kits, blankets and stores will be collected by the Transport Officer after the Brigade has moved off, and will be carried on the lorries detailed to accompany the Transport. One policeman will be left in charge of the lorries.

5. Transport will join "B" Echelon Cavalry Corps at HEM Station under orders from Brigade Transport Officer.

6. Ammunition, rations, etc. have been issued.

7. Reports to head of Battalion on the move after 7.a.m.

8. Battalion Headquarters will close at BRAY at 7.a.m and re-open at the head of the column (A) at that hour.

                    (signed) C. GERARD - Captain,
Issued at 00.30. a.m.x   Adjutant 4th.Bttn:Grenadier Guards.

Copies to:-

    1. No. 1(double) Coy.   2. No. 2(double) Coy.
    3. Quartermaster.   4. Transport Officer.
    5. Intllgce. Officer.   6. M.T.P., 4th. G.G.
    7. 4th. Guards Bde.   8. Sergt. Major.
                    9. Retained.
              /10/11. War Diary.

SECRET

App. 243.

No. 1 Coy
No. 2 Coy.
2nd in Command
Quartermaster
Transport Officer
[Signals?] Officer
M.T.O. & [C.C.]
[S.?] [Major?]
[H.Q.?] [guard?] B[n?]

(a) The Battalion will move to COMBLES [about?] [noon?] 16 Oct.
(b) VENDHUILE (South via Sugar factory) – LEMPIRE – EPEHY – VILLERS FAUCON – LONGAVESNES – TEMPLEUX-LA-FOSSE – MOISLAINS – BOUCHAVESNES – COMBLES
(c) The Battalion (less transport and [shops?]) will be [embussed?] and ready to move off at [ ]
(d) 25 [cwt?] lorries [to form?] convoy in COMBLES.

(2)

2. Blankets, packs, caps, coy. stores, officers kits, bivouac sheets and tents will be loaded on to the lorries with the men.

3. A billeting party under Capt. L. NAIRN will parade at B.H.Q. at 01.20 hrs.

4. Transport and shops will proceed to COMBLES subarea under orders from the Bde Transport Officer.

5. B.H.Q will close at Coy A at 09.30 hrs and reopen at the head of Coy A at the same hour.

map] VALENCIENNES
   ] ST. QUENTIN
   ] AMIENS LENS

15/10/18
23.30 hrs.

G. Lyward Capt.
Adjutant 4th Batt.
Grenadier Guards.

"A" Form.
MESSAGES AND SIGNALS.

Army Form C.2121 (in pads of 100).

TO — No 1 Coy. Quartermaster. Intelligence Officer.
No 2 Coy. Transport Officer. 4th Gds. Bde.
2nd in Command. Sgt Major. War Diary. Retained.

Day of Month: 18th.   AAA

Order No 1 AAA Companies will parade tomorrow on the road outside their billets ready to move off at [?]00 hrs AAA Dress Fighting Order with picks and shovels (greatcoats and haversacks will not be taken) AAA Company Commanders will be mounted AAA Buses will not be used AAA Only Maps required LENS 1/100,000 AAA Dinners on return to Camp about 1400 hours.

From: Adjutant, 4th Battn. Grenadier Guards.
Time: 2000 hours. 17th October.

SECRET. Copy No...11..

4th Battalion Grenadier Guards   Order No. 175.

Ref. Maps. LENS.   )
         AMIENS.   ) 1/100,000.
         ABBEVILLE.)   24th October 1918.

---

1. (a) The Battalion will move to the CRIEL area tomorrow, 25th inst., by lorry and train.
   (b) The Battalion will be embussed and ready to move off at 1200 hours.
   (c) Train leaves BAPAUME 1445 hours, detraining at EU on arrival.
   (d) ROUTE:-   via LE TRANSLOY.
   (e) DRESS:-   S.D.M.O.
   (f) Dinners from the cookers on arrival at BAPAUME.

2. (a) Transport will move off from Camp at 0830 hours.
   (b) No 2 Company will provide a loading party of 50 men under an officer to be detailed by O.C. No 2 Company: this party will parade at Battn. H.Qrs at 0900 hours and will be conveyed to BAPAUME by lorry.

3. A billeting party consisting of Captain the HON. A.HARDINGE. MC., the Quartermaster, Drill Sgt DAY, 1 C.Q.M.Sgt per double Company, and 1 N.C.O. from the Transport, will proceed to H.Q. 2/I.G. at CRIEL PLAGE, leaving Battn. H.Qrs. at 0830 hours by tender, and will report to the Staff Captain at 1300 hours.

4. (a) The lorries at present attached to the Battalion will leave for HESDIN at 0800 hours.
   (b) Lorries for the conveyance of the Battalion to BAPAUME will arrive at approximately 0830 hours.
   (c) Only the lorries to be loaded up with kit will be brought into the area of the Camp: the remainder of the column will be drawn up on the COMBLES-LE TRANSLOY road.
   (d) All kit will be loaded by 1100 hours.

5. Battn. H.Qrs will close at COMBLES at 1200 hours, and re-open in the CRIEL area on completion of the move.

                                                        Captain.
                            Adjutant, 4th Battalion Grenadier Guards.

Copies issued to:-

   1. No 1 Coy.   2. No 2 Coy.
   3. 2nd in Command.   4. Quartermaster.
   5. Transport Officer.   6. 4th Guards Brigade.
   7. M.T.O.   8. Intelligence Officer.
   9. Sgt Major.   10 & 11. War Diary.

War Diary.

4th Battalion Grenadier Guards.

List of Draft proceeding to join 2nd Bn. Grenadier Guards.

Reg.No.	Rk.	Name.	Courses.	Reg.No.	Rk.	Name.	Courses.
15019.	L/C	Lane	T.	17752.	L/C	Cook	G.
31631.	Pte	Davidson	T. L.Gun *	32464.	Pte	Felgate	E. L.Gun *
31787.	"	Hooper	G. L.Gun *	34427.	"	Haddock	A. L.Gun *
31065.	"	Jessup	G. L.Gun *	31632.	"	Proctor	R. L.Gun *
31791.	"	Wright	B. L.Gun *	32340.	"	Holland	G. L.Gun *
31781.	"	Downing	F. L.Gun *	31792.	"	Davies	H. L.Gun *
31743.	"	Gorn	D. L.Gun *	32222.	"	Charlton	D.
31638.	"	Freer	A.	31904.	"	Pitchford	A.
31906.	"	Wright	E.	32426.	"	Hill	A.
32033.	"	Harper	E.	32006.	"	Jackson	D.
31717.	"	King	G.	31640.	"	Lockley	T.
31693.	"	Lawrence	S.	31908.	"	Newell	H.
32438.	"	Pettitt	F.	31845.	"	Parker	R.
31636.	"	Young	F.	31742.	"	Sayer	E.
31953.	"	Archer	R.	31647.	"	Allen	A.

L.Gun *. These men have all fired a short course in the L.Gun, but are not 'A' Lewis Gunners.

4th Battalion Grenadier Guards.

List of Draft proceeding to join 3rd Bn. Grenadier Guards.

Reg.No.	Rk.	Name.	Courses.	Reg.No.	Rk.	Name.	Courses.
22087.	L/C.	Starbuck	W.	31622.	Pte.	Rogers	H. L.Gun *
32355.	Pte.	Richardson	E. L.Gun *	31924.	"	Schofield	H. L.Gun *
31831.	"	Warren	T. L.Gun *	31712.	"	Bearman	G.
32447.	"	Bowden	V.	31947.	"	Brown	H.
32022.	"	Butler	A.	31902.	"	Warndon	A.
31967.	"	Goodchild	J.	31969.	"	Gilbertson	W.
31627.	"	Green	G.	32331.	"	Godfrey	G.
32296.	"	Hampton	W.	31756.	"	Hines	G.
29003.	"	Holmes	T. Servt.	32360.	"	Muscutt	G. L.Gun *
31737.	"	Mirren	A. L.Gun *	32077.	"	Price	A.
31842.	"	Steedman	J. L.Gun *	31907.	"	Smith	S.
32380.	"	Sheward	R.	31909.	"	Upton	A.
31949.	"	Watts	H. L.Gun *	31903.	"	West	W.
31232.	"	Wherlock	H.	31950.	"	Wallis	R.
31919.	"	Wright	F. L.Gun *	32333.	"	Fynn	E.
32544.	"	Enerfer	E.				

L.Gun *. The men have all fired a short course in the L.Gun, but are not 'A' Lewis Gunners.

4th Battalion Grenadier Guards.

List of Draft proceeding to join 1st Bn. Grenadier Guards.

Reg.No.	Rk.	Name.		Courses.	Reg.No.	Rk.	Name.		Courses.
15111.	L/S.	Norman	H.		31701.	Cpl	Lowen	H.	
13023.	Cpl.	Ward	H.		27876.	Pte	Arthurs	J.	L.Gun.
31619.	Pte.	Archer	S.	L.Gun.	32288.	"	Allen	S.	L.Gun.
27374.	"	Burford	A.	L.Gun.	32129.	"	Forrest	R.	L.Gun.
32036.	"	Fleming	J.	L.Gun.	31929.	"	Langridge	P.	L.Gun.
31895.	"	Neilson	J.	L.Gun.	32393.	"	Baldwin	C.	L.Gun.*
32443.	"	Cox	L.	L.Gun.*	32374.	"	Darch	F.	L.Gun.
32444.	"	Ripley	J.	L.Gun.*	31643.	"	Stretton	J.	L.Gun.*
31662.	"	Tustin	W.	L.Gun.*	32442.	"	Talbot	B.	L.Gun.*
33006.	"	Watson	R.	L.Gun.*	31633.	"	Stray	H.	L.Gun.
31970.	"	Titcombe	F.	L.Gun.	32324.	"	Titt	F.	L.Gun.
32292.	"	Watson	G.	L.Gun.	37690.	"	Amos	W.	
32033.	"	Broomhead	J.		32359.	"	Buckland	H.	
32017.	"	Bradford	J.		31212.	"	Browell	G.	
31182.	"	Bolt	J.		31634.	"	Carr	J.	
31626.	"	Chetwynd	F.		31615.	"	Elliott	F.	
31365.	"	Jarrett	T.		31621.	"	Hall	C.	
31199.	"	Haley	J.		35359.	"	McKnight	A.	
33703.	"	Hornsey	J.		31707.	"	Menzies	H.	
31296.	"	Nesbit	W.		35041.	"	Walsh	J.	
33081.	"	Bushby	J.		31933.	"	Creigh	J.	
31073.	"	Carter	S.		31650.	"	Chapman	F.	
35074.	"	Dore	T.		32281.	"	Fearn	T.	
32461.	"	Heaton	G.		32276.	"	Haines	E.	
31428.	"	Humphriss	G.		31637.	"	Marsh	E.	
32081.	"	Morris	J.		31748.	"	McLaren	J.	
31857.	"	Royle	S.		31629.	"	Summersell	L.	
30691.	"	Wheeler	S.		31697.	"	West	J.	
34178.	"	Wallace	S.		31705.	"	Ayling	H.	
32441.	"	Brown	L.		32003.	"	Briggs	T.	

L.Gun.*   These men have all fired a short course in the L.Gun, but are not 'A' Lewis Gunners.

4th Battalion Grenadier Guards.

TRAINING SCHEME.

MONDAY.

0830 - 0930 hours.   Adjutant's Parade.
                     All Subaltern Officers, and N.C.Os and men on
                     courses will attend.
0930 - 1230 hours.   Musketry Instruction.
                     P. & B.T.Training.
                     Extensions.
                     Bombing.
                     Lewis Gun firing.
                     Bayonet Training Course is available between the
                     hours of 1030 and 1230. Company Commanders will
                     make arrangements between themselves as to what
                     time they make use of it.

TUESDAY.

0830 - 1230 hours.   Tactical Training on MONT JOLIBOIS.
                     It will include Company Commanders giving their
                     N.C.Os schemes to carry out on the ground.

WEDNESDAY.

                     Battalion Route March.
                     Not less than 10 miles.
                     Employed men, Lewis Gun course and N.C.Os' Course
                     will attend.

THURSDAY.

0830 - 0930 hours.   Adjutant's Parade.
                     All Subaltern Officers, and N.C.Os and men on
                     courses will attend.
0930 - 1230 hours.   Musketry Instruction.
                     P. & B.T.Training.
                     Extensions.
                     Bombing.
                     Lewis Gun firing.
                     Bayonet Training Course is available between the
                     hours of 1030 and 1230. Company Commanders will
                     make arrangements between themselves as to what
                     time they make use of it.
1400 - 1500 hours.   Lewis Gun firing.

FRIDAY.

0830 - 1230 hours.   Tactical Training on MONT JOLIBOIS including OUTPOSTS.
Afternoon.   N.C.Os' Course on Rifle Range.

SATURDAY.

0830 - 1230 hours.   POLYGONE Rifle Range.
                     The following practises will be fired:-

                        100 Yards Grouping.
                        200 Yards, 5 rounds, Application, Bayonets Fixed.
                        200 Yards, 10 rounds, Rapid, Bayonets Fixed.
                        5 rounds at Silhouettes - 4 seconds allowed
                        for each.

NOTES.-

1. A Lewis Gun Class of 10 men per Company will be formed on the 31st
   inst. under Lieut O.E.KIRBY.MG.
   A N.C.Os' Class (Scheme for training attached) will be formed under
   the Serjeant Major. 6 N.C.Os from each Company will report to him
   after Adjutant's Parade on Thursday, the 31st.

2. Companies will train and fire all their men in the Lewis Gun, so
   that they can pass the "B" test.
   The YAUVILLE RANGE - Right Sector - is available on the following
   days:-

        Monday morning.
        Tuesday afternoon.
        Thursday afternoon.
        Friday morning.
        Saturday - all day.

3. The following Targets are available at the Brigade Pioneer Shop, and
   can be drawn when required:-
        (a) Small Frame Bulls-Eye Targets.
        (b) Medium Frame Figure Targets.
        (c) Large Frame Figure Targets.
        (d) Silhouettes.
        (e) Four Lewis Gun Traversing Targets.
   In addition, Red Flags, Marking Discs and Patching will be issued
   with the Targets.
   Paste and Brushes will be drawn from the Battalion Pioneers Shop.
   Targets drawn from the Brigade will be returned after use.

4. Companies are responsible for taking the usual precautions when
   firing live ammunition.
   Red Flags to be erected at the edge of the cliffs to warn Shipping.

5. Subaltern Officers will attend 2/Lieut H.V.GILLETT'S Lecture with
   the N.C.Os' Course.

6. Lieut J.E.GREENWOOD will be required to take the N.C.Os' Class from
   0930 to 1030 hours on Mondays and Thursdays.

7. 2/Lieut H.V.GILLETT will lecture as per N.C.Os' Scheme.

8. The following N.C.Os will be required:-

        For LEWIS GUN CLASS.

            Sgt. Weatherley   B.
            Sgt. Newell   B.
            L/C. Eager   A.
            L/C. Blake   H.

For N.C.Os! COURSE - when detailed by the Sgt. Major.
MUSKETRY.

    C.S.M. Brown   C.
    Sgt. Morris   A.
    Sgt. Lancaster   F.

For P. & B.T. TRAINING - to assist Lieut J.E.GREENWOOD

    Cpl. Mason   B.
    Cpl. Coomer   H.

[signature]
Captain.
Adjutant, 4th Battalion Grenadier Guards.

Copies issued to:-

    O.C. No 1 Company.
    O.C. No 2 Company.
    2nd in Command.
    Lieut J.E.GREENWOOD.
    2/Lieut A.V.GILLETT.
    B.H.Q.Mess.
    4th Guards Brigade.
    War Diary (2).
    Retained. (3).

4th Battalion Grenadier Guards.

N.C.Os' COURSE OF INSTRUCTION.

THURSDAY – 31st OCT.
0830 – 0930. Adjutant's Parade.
0930 – 1030. Bayonet Fighting etc.
1030 – 1130. Lecture – 'Discipline'.
1130 – 1230. Squad Drill.

FRIDAY – 1st NOV.
0830 – 0930. Shouting and Arm Drill.
0930 – 1030. Squad Drill.
1030 – 1130. Lecture – 'Duties on Guard'.
1130 – 1230. Musketry.
1400 – 1500. Firing on POLYGONE Range.

SATURDAY – 2nd NOV.
0830 – 0930. Shouting and Arm Drill.
0930 – 1030. Squad Drill.
1030 – 1130. Guard Mounting and Dismounting.
1130 – 1230. Extended Order Drill.

MONDAY – 4th NOV.
0830 – 0930. Adjutant's Parade.
0930 – 1030. Bayonet Fighting etc.
1030 – 1130. Musketry.
1130 – 1230. Squad Drill.

TUESDAY – 5th NOV.
0830 – 0930. Shouting and Arm Drill.
0930 – 1030. Squad Drill.
1030 – 1130. Lecture – 'Duties of N.C.Os in Waiting'.
1130 – 1230. Extended Order Drill.
1400 – 1500. Lecture – 'Map Reading'.

WEDNESDAY – 6th NOV.   Battalion Route March.

THURSDAY – 7th NOV.
0830 – 0930. Adjutant's Parade.
0930 – 1030. Bayonet Fighting etc.
1030 – 1130. Musketry.
1130 – 1230. Squad Drill.

FRIDAY – 8th NOV.
0830 – 0930. Shouting and Arm Drill.
0930 – 1030. Squad Drill.
1030 – 1130. Lecture – 'Duties of N.C.Os in Waiting'.
1130 – 1230. Guard Mounting and Dismounting.
1400 – 1500. Firing on POLYGONE Range.

SATURDAY – 9th NOV.
0830 – 0930. Shouting Drill.
0930 – 1030. Written Examination on Duties of N.C.Os in Waiting.
1030 – 1130. Squad Drill.
1130 – 1230. Musketry.

MONDAY – 11th NOV.
0830 – 0930. Adjutant's Parade.
0930 – 1030. Bayonet Fighting etc.
1030 – 1115. Squad Drill.
1115 – 1230. Written Examination on Duties of N.C.Os in Waiting.

TUESDAY – 12th NOV.   Map Reading – Tactical Scheme.

4th Battalion Grenadier Guards

Officers present with Battalion
31/10/18.

Lt.Colonel W.S.Pilcher, D.S.O.
    Major J.S.Hughes, M.C.
    Captain Hon.F.E.Needham. (No 1 Officers' Camp)
    Captain R.Wolrige Gordon, M.C.
    Captain C.R.Gerard, D.S.O.
    Captain I.H.Ingleby.
    Captain Hon.A.H.L.Hardinge, M.C.
    Captain E.H.Tuckwell, M.C. (4th.Gds.Bde.H.Q)
    Captain B.C.Layton..(Sick)

    Lieut. H.G.Wiggins, M.C.
    Lieut. C.E.Irby, M.C.
    Lieut. G.W.Selby Lowndes
    Lieut. M.P.B.Wrixon, M.C.
    Lieut. J.E.Greenwood.
    Lieut. R.L.Murray Lawes.

    2/Lieut.P.G.S.Gregson Ellis.
    2/Lieut.W.R.Wearne
    2/Lieut.H.V.Gillett.
    2/Lieut.A.G.Snelling.
    2/Lieut.M.C.StJ.Hornby.

App. 249.

4th Battn Grenadier Guards

Strength Return -- October 1918

	O	OR
October 1st	19	290
Increase to 5/10	17	162
	2	6
WE October 5th	19	458
Decrease to 12/10	---	1
Increase to 12/10	1	---
WE October 12th	20	457
Decrease to 19/10	---	2
WE October 19th	20	455
Decrease to 26/10	---	1
Increase to 26/10	1	22
WE October 26th	21	476
Decrease 26/31st	1	124
Present Strength	20	352

Evans Division
4th Pcn Bde
4 st Br Gen. Ser
June — Oct. 1918

www.ingramcontent.com/pod-product-compliance
Lightning Source LLC
Chambersburg PA
CBHW082012220426
43670CB00014B/2606